DISCOVER
Death Valley

DISCOVER
Death Valley

Death Valley may be as close as you get to visiting another planet. Its sculpted sand dunes, crusted salt flats, towering rocks, and polished marble canyons will make you consider your place in the universe.

Declared a national monument in 1933, then signed into national park status in 1994, Death Valley is the largest national park in the Lower 48 states. Located within the northern Mojave Desert, the park is named after the prominent valley within the region and boasts extremes of temperatures and elevation. One early travel advertisement promised "all the advantages of hell without the inconveniences." From the oppressive glaring salt flats of Badwater Basin 282 feet below sea level to the snow line at Telescope Peak 11,043 feet above, a complex and varied geology spans eras of seas and volcanoes, tectonic forces, and fault lines.

Death Valley holds spectacular sights for all to see, but its secrets are not so easily given up. Dotting the landscape are hidden springs, mining camps and ghost towns, petroglyphs and the sacred spots of indigenous people who call the valley home. Decaying or preserved, battered by wind or watered by secret oases, these places stand as a testament to the frenzy of human hopes and the

Clockwise from top left: railroad tracks in an old talc mining district; rock art in Coso Canyon; deep springs at Ash Meadows National Wildlife Refuge; hiking in Red Wall Canyon; equipment at the Borax Museum; a Desert Five Spot flower.

fury of imagination. Get out of the car to walk the twisting canyons, search for waterfalls or petroglyphs, and listen to the wild landscape.

This was and still is a place for dreamers—pyramid schemes and tall tales abound. Thousands came here to seek their fortunes. Some remain etched into popular history, while others have faded into local lore. Come to be awed and humbled, dazzled and pushed out of your comfort zone. You'll wonder whether the searing heat and whipping cold are creating a mirage—or lifting the scales from your eyes.

Clockwise from top left: Rhyolite; Scotty's Castle; The Racetrack; Surprise Canyon.

Planning Your Trip

Where to Go

Furnace Creek and the Amargosa Range

Iconic views, short hikes, and easy access make Furnace Creek and the Amargosa Range an excellent introduction to Death Valley. The village of **Furnace Creek** serves as the park headquarters, with a plethora of services—**lodging, campgrounds, restaurants,** and even gas. The most popular sights are in this region, including **Badwater Basin, Artist's Drive, Devil's Golf Course,** and **Natural Bridge.**

The Amargosa Range provides opportunities for in-depth **hiking, biking,** and **rock climbing.** Dig into Death Valley's mining past by traveling the **West Side Road** to the rugged canyons of the Panamint Range, the orchards of **Hungry Bill's Ranch,** or the bubbling oases of

Hanaupah Canyon. An easy two-hour drive to the park's lightly visited **Southeastern Corner** yields scenic springs, ghost mines, and pristine dunes.

Stovepipe Wells and the Nevada Triangle

Stovepipe Wells and the Nevada Triangle are home to steep alluvial fans that lead to the wind-sculpted and colorful canyons of the Cottonwood and Grapevine Mountains, including **Marble Canyon.** The tiny visitor hub of **Stovepipe Wells** occupies a central location on Highway 190, with the scenic **Mesquite Flat Sand Dunes** within sight.

The Nevada Triangle serves as a jumping off point to the spectacular—and popular—**Titus Canyon** drive, as well as the haunting ghost town

The vast salt flats of Badwater Basin are the lowest point in North America at 282 feet below sea level.

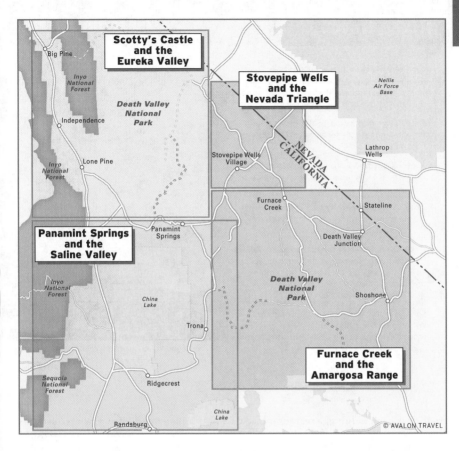

of **Rhyolite.** Nearby **Beatty, Nevada,** offers services in this tiny corner of the park.

Scotty's Castle and the Eureka Valley

The Eureka Valley is the most **lightly visited** park region. There are **no services,** so a trip here means roughing it, but you'll be rewarded with solitude and natural wonders. The exception is popular **Scotty's Castle;** thousands of visitors come to this 1920s mansion tucked in the folds of the Grapevine Mountains.

The **Eureka Dunes** are the main draw in the Eureka Valley, towering more than 600 feet above the valley floor. In the secluded Racetrack

Valley, hardy souls make the long, difficult drive to **The Racetrack,** a dry lake bed scattered with the mysterious trails of rocks that skate across its surface.

Panamint Springs and the Saline Valley

Panamint Springs and the Saline Valley are filled with creeks and springs, historic mining roads and camps. Old cabins and ghost towns, like **Skidoo** and **Panamint City,** are scattered through the wrinkled folds of the western Panamint Mountains, which are home to **Telescope Peak,** the highest peak in Death Valley. The village of **Panamint Springs** is the

If You Have...

- **Two Hours:** Drive Badwater Basin Road south from Furnace Creek to see iconic Death Valley sights: Badwater Basin, the Devil's Golf Course, the Artist's Drive, and Zabriskie Point.

- **One Day:** Add a visit to the ghost town of Rhyolite, and take the scenic drive through Titus Canyon.

- **Two Days:** Add a stop at the Mesquite Flat Dunes near Stovepipe Wells, then drive up to Scotty's Castle.

- **Three Days:** Make the adventurous trek out to The Racetrack; consider spending all three days dry camping in the Racetrack Valley.

- **Four Days:** Attempt the rugged Saline Valley Road and spend four days camping in the Saline Valley. Alternatively, add a trip to the remote Eureka Dunes.

- **One Week:** Base yourself in the Panamint Springs region and explore the Emigrant and Wildrose Canyons, hike Wildrose Peak and Telescope Peak, and backpack to Surprise Canyon and Panamint City.

a double rainbow over Stovepipe Wells

region's hub, with **lodging,** a **restaurant,** and few services.

The Saline Valley brings it back to the basics with sheer quiet remoteness. The long washboard **Saline Valley Road** offers rough access to the **Lee Flat Joshua Tree Forest,** rarely visited **Saline Valley Dunes, hot springs,** and the remains of the Salt Tramway.

When to Go

Death Valley's steep mountains and low valleys mean that temperatures fluctuate wildly depending on where you are at what time of year. High elevations are cooler and low elevations are hotter.

High Season (mid-Oct.-mid-May)
The most popular time to visit Death Valley is **spring** (March, April, and May) for its **wildflowers** and mild temperatures at all elevations. **Fall** is also lovely and moderate, however, a few businesses, especially those beyond the boundaries, may be closed.

Winter is a great time to visit—there are few crowds and the temperatures are pleasant at lower elevations, such as Furnace Creek. Winter brings snow to higher elevations, such as Wildrose and Telescope Peaks in the Panamint

These beautiful architectural kilns were used to make charcoal for the mines in the area.

Mountains. **Roads may close;** check road conditions and carry chains.

Off-Season (mid-May-mid-Oct.)

Death Valley may be a year-round destination, but **summer** is the off-season due to extreme heat. **Services are limited** and it can be brutally hot everywhere, particularly in the valleys. **Hiking is strongly discouraged** at low elevations in summer. Still, many visitors come to the park in summer despite the heat.

Before You Go

There are **limited services** within Death Valley. Stock up on water, food, and any necessary supplies before entering the park. Gas, ice, and limited food and supplies are available at **Furnace Creek, Stovepipe Wells,** and **Panamint Springs.**

Park Fees and Passes

The park entrance fee is **$20 per vehicle,** good for seven days; an **annual pass** is available for $40. **Furnace Creek**, accessed via **Highway 190,** serves as the main park entrance station. Fees can also be paid at the Furnace Creek Visitors Center, Scotty's Castle, the Stovepipe Wells Ranger Station, and at self-pay kiosks located within the park.

Reservations

Spring, fall, and **holiday weekends** can be competitive times for lodging. Make reservations a few weeks to several months in advance if you want to stay inside the park. If all park lodging is booked, your next option is in one of the gateway towns such as Lone Pine, California or Beatty, Nevada.

Furnace Creek Campground (Furnace Creek, 877/444-6777 or www.recreation.gov, Oct. 15-Apr. 15) is the only park campground that accepts reservations. All other park campgrounds are first-come, first-served.

In-Park Lodging

	LOCATION	PRICE	SEASON	AMENITIES
Sunset Campground	Furnace Creek	$12	Oct.-May	tent and RV sites
Texas Spring	Furnace Creek	$14	Oct.-May	tent and RV sites
Furnace Creek RV Park and Fiddlers Campground	Furnace Creek	$18-38	year-round	tent and RV sites
Furnace Creek Campground	Furnace Creek	$18	year-round; reservations Oct.-Apr.	tent and RV sites
Furnace Creek Ranch	Furnace Creek	$215-270	year-round	motel rooms, cabins, restaurants
Inn at Furnace Creek	Furnace Creek	$400-450	mid-Oct.-mid-May	hotel rooms, restaurants
Stovepipe Wells Campground	Stovepipe Wells	$12	Sept. 15-early May	tent and RV sites
Stovepipe Wells RV Park	Stovepipe Wells	$32.75	year-round	RV sites
Stovepipe Wells Hotel	Stovepipe Wells	$117-175	year-round	motel rooms
Mesquite Spring	Scotty's Castle	$12	year-round	tent and RV sites
Eureka Dunes Dry Camp	Eureka Valley	free	year-round, weather permitting	primitive sites
Homestake Dry Camp	Racetrack Valley	free	year-round, weather permitting	primitive sites
Panamint Springs Resort Campground	Panamint Springs	$10-65	year-round	tent sites, RV sites, tent cabins
Panamint Springs Resort	Panamint Springs	$79-169	year-round	motel rooms, cottage, restaurant
Emigrant Campground	Emigrant Canyon	free	year-round	tent sites
Wildrose Campground	Wildrose Canyon	free	year-round	tent sites
Thorndike Campground	Wildrose Canyon	free	Mar.-Nov.	tent sites
Mahogany Flat Campground	Wildrose Canyon	free	Mar.-Nov.	tent sites

In the Park

Visitors Center

The **Furnace Creek Visitors Center** (Furnace Creek Ranch, Hwy. 190, 760/786-3200, www.nps.gov/deva, 9am-5pm daily Oct.-mid-June, 9am-6pm daily mid-June-Sept.) serves as the main park hub year-round.

Where to Stay

There are only four accommodations options within the park. If you're not staying at one of these, you're camping.

- **Furnace Creek Ranch** (Furnace Creek, 800/236-7916, www.furnacecreekresort.com, year-round)
- **Inn at Furnace Creek** (Furnace Creek, 800/236-7916, www.furnacecreekresort.com, mid-Oct.-mid-May)
- **Stovepipe Wells Village** (Stovepipe Wells, 760/786-2387, www.deathvalleyhotels.com, year-round)

- **Panamint Springs Resort** (Panamint Springs, 775/482-7680, www.panamintsprings.com, year-round)

There are **12 campgrounds** in the park; with the exception of Furnace Creek Campground, all are **first-come, first-served.** Finding an open site is rarely a problem; however, Texas Spring Campground, in Furnace Creek, may fill during spring weekends.

Campgrounds are open seasonally (either Oct.-May or May-Oct.) depending on their elevation. There are also primitive campgrounds and many opportunities for backcountry camping.

Getting Around

Most visitors fly into Los Angeles or Las Vegas and rent a car to drive to Death Valley. There are no park shuttles or public transportation available within the

Furnace Creek welcomes visitors.

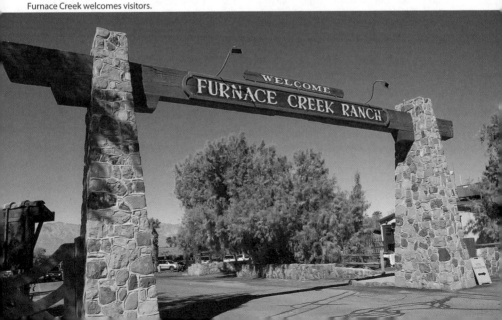

Panamint Springs Resort offers food and lodging on the edge of Death Valley.

park—**you will need your own vehicle**. For back-road excursions, **4WD rentals** are available through **Farabee's** (Furnace Creek, 760/786-9872, www.farabeesjeep-rentals.com, mid-Sept.-mid-May); advance reservations are recommended during high season.

Gas is available within the park, but it's best to fill up at one of the gateway or service towns instead, as distances are great and gas prices are expensive. If entering from the south, fill up at **Ridgecrest** or **Trona;** from the west, stop in **Olancha** or **Lone Pine;** if entering from Nevada, **Beatty** has gas; on the south-eastern route into the park, gas is available in **Shoshone.**

The Best of Death Valley

Day 1

Fly into **Las Vegas, Nevada** and rent a car for the road trip to Death Valley. From Las Vegas, travelers will access the eastern side of the park, a drive of about 2.5-3 hours (150 miles) to the park hub of Furnace Creek.

Day 2

Set yourself up in **Furnace Creek,** the main park hub, to enjoy Death Valley's most iconic sights. The casual Furnace Creek Ranch and the upscale Furnace Creek Inn are your only accommodation options. Texas Spring is the most scenic campground, but it can get crowded; make sure you've lined up your space early.

Just south of Furnace Creek, **Badwater Basin Road** offers a scenic driving tour. Fill up with breakfast at The Wrangler or the 49'er Café in Furnace Creek before heading out. Your first stop is **Golden Canyon,** where you can beat the heat (and the crowds) with a lovely morning hike.

Continuing south along Badwater Basin Road, the **Devil's Golf Course** surprises with its bizarre salt formations, but you can only see these if you stop and get up close. Two miles south is the turnoff to an easy stroll through impressively large **Natural Bridge.** Continue four miles south on the park road to admire **Badwater Basin's** surreal salt flats, 282 feet below sea level and the lowest point in North America.

From Badwater, turn around and retrace your route north. Make a quick side trip to enjoy the relaxing and scenic drive along **Artist's Drive** and through the colorful **Artist's Palette.** Back on Badwater Basin Road, continue north to the junction with Highway 190 and turn right (east). Finish your scenic driving tour at **Zabriskie Point** for spectacular views of the valley below.

Leave yourself enough time to enjoy the warm spring-fed pool at the Furnace Creek Ranch before heading to dinner. Reserve a table at the **Furnace Creek Inn** for a sunset meal at one of the outdoor tables or in the historic dining room.

A paved road winds through colorful Artist's Drive in the Black Mountains.

The towering sand of the Eureka Dunes contrasts with the dark backdrop of the Last Chance Range.

The Inn also has a cocktail lounge where you can enjoy the same view.

Day 3

Today, explore the Stovepipe Wells and Nevada Triangle region. The short hike through **Mosaic Canyon** is a great introduction to the canyons—wander through polished marble, colorful mosaic stone, and satisfying narrows. Just across Highway 190, the sculpted sand dunes of **Mesquite Flat** are visible from Stovepipe Wells, but are definitely worth a closer view.

From Stovepipe Wells, head east for 26 miles along Daylight Pass Road to **Beatty, Nevada,** the jumping-off point for your next adventure. Beatty is a good place to fill up on gas and food. Try the **Happy Burro Chili & Beer,** a charming saloon-style bar and restaurant with an outdoor patio.

The ghost town of **Rhyolite** is just four miles west of Beatty. Wander the impressive ruins of this once-rich gold mining town, then stop at the **Goldwell Open Air Museum** next door to peruse the hauntingly beautiful outdoor art exhibits set incongruously against the desert backdrop.

The crowning point of your day will be driving the **Titus Canyon Road**—the most popular backcountry route in Death Valley. The one-way access point begins 2.1 miles south of Rhyolite, just off Daylight Pass Road. The washboard road winds 27 miles past rugged rock formations, sweeping canyon views, petroglyphs, and even a ghost town to eventually end at Scotty's Castle Road, 20 miles north of Stovepipe Wells.

End your day with a celebratory drink at the **Badwater Saloon** back in Stovepipe Wells Village. Enjoy a dip in the pool or a casual dinner before retiring to one of the basic motel rooms.

Day 4

You'll need an early start to explore Scotty's Castle and Eureka Valley. Pack your car with all the food and water you'll need for a full day, and bring your camp gear.

The first stop is **Scotty's Castle,** a Spanish colonial-style mansion set in the rocky twists of the Grapevine Mountains. Take a self-guided tour of the well-watered and shady grounds, or book a guided tour of the interiors, with its fascinating architecture and period furnishings. This is popular spot, so make **tour reservations in advance** online, as it can get very busy on spring and holiday weekends.

Continue north to the **Eureka Dunes,** a drive of nearly 50 miles. It's a two-hour haul to the northernmost destination in the park, but it's well worth it to enjoy the isolated and pristine setting. The Eureka Dunes are the tallest dunes in Death Valley, rising from the Eureka Valley floor and framed by the Last Chance Range.

When you've had your fill, head back down to Scotty's Castle Road (a one-hour drive) and camp at **Mesquite Spring.** The sites at this quiet, pretty campground are dotted with its namesake trees sheltered along a wash. If you're not camping, Stovepipe Wells has the closest accommodations, but this will add an extra hour of driving.

Day 5

Today's destination is the Racetrack Valley. (If you've camped at Mesquite Spring, you're well positioned for this trip.) The long, gravel high-clearance Racetrack Road begins just beyond **Ubehebe Crater.** Make a quick pit stop at this colorful volcanic overlook before heading south

toward the Racetrack Valley. The destination for most people is the Racetrack, 26 miles in.

At 19 miles, the colorful **Teakettle Junction** signpost comes into view. Take a left turn at Teakettle Junction for a quick detour to the picturesque and weathered cabin of the **Lost Burro Mine** (at 3.2 miles, you will reach a four-way junction; park and walk along the right spur, which ends at the Lost Burro Mine in 1.1 miles).

Head back to Racetrack Valley Road and turn left to continue to **The Racetrack.** This dry lake bed, or playa, is famous for its moving rocks, which glide across the surface and leave mysterious trails. Soak in the surreal sight, then tackle the ambitious hike to **Ubehebe Peak.** The trail starts at **The Grandstand** parking area, then switchbacks up the side of the mountain with increasingly spectacular views of the Racetrack and the surrounding valley. Leave enough time for the hike back down and the long drive back out.

Spend another night camping at Mesquite Spring, or drive the 66 miles (1.5 hours) south to the **Panamint Springs Resort** on Highway 190. Tuck into a rustic cabin, motel room, or campsite and enjoy a relaxing dinner on the stone

Teakettle Junction points the way in the Racetrack Valley.

The Best in One Day

If you only have one day to spend, this driving tour of the park will help you experience some of the most iconic sights, stretch your legs, and even enjoy a back-road adventure. Fill your gas tank before entering the park, and be sure to have plenty of food and water on hand, as services are limited.

- Start the day at **Furnace Creek**, a tourism outpost since 1933. Orient yourself at the **Furnace Creek Visitors Center** (page 31), where you can pick up a park map and pay the entrance fee. Furnace Creek is also home to a few restaurants and a general store; this is a good place to fill up on breakfast or lunch before hitting the road.

- Drive south along Badwater Basin Road to **Badwater Basin** (page 37), a Death Valley classic. The lowest point in North America, these vast salt flats lie 282 feet below sea level and encapsulate the mesmerizing yet unforgiving landscape of Death Valley. Walk out onto the salt flats to look for delicate salt crystal formations.

- Head north, back to Highway 190, and continue past Furnace Creek to the **Mesquite Flat Sand Dunes** (page 74) near Stovepipe Wells. These sculpted, windswept dunes sit perched on a slope of the valley floor and are the most popular dunes in the park.

- Venture east along Daylight Pass Road to the ghost town of **Rhyolite** (page 76). Wander the ruins of this once-flourishing town whose crumbling banks burst with gold.

The impressive drive along Titus Canyon Road winds through red rock formations.

- Two miles east of Rhyolite, **Titus Canyon Road** (page 75) begins. The 27-mile one-way dirt road is one of the most popular backcountry routes in the park. It sweeps past rugged rock formations and a ghost town before the grand finale, the canyon narrows. The narrows tower overhead, barely allowing a car to squeeze through before they open wide to reveal the salty and barren Death Valley floor.

patio. Swap stories of your day's adventure with the other visitors at this friendly outpost on the western side of the park.

Day 6

Fill up on breakfast at Panamint Springs before heading out for a full day of exploring and hiking in the **Emigrant and Wildrose Canyons** on the western side of the Panamint Range. The first stop is the historic **Charcoal Kilns.** Once used to make charcoal for the mining efforts in

the area, they now stand as works of hand-engineered beauty.

The **Wildrose Peak** trail starts from the Charcoal Kilns parking area. This colorful forested trail leads through juniper trees to a big payoff at Wildrose Peak and its panoramic views.

Wind down with two final stops on your way back to Panamint Springs Resort. Located off Aguereberry Road, **Aguereberry Camp** provides a great perspective of a small mining camp and life in the desert. Enjoy the spectacular views from **Aguereberry Point** across Death Valley below.

You've definitely earned your relaxing dinner at Panamint Springs Resort after this day. If you're camping, **Wildrose Campground** is a great choice, tucked away in Wildrose Canyon.

Day 7

From Panamint Springs, it's about 50 miles west to **Lone Pine,** an outpost of civilization on U.S. 395 and your western exit from Death Valley. Spend a few hours exploring the town before driving south to **Los Angeles** (3 hours, 200 miles) or return to **Las Vegas** (5 hours, 300 miles) for your flight home.

Best Hikes

While there are few maintained trails in the park, old mining roads, narrow canyons, and natural features offer spectacular hiking opportunities.

Gower Gulch and Golden Canyon

Hike through glowing **Golden Canyon** (page 39) and past historic borax mining ruins to the spectacular views from **Zabriskie Point,** the stunning halfway point on this **6-mile round-trip** trek. Shorter destinations include equally striking **Red Cathedral.**

Hungry Bill's Ranch

Historic **Hungry Bill's Ranch** (page 44) was tied to one of the biggest silver rushes in the area. The **3.3-mile round-trip** hike is via **Johnson Canyon,** one of the most-watered canyons in Death Valley. Gorgeous canyon views and hand-built rock walls make this well worth the effort it takes to drive the rough, 4WD-only road to get here.

Ashford Canyon

Colorful **Ashford Canyon** leads to the tucked away and well-preserved **Ashford Mine Camp** (page 46). Gold mining caught on in the area in 1907; the Ashford Mine was worked until the 1940s, when it was finally abandoned, leaving behind cabins, underground rooms, and the trappings of camp life. The steep **4.2-mile round-trip** hike follows the canyon and pieces of the old mining road.

Mosaic Canyon

Mosaic Canyon (page 82) is a popular hiking destination. This **2.8-mile round-trip** trek through the canyons of the **Cottonwood Mountains** wanders through polished marble and colorful mosaic stone. The trailhead is just outside Stovepipe Wells.

Marble Canyon

The sculpted narrows of **Marble Canyon** (page 83) offer a cool respite from the valley's heat. The rough drive (high-clearance and 4WD) into the **Cottonwood Mountains** leads to this **3.2-mile round-trip** hike through two sets of twisting canyon narrows.

Ubehebe Peak

Unlike other Death Valley hikes, there is an actual trail to **Ubehebe Peak** (page 103); miners built it as a mule trail to haul out copper ore. A difficult **6-mile round-trip** climb rewards with sweeping views of **The Racetrack** and the **Saline Valley.**

Telescope Peak

At 11,331 feet, **Telescope Peak** (page 140) is the highest point in Death Valley. Covered in snow most of the year, this **13-mile round-trip** hike is strenuous but worth it. Plan your attempt in **May or June** for premium views.

Wildrose Peak

The steep hike to 9,064-foot **Wildrose Peak** (page 141) leads through conifer forests, offering some welcome shade for hiking. The limber and bristlecone pine-studded trail stretches **9-miles**

Ancient pines and views of Death Valley make Wildrose Peak worth the effort.

round-trip, but pays off with impressive views of Death Valley Canyon and Trail Canyon.

Surprise Canyon to Panamint City

The silver boom ghost town of **Panamint City** (page 138) can only be reached via a long, strenuous hike through the scenic and well-watered **Surprise Canyon** (page 137). This **10-mile round-trip** hike is best done as a backpacking trip: plan one day to hike in, a day to explore, and a day to hike out.

Hidden Springs and Desert Oases

The most surprising feature in Death Valley may be the presence of wetlands. These rare environments support distinct fish populations and provide life-giving watering holes for plants, animals, and humans.

Salt Creek

Salt Creek supports its own species of **pupfish** in the delicate riparian environment. A short walk along the wooden **wheelchair-accessible trail** (page 74) and the incongruous sight of a rushing creek in the tortured expanse of the valley floor give this place a lot of bang for the easy effort to get here.

Johnson Canyon

The energetic creek here has literally shaped **Johnson Canyon** (page 44), carving out the sheer walls that tower above. Stroll along the creek's edge or hike the steep ridge of the canyon to look down on this powerful thicket.

Hanaupah Canyon

A short hike leads to a charming creek and the historic site of **Shorty Borden**'s camp (page 43),

Mining Camps and Ghost Towns

From small Western towns that refused to die to forgotten mining camps, these destinations tell Death Valley's history, geology, and human experience.

- **Ashford Mine Camp** (page 47): Gold mining caught on in Ashford Canyon in 1907, and the Ashford Mine was worked until the 1940s. The well-preserved Ashford Mine Camp is home to abandoned cabins and the remnants of camp life.

- **Ballarat** (page 127): Sole resident Rocky Novak runs the general store, keeping Ballarat from ghost-town status. The town had its heyday between 1897 and 1905; original adobe structures and wood cabins remain.

- **Gold Point** (page 113): Gold Point was a mining camp in the 1860s. The abandoned property was bought and rehabilitated in the early 1980s, resulting in a Wild West gem.

- **Inyo Mine Camp** (page 33): Inyo Mine is a bona fide ghost town, with a boarding house, cookhouse, several cabins, and mine works.

- **Lost Burro Mine** (page 100): Hidden in a corner of the Racetrack Valley, the Lost Burro Mine's camp and hand-painted sign are especially picturesque.

- **Panamint City** (page 138): The silver-boom ghost town of Panamint City is scenic and well preserved, with cabins, a mill, and artifacts for days.

- **Randsburg** (page 152): What started as a gold mining camp in 1895 has evolved into a humble tourism destination with a saloon, a main street, a church, and cabins scattered over the hills.

The Lost Burro Mine was discovered by a prospector rounding up his burros.

- **Rhyolite** (page 76): At its peak, Rhyolite was home to 3,500-5,000 people; by 1920, only 14 remained. Today you can walk the main road past crumbling two-story bank ruins, a red-light district, a cemetery, and mine remains.

- **Saratoga Mines** (page 53): A peaceful walk along the Ibex Hills follows a former mining road that served several groups of talc mines in the hillsides.

a friendly prospector who made a name in Death Valley history. The creek is fed by snow from the Panamint Mountains, and the hike is scenically framed by views of Telescope Peak.

Warm Springs Camp

Nestled within **Warm Spring Canyon**, a luxurious spring was the site of the **Warm Springs Camp** (page 39), a mining camp established in the 1930s by Louise Grantham. Wandering amid the abandoned buildings, you'll come across the last thing you might expect—a swimming pool (now drained) which was fed from the spring's source behind the camp.

Hundreds of miles of unmaintained 4WD roads in the park that provide access to remote destinations. **Farabee's Jeep Rentals** in Furnace Creek rents 4WD vehicles and has up-to-date backcountry road information. Check the visitors centers and ranger stations to confirm current road conditions, which can change from one day to the next.

· **Cottonwood Canyon Road** (page 73): This 19-mile primitive road travels deep into the Cottonwood Mountains. The road starts off spitting through semi-deep sand, eventually becoming more solid (washboard and gravel) then much rougher as it enters Cottonwood Canyon wash.

· **Echo Canyon to Inyo Mine** (page 33): The 19-mile (round-trip) drive is popular for its scenic, winding canyon and ghost camp ruins. Access starts from Highway 190, east of Badwater Road, and requires a high-clearance vehicle for the 3 miles to the canyon mouth and 4WD beyond to the mining camp.

· **Pleasant Canyon to Rogers Pass** (page 124): This rugged road requires a 4WD vehicle through Pleasant Canyon. You will be driving directly in the creek en route to backcountry cabins and historic mining camps in the Western Panamint Mountains.

· **Racetrack Valley Road** (page 95): High-clearance vehicles can make the long, white-knuckle drive 26 rocky miles into the Racetrack Valley, but 4WD may be necessary at times.

· **Saline Valley Road** (page 123): This rough

an innovative gold mill in Warm Spring Canyon

yet graded dirt road travels 78 lonely miles from Highway 190 to Big Pine Death Valley Road. Although a high-clearance vehicle is suitable during good weather, 4WD may be necessary at times to access the remote Saline Valley.

· **Warm Spring Canyon to Butte Valley** (page 33): The lower canyon is easily accessible, following a good graded road the first 11 miles to Warm Springs Camp. The upper canyon is harder to reach and requires 4WD into Butte Valley.

Ash Meadows National Wildlife Refuge

This magical swatch of open desert in the **Amargosa Valley** (page 60) contains crystal-blue pools of warm water, its own fish population, and the **Devil's Hole,** a deep window into an ancient aquifer system.

Amargosa River

The elusive **Amargosa River** surfaces in only two places during its 185-mile length. It makes one of its rare appearances at the **China Ranch Date Farm** (page 64), near **Tecopa,** creating valuable habitat for migratory birds and other animals.

Saratoga Spring

These **springs** (page 53), hidden away in the **park's southeast corner,** quietly mirror the desert sky. Surrounded by reeds and desert

The Saratoga Spring feeds these shining ponds in a remote corner of Death Valley.

grasses, they provided water for mining camps in the area and formed the backbone of a short-lived but enterprising water-bottling plant.

Cottonwood Canyon

The luxuriant springs of **Cottonwood Canyon** (page 73) are the crowning set of wonders along an action-packed 4WD trail. The first spring begins just beyond the end of the road as an energetic desert stream. Two more springs beyond give rise to the canyon's signature cottonwood trees and a shady oasis, a miracle of desert life that's surprising in this rugged canyon.

McElvoy Canyon

The spur road to **McElvoy Canyon** (page 135) is a faint track off the dusty Saline Valley Road that has you trudging over a hot alluvial fan until you hit the clear luscious creek. Following it to the canyon mouth will take you to a grotto waterfall, cool with hanging ferns. A second waterfall lies beyond if you're up for a short rock climb.

Furnace Creek and the Amargosa Range

The Amargosa Range rides the eastern boundary of Death Valley National Park, from the California-Nevada border south to the Amargosa River in the southeastern corner of the park.

The Grapevine, Funeral, and Black Mountains roll down into alluvial fans as the valley trends north in a wash of salt-crusted desert floor the length of the park. At its most extreme, the valley sinks below sea level, generating hot winds that lick at the mountain slopes. Shimmering heat and the unrelenting blue sky inspire wonder at the resourcefulness of the indigenous people who called this area home. How did pioneers cross this expanse with their lives intact?

The park hub of Furnace Creek provides a good introduction for first-time visitors and includes many of the park's highlights: Zabriskie Point, Badwater Basin, and Artist's Drive. Wander among alien salt formations, red canyons, pioneer camps, or muted mineral tones with the mountains as canvas.

Like the chaotic geography that makes Death Valley famous, this area bucks easy categorization. Heading away from the magnetic pull of the valley's center reveals pristine sand dunes, bubbling oases, and forgotten mines.

PLANNING YOUR TIME

Furnace Creek is the park hub, an outpost of comfort and civilization with a visitors center, accommodations, campgrounds, restaurants, and even gas. This is the only area of the park where you will regularly encounter crowds, but even here, solitude is easy to achieve.

The two main, paved roads in the park—**Highway 190** and the **Badwater Basin Road**—intersect at Furnace Creek. A drive here is a pretty straightforward experience if you plan to stay on paved roads and see the popular destinations within an easy day-trip from Furnace Creek. Most visitors concentrate their time on the sights along **Badwater Road,** touring the highlights in an afternoon; adding a hike can turn the trip into a full day.

Set aside **two days** to travel the length of the road, visit all the sights, and complete several hikes. Exploring some of the more rugged hikes and drives accessed from the graded, dirt West Side Road can add an additional

Previous: Johnson Canyon; talc mine headframe near Saratoga Spring. **Above:** a slot canyon in the Amargosa River Natural Area.

Look for ★ to find recommended
sights and activities.

Highlights

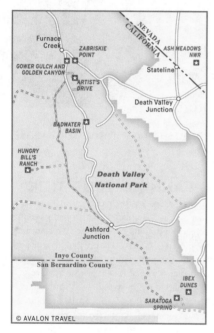

© AVALON TRAVEL

★ **Zabriskie Point:** A popular stop for photographers and visitors, this iconic Death Valley view overlooks eroded badlands from a central vantage point. The colors kindle at sunrise and sunset, revealing the magnificent desolation of the valley (page 35).

★ **Artist's Drive:** Named for its shifting palette of colors, this gentle drive rises along an alluvial fan fed by the Black Mountains, proffering a chaotic jumble of hues from oxidized metals (page 37).

★ **Badwater Basin:** The lowest point in North America at 282 feet below sea level, these vast salt flats encapsulate the mesmerizing yet unforgiving landscape of Death Valley (page 37).

★ **Gower Gulch and Golden Canyon via Zabriskie Point:** The eroded hills of the badlands, glowing Golden Canyon, and historic borax mining ruins are the highlights of this rewarding hike (page 39).

★ **Hungry Bill's Ranch:** If you have a high-clearance 4WD vehicle, this canyon is worth braving every boulder and washout in the remote and wild Panamint Mountains (page 44).

★ **Ibex Dunes:** The Ibex Dunes are secluded, pristine sand scapes. Admire the dunes from a distance against the sharp backdrop of the Saddle Peak Hills or hike one mile to their steep slopes (page 52).

★ **Saratoga Spring:** These beautiful ponds, tucked away in the often overlooked southeastern section of the park, are a rare sight in Death Valley (page 53).

★ **Ash Meadows National Wildlife Refuge:** Fossil water, melted from the last ice age, supplies this largest remaining oasis in the Mojave Desert, home to nearly 30 endemic plant and animal species (page 60).

Furnace Creek and the Amargosa Range

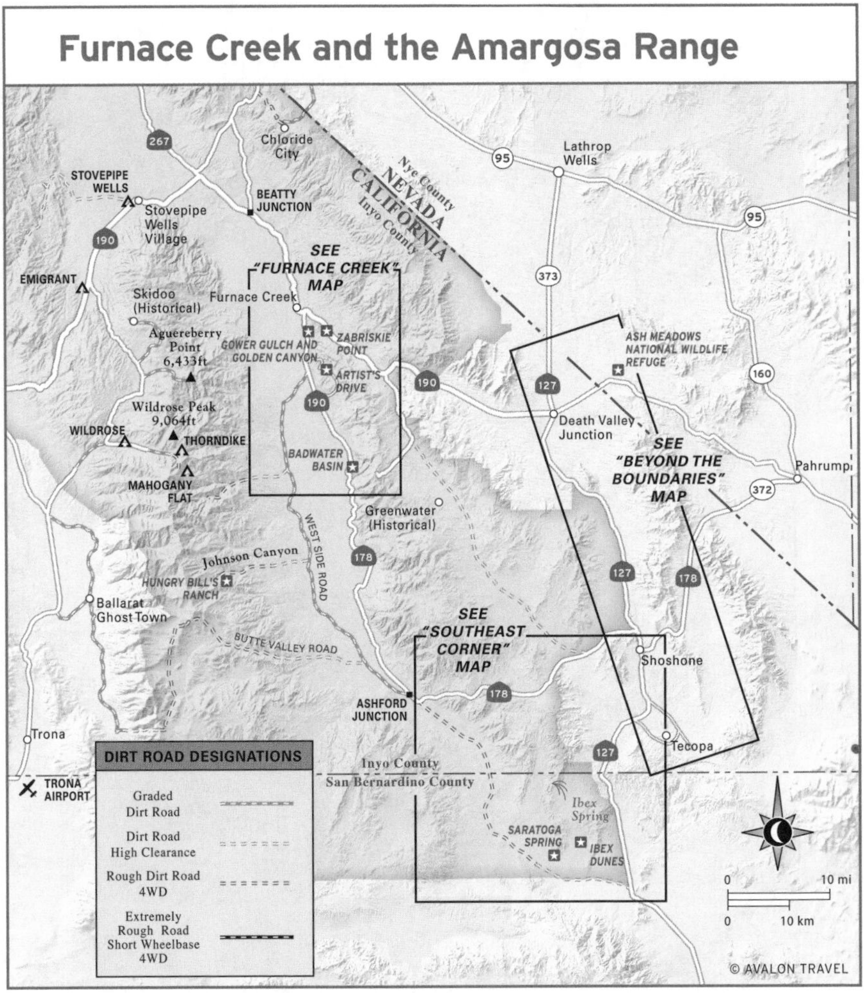

day or two. To visit the southeastern section of the park with its cluster of natural and historic sights, allow an extra day.

When to Go

Furnace Creek Village lies 190 feet below sea level, making it an inferno in summer with temperatures soaring to well over 100°F and dropping by as much as 40 degrees at night. The heat and wind of the valley floor are omnipresent. Certain times of the day and year are lovely, but prepare for extreme fluctuations in temperature and oppressive heat from **mid-May to the beginning of October.** Most services remain open in summer, but the Furnace Creek Inn closes for the season, and business hours may fluctuate in off-season. Hiking is strongly discouraged at lower elevations during summer.

Spring is the peak season to visit—daytime temperatures are pleasantly warm and nighttime temperatures are moderate. Seasonal businesses are open, and there may even be wildflowers during wetter years. **Fall**

Furnace Creek

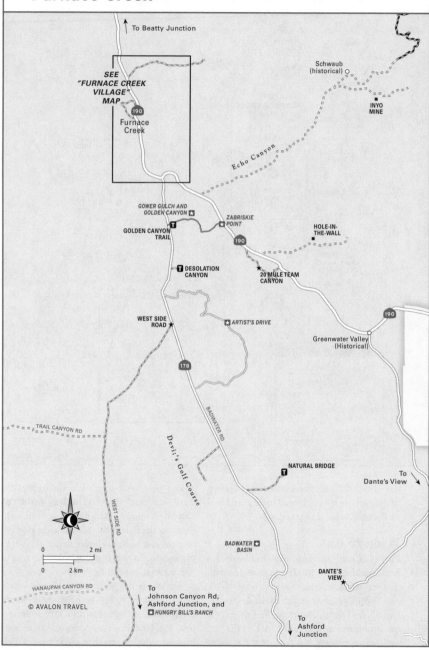

To Beatty Junction

SEE "FURNACE CREEK VILLAGE" MAP

190 Furnace Creek

Schwaub (historical)

INYO MINE

Echo Canyon

GOWER GULCH AND GOLDEN CANYON

ZABRISKIE POINT

GOLDEN CANYON TRAIL

190

HOLE-IN-THE-WALL

DESOLATION CANYON

20 MULE TEAM CANYON

WEST SIDE ROAD

ARTIST'S DRIVE

190

Greenwater Valley (Historical)

178

BADWATER RD

TRAIL CANYON RD

Devil's Golf Course

NATURAL BRIDGE

To Dante's View

0   2 mi

0   2 km

WEST SIDE RD

BADWATER BASIN

DANTE'S VIEW

HANAUPAH CANYON RD

© AVALON TRAVEL

To Johnson Canyon Rd, Ashford Junction, and HUNGRY BILL'S RANCH

To Ashford Junction

Where Can I Find...?

Furnace Creek provides several basic visitor services. For more information, call 760/786-2345.

- **ATMs:** Located at Furnace Creek Ranch.

- **Cell phone reception:** The village of Furnace Creek, including the Furnace Creek Ranch and Inn, has the only cell reception in the park. Wi-Fi is available to all registered hotel guests and to others for a fee.

- **Gas and auto repair:** The gas station at Furnace Creek Ranch performs basic auto repairs. For major repairs or towing, services will come from Beatty or Pahrump, Nevada.

- **Gift shops:** Furnace Creek Inn and Furnace Creek Ranch (760/786-2381).

- **Laundromat:** Furnace Creek Ranch (daily).

- **Post Office:** Furnace Creek Ranch (760/786-2223, 10am-5:30pm Mon.-Fri.).

- **Showers:** Furnace Creek Ranch (day pass $5).

- **Supplies:** Furnace Creek Ranch General Store (760/786-2381, 7am-10pm daily) sells basic camp supplies.

has equally lovely temperatures and is generally less crowded. **Winter** can be a great time to visit the lower elevations around Furnace Creek. There are fewer crowds, and skies are often clear. However, some park roads may be closed due to snow.

Exploring the Park

The Amargosa Range owes its creation to the Northern Death Valley Fault Zone, but despite its tumultuous formation, this is the most visited and accessible area of the park. The Grapevine, Funeral, and Black Mountains roll down into alluvial fans, and the popular Badwater Basin Road will take you past the famous sights: the haunting and eroded Zabriskie Point badlands, stifling and strange Badwater Basin, and the colorful mineral palette of Artist's Drive.

The village of Furnace Creek offers lodging, dining, gas, souvenirs, supplies, a post office, restrooms, a park museum, the Borax Museum, and a golf course. Visitors casually gather around outdoor seating, gas fire rings, and a saloon porch with the smell of fresh barbecue wafting over the scene, depending on the season and time of day.

VISITORS CENTER

The **Furnace Creek Visitors Center** (Hwy. 190, 760/786-3200, www.nps.gov/deva, 9am-5pm daily Oct.-mid-June, 9am-6pm daily mid-June-Oct.) is located within the Western-themed village of Furnace Creek and provides information on park sights, activities, and programs, as well as camping and hiking. Interpretive displays offer an overview of the park's natural and cultural history. Park passes, permits, and information are available here. Park passes are also available from a cash or card kiosk outside the Visitors Center as well as at strategic locations in the park.

The **Death Valley Natural History Association** (http://dvnha.org) maintains an outlet filled with books on the natural and cultural history of the park. Take a few minutes to stroll through the Visitors Center's museum exhibits, which take a fresh and

Driving Distances

From Furnace Creek to:	Distance	Duration
Stovepipe Wells	25 mi	30 min
Scotty's Castle	54 mi	1 hr 10 min
Panamint Springs	55 mi	1 hr
The Racetrack	83 mi	3-4 hr
Eureka Dunes	97 mi	3 hr
Southeast Corner	80 mi	2 hr
Death Valley Junction	30 mi	30 min
Shoshone	56 mi	1 hr
Tecopa	68 mi	1 hr 10 min
Olancha	102 mi	2 hr
Baker	112 mi	2 hr

engaging approach to give background on the area's cultural and natural history and phenomena. Restrooms are available outside the Visitors Center, and water is available to refill reusable water bottles.

PARK ENTRANCES

Highway 190 leads to the park hub at Furnace Creek; it is the most popular and efficient way to access the park's most-visited sights. The road is fully paved, and if you are visiting for the first time, the Visitors Center can be a source of helpful information.

Highway 190 can be accessed from the **east** via **Death Valley Junction** and Highway 127, a distance of approximately 30 miles (30 minutes). Furnace Creek can also be accessed from the **west** via Highway 190, which connects with U.S. 395 at the town of **Olancha** (100 miles, 1 hour and 45 minutes).

Aside from Furnace Creek, there are no other entrance stations; however, there is an automated **kiosk** on Highway 190 across from Dante's View Road. The kiosk accepts cash and major credit cards. Visitor guides with basic park maps and information are available for free.

Gas and Services

While Furnace Creek is conveniently located and a good place to explore this popular region of the park, the food, supplies, and accommodations here can be pricey. Plan ahead to stock up on gas and other supplies at larger towns outside the park.

Gas and limited supplies are available in **Shoshone,** 57 miles southeast of Furnace Creek at the junction of Highways 190 and 178. Outside the park boundaries, gas and supplies are available 56 miles farther south in the town of **Baker,** at the junction of I-15 and State Route 127.

DRIVING TOUR

Many visitors treat a visit to Death Valley as a car-only tour, an approach that makes sense during summer due to the extreme heat. But during spring, fall, and winter, you can experience the nuance of the desert and enjoy your own little piece of it by hiking some of the canyons or taking one of the many lightly traveled roads.

Dirt roads vary in their accessibility. Some roads require only high clearance and may be passable with a passenger car, while others require a serious 4WD vehicle. Several of the dirt roads in this area, including the **West Side Road** and the **Greenwater Valley Road,** are graded and easily passable with a passenger car. A 4WD vehicle opens up your possibilities for canyon or other more remote exploration.

West Side Road

West Side Road visits the rugged canyons of

the Panamint Range; experience the orchards of **Hungry Bill's Ranch** or the bubbling oases of **Hanaupah Canyon**. There are plenty of backcountry campsites and hikes where you can enjoy the intense quiet of the desert and the translucent glow of the night sky from the salt-crusted valley floor.

The West Side Road is a graded dirt road; high clearance is recommended due to washboards and pockets of soft dirt. There are two access points: from the junction of Highway 190 and Badwater Road, the northern access is 6 miles south; the southern access is 39.2 miles farther south. West Side Road runs for 37 miles and takes about **one hour to drive,** depending on road conditions. Note that the West Side Road may be closed in summer due to extreme heat.

Southeastern Corner

Located at the southern end of the Amargosa Range, the southeastern corner yields scenic springs, ghost mines, and pristine dunes. **Ibex Spring Camp** and **Saratoga Spring** offer a rare look into desert wetlands and the endemic plant and animal species.

From Furnace Creek, take Highway 190 east for 30 miles to Death Valley Junction and Highway 127. Continue south on Highway 127 for 44 miles to the Ibex Spring Road; plan **1 hour and 45 minutes** for the drive. Another option is to access Highway 127 via the Badwater Road and Highway 178, a drive of about 2.5 hours.

Scenic Four-Wheel Drives
ECHO CANYON TO
INYO MINE CAMP

The Echo Canyon drive (19 miles round-trip) is popular for its scenic and winding canyon, stone arch, and ghost camp ruins. **Echo Canyon** starts from Highway 190, at an inconspicuously signed junction 2.5 miles east of Badwater Road. For the first couple of miles, as the road crawls toward the canyon mouth, it may be passable with a high-clearance vehicle or even a passenger car. Once the road approaches the mouth of the

canyon, things change—from here to the mining camp, a high-clearance 4WD vehicle is required.

After entering the canyon mouth, the road winds through canyon narrows, reaching the **Eye of the Needle**, a sharp stone arch that juts into the canyon, at 4.8 miles. The canyon broadens into a valley that may be filled with flowers in springtime. Another 4.3 miles past Eye of the Needle (9.1 miles into the drive), a signed junction marks a small triangular intersection. Continue right toward the **Inyo Mine Camp.** The road leads to a small parking area below the mine. There are enough buildings here to elevate the site beyond the level of camp to a bona fide ghost town with a boarding house, cookhouse, several cabins, and, of course, the mine works.

WARM SPRING CANYON
TO BUTTE VALLEY

This scenic drive leads through Warm Spring Canyon to Butte Valley (44.6 miles round-trip). The drive begins on Warm Springs Canyon Road, accessed from the West Side Road 2.9 miles from its southern end or 33 miles from its northern entrance. A good graded road leads 11 miles to **Warm Springs Camp.** While lower Warm Spring Canyon is easily accessible, the upper canyon is harder to reach, requiring a 4WD vehicle to access remote springs, secluded cabins, and the lovely geology of **Butte Valley.**

From Warm Springs Camp, the road spurs to the northwest at 4.4 miles (15.4 miles into the drive) to **Arrastre Spring** and the **Gold Hill** area; little remains from its brief time as a gold mining location. Arrastre Spring was named for the stone *arrastres* (now obscured by willows) used to grind gold. It is most famous as the spot where some historians think the infamous Bennett-Arcane party spoke the words "Good-bye, death valley" as they escaped their near-death ordeal.

The road continues as Butte Valley Road. The road condition worsens, but the scenery improves as the road drops into Butte Valley at 17.8 miles. The impressive **Striped**

Butte, an unmistakable geologic feature for which this area was named, is straight ahead. Access to Striped Butte is via a northwest road into **Redlands Canyon** at 20.3 miles. Continuing on Butte Valley Road will take you to **Anvil Spring Junction** at 22.3 miles (look for an unsigned but obvious junction). From here, a right turn leads to Anvil Spring and the well-known **Geologist's Cabin.** A left turn leads to **Willow Spring.** Straight on, the road continues to **Russel's Camp,** Mengel Pass, and Goler Wash. Historic interest groups, the public, and the National Park Service maintain **cabins** in the area. They are available to camp in on a first-come basis; treat them

with respect and leave them in a better condition than you found them. (Also, be aware of the threat of hantavirus that exists in any old building.)

To complete the drive, turn around in Butte Valley and head back out the way you came in. From Anvil Spring Junction, it is a 22.3-mile drive to return to the West Side Road. **Allow at least three hours** for the drive back. (It is sometimes possible to continue via Mengel Pass into Goler Wash and the western side of the Panamint Mountains, but this is one of the worst and most dangerous drives in the park. The road is often impassable and should not be attempted if you are not an experienced 4WD driver.)

Sights

FURNACE CREEK VILLAGE

With its Wild West theme and visitor-friendly amenities, the village of **Furnace Creek** (Hwy. 190) could fool you into thinking it has never been anything more than that. In reality, the site of Furnace Creek Ranch has some serious park cred when it comes to history.

Located at the mouth of Furnace Creek, the site was a working ranch from the 1870s on, growing alfalfa, dates, produce, and later livestock for distribution to nearby mining camps. More importantly, it provided relief from the relentless sun and loneliness of travelers and prospectors making their way against the merciless salt and sky, seeking riches but more often just scraping a living. Even after Furnace Creek became a homestead and ranch, it remained a meeting point for three different Native American groups: the Shoshone from the north, the Southern Paiute from east of the valley, and the Kawaiisu from southern Death and Panamint Valleys. Currently, the Timbisha Shoshone Band of California has a community here.

The Pacific Coast Borax Company took a big role in steering the historical course of the

ranch when it took over sometime after 1889. The ranch served as terminus for the famous 20-mule team runs, distributing borax from major mines in the region. In the 1920s the company added tourism to their repertoire in Death Valley. They commissioned the building of the elegant Furnace Creek Inn, which opened to visitors in 1927. Furnace Creek Ranch opened as a tourist destination in 1933.

Today the village of Furnace Creek refers to both the inn and the ranch, located one mile apart. **Furnace Creek Ranch** is home to a cabin and motel complex as well as restaurants, a general store, saloon, post office, golf course, the **Borax Museum,** horse stables, a **gas station,** park headquarters, and a **visitors center.** The **Furnace Creek Inn** is terraced into a hillside near the ranch, with its own restaurant and hotel amenities. **Jeep rentals** are available across from the inn.

BORAX MUSEUM

The **Borax Museum** (760/786-2345, www.furnacecreekresort.com, 9am-9pm daily, donation), located at Furnace Creek between the restaurants and golf course, is housed in a building that has a reputation for being

Furnace Creek Village

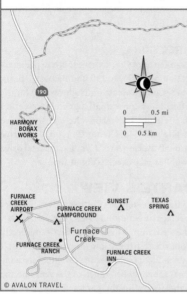

190

HARMONY
BORAX
WORKS

0   0.5 mi
0   0.5 km

FURNACE
CREEK
AIRPORT   FURNACE CREEK
                 CAMPGROUND
                                SUNSET   TEXAS
                                                SPRING

                 Furnace
                 Creek
FURNACE CREEK
RANCH
                            FURNACE CREEK
                            INN

© AVALON TRAVEL

west. It was here that mostly Chinese laborers lived in tent communities, harvesting borate, which they raked into mounded "haystacks" for processing. Mercifully, the temperatures were too hot in Furnace Creek for the operations to continue in summer.

It is possible to see the faint eroded remains of some of the **borax haystacks** on a 1.5-mile walk across the salt pan. From the parking area, drive the graded road as it begins to veer right into Mustard Canyon. Park here and walk 1.5 miles westward across exposed open desert, passing strange salt formations and eventually hitting the rows of haystacks, which run north and south. The salt flats form a shallow seasonal lake, making this walk impossible at times. Even when it is passable, mud can make the passage difficult, and footprints can remain for years. Do not walk through the haystacks; instead, enjoy them from a safe distance. Do not attempt this in summer due to the extreme heat or after a rain.

the oldest house in Death Valley. Built in 1883, it was once the assay office for the Monte Blanco Mine in what is now the 20-Mule Team Canyon. It was moved to Furnace Creek, where it packs in exhibits on Native Americans in Death Valley as well as mining history and the history of borax, the "white gold" of the valley. The outdoor exhibits include a 60-ton oil-burning locomotive that hauled borate, which gives some idea of the brute force it took to tackle mining in the harsh environment.

HARMONY BORAX WORKS

Just one mile north of Furnace Creek, a short paved path leads to the site of the **Harmony Borax Works.** A 20-mule team wagon, the remains of a borax refinery, and interpretive signs tell the textbook history of the site as a base of operations for borax mining and processing from 1883 to 1888. The deeper history may well be in the harsh, exposed salt flats that extend in a white glare north and

★ ZABRISKIE POINT

Iconic **Zabriskie Point** overlooks otherworldly and eroded badlands from a vantage point just off Highway 190, seven miles south of Furnace Creek. A popular stop for photographers and other visitors, the colors kindle at sunrise and sunset, capturing the magnificent desolation of the valley.

Manly Beacon, a rock outcropping to the north, commemorates William L. Manly, who, along with John Rogers, guided a group of 49ers, migrant pioneers headed to the California gold fields, out of danger during an 1849 crossing of Death Valley. The site was once ancient Lake Manly, and the hills began eroding into the shape seen today by the formation of the Black Mountains to the west. The darker ridgelines are formed by lava.

This is a beautiful and haunting place to soak it all in, and an excellent hiking destination (or starting point) for hikes through **Golden Canyon** and **Gower Gulch** to experience the splendid desolation on a closer scale.

20-MULE TEAM CANYON

A short, graded dirt road leads three miles through a mudstone canyon past badlands and the site of historic mining prospects at **20-Mule Team Canyon.** The road is not accessible to vehicles over 25 feet long and the route is prone to washouts, so check to make sure it's open before you make the trip.

At 1.8 miles, **20-Mule Team Canyon Road** veers to the right, but if you look to the left, you will see the site of the **Monte Blanco assay office,** a large wooden house built in 1883 to serve miners. (The building was moved and now houses the Borax Museum at Furnace Creek Ranch.) The area was never extensively mined, but old adits (tunnels) are visible.

Although the name of the canyon evokes the big wagon teams from tales of the Wild West, the Monte Blanco mining district was never fully developed and might not have seen the big wagon teams. Instead, look toward the gold-and-white hills to understand what all the fuss was about. The white striations are borate ore. Although not as romantic as gold, borax was Death Valley's bread and butter.

It's never a good idea to climb into mining tunnels. If you are itching to do some exploring, there are more tunnels as well as other borax-mine remains a short hike into the canyon, starting at the site of the old assay office.

DIRECTIONS

From Furnace Creek, drive south to the intersection of Highway 190 and Badwater Basin Road. Continue east on Highway 190 for 4.7 miles. Look for a small signed intersection on the right indicating the one-way drive through 20-Mule Team Canyon. The drive through the canyon is 2.7 miles; the total drive from Furnace Creek is about 16 miles.

DANTE'S VIEW

As the name suggests, **Dante's View** provides spectacular panoramic views of Death Valley. The Panamint Mountains rise dramatically from the stiflingly low Badwater Basin salt flats at 282 feet below sea level to Telescope Peak, snow-capped much of the year and the highest point in the park at 11,331 feet. On a clear day you can see Mount Whitney, the highest point in the contiguous 48 states in the same view. The Owlshead Mountains to the south, the Funeral Mountains to the north, and the Greenwater Mountains to the east make this a good place to get your bearings

Impressive equipment at the Borax Museum shows what it took to mine in remote locations.

and be dazzled at the same time. Visit at sunrise to see the whole valley suffused with morning light. Some people bring telescopes out at night for unparalleled **stargazing**.

DIRECTIONS

From Furnace Creek, drive south to the intersection of Highway 190 and Badwater Basin Road. Follow Highway 190 east for 10.7 miles, then turn right onto Furnace Creek Wash Road. At 7.5 miles, continue onto Dante's View Road. Drive 5.5 miles to the parking area and overlook. The total drive from Furnace Creek is about 24 miles.

★ ARTIST'S DRIVE

Named for the shifting palette of colors, gentle **Artist's Drive** rises along an alluvial fan fed by the Black Mountains. The colors, caused by the oxidizing of different metals on the volcanic rock, proffer a chaotic jumble of hues, including green, rose, yellow, purple, and red. The **scenic, paved nine-mile loop** is a one-way road starting on Badwater Road, five miles south of Furnace Creek. There are plenty of places to pull over for the many pictures you will want to take.

As with many good things in Death Valley, they get even better once you step out of your car. It's possible to explore **one short, colorful canyon** 3.5 miles in, at the second dip in the road. There is a small turnout at the top of the rise on the right side where you can park. Hike up the wash at the bottom of the dip about 50 yards, where a pink fall marks the entrance to the canyon. Look for mud drippings and slickensides (rocks polished smooth by movement along a fault) and enjoy the scramble over several boulder jams. If you haven't given up before this, the last stretch of the canyon is a vertical narrows that ends at a 20-foot fall.

Artist's Palette

A popular stop is the **Artist's Palette,** a scenic viewpoint 4.5 miles into the drive. The low hills right next to a small parking area show heavy signs of use from visitors walking out

onto them. This doesn't actually give you a better view of the hills, and it also damages the fragile hillsides. If you want to be part of the landscape, you can instead hike out into one of the two washes leading from the hills. The farthest wash eventually leads to an ocher canyon ending after about 0.6 mile at a high fall.

DEVIL'S GOLF COURSE

You'll want to put your camera on the macro setting to capture the controlled chaos of the **Devil's Golf Course** (Badwater Rd., 11 miles south of Furnace Creek). Located on the northern end of the eerie, stark salt flats of Badwater Basin, Devil's Golf Course is filled with spiky salt crystals that you have to see close up to appreciate. Groundwater seeps up to the surface, prompting the jagged pinnacles.

It's extremely difficult to walk out here. Take the graded dirt road to a small parking lot, where you can see the formations at closer range. If you step out into them, place your feet carefully between the pinnacles. A few awkward steps into the frenetic landscape will reveal tiny salt crystals, sprouting wildly in the barbed ground.

★ BADWATER BASIN

Badwater Basin (Badwater Rd., 16 miles south of Furnace Creek) is a Death Valley classic. If you're going to visit one place in Death Valley, this is it. The lowest point in North America at 282 feet below sea level, these vast salt flats encapsulate the mesmerizing yet unforgiving landscape of Death Valley. Walk out onto the salt flats to feel the sea of air and look for delicate salt-crystal formations. The blinding glare, emanating heat, and scale of humans next to the surrounding Black Mountains puts our existence into perspective and gives us a sense of the earth's extremes.

WEST SIDE ROAD

This **graded gravel road** runs along the west side of Badwater Basin, skirting the foot of the Panamint Range and offering a unique perspective of the Death Valley floor from the more heavily traveled Badwater Road to the east. West Side Road crosses the **Devil's Golf Course** to head south, skirting the shimmering oven of the Badwater salt pan. It is generally used as an access road to the rugged and scenic canyons on the eastern side of the Panamint Mountains. Rugged roads that demand high-clearance and 4WD vehicles cross the alluvial fans to a series of deep and scenic canyons with hidden streams, mining ruins, and beautiful canyon walls.

Unlike the valley floor from Badwater Basin Road, the West Side Road parallels a wide swath of vegetation supported by the four main springs: **Tule Spring, Shorty's Well, Eagle Borax Spring,** and Bennett's Well, at the **Bennett-Arcane Long Camp.** The mesquite trees and other tenacious vegetation have adapted to the saline environment and offset the white austerity of the salt playa and mountain backdrop.

DIRECTIONS
The **West Side Road** starts on Badwater Road, opposite the Artist's Drive loop, and continues south for 37 miles, ending just before the ruins of Ashford Mill. The road has a few rough patches, and a **high-clearance**

vehicle is generally recommended. At times the road may be passable in a passenger car, but conditions change, especially after rain, when the water creates mud and washouts. The road may close during summer due to extreme heat. Check at the visitors center or online for road conditions.

To reach the northern entrance from Furnace Creek, drive six miles south on Badwater Road and turn right at the signed junction.

Eagle Borax Works
The **Eagle Borax Spring** (12.6 miles) is the site of the Eagle Borax Works and its historic remains are worth a quick stop. The area includes the **Bennett-Arcane Long Camp** (15.6 miles), where a famous group of 49ers, migrant pioneers headed to the California gold fields in 1849, set up a desperate camp after nearly dying on an ill-fated shortcut through Death Valley. Members of the party who went to seek supplies on foot eventually returned to rescue them. Upon leaving, one of the members of the party was said to have turned for a last look at their narrow escape and said, "Good-bye, death valley," even though only one of the party actually died. Understandably, the name stuck.

fields of salt spires at the Devil's Golf Course

Warm Spring Canyon

It seems like it should be much more difficult to visit the wealth of talc mining ruins and the aptly named **Warm Springs,** flowing freely out of the cliff above the abandoned Warm Springs Camp. The lower canyon is easily accessible via Warm Spring Canyon Road (access is from West Side Road, 2.9 miles from its southern end or 33 miles from its northern end).

Warm Spring Canyon Road is a well-maintained graded road suitable for any **high-clearance vehicle** (and possibly passenger vehicles, depending on road conditions). Along the 11 miles to Warm Springs Camp, the road passes many mining claims; those on the north side are older and more historic.

WARM SPRINGS CAMP

Dating from the 1880s, miners used the region around the spring as a camp. In the early 1930s, Louise Grantham established **Warm Springs Camp** to serve her mines. Grantham was one of the most famous and financially successful women miners in Death Valley. She moved here from Ohio at age 25 and began staking claims in Warm Spring Canyon in the early 1900s. Her camp was a step above many of the rough subsistence camps elsewhere and included her private residence, a mess hall, a shop, a dormitory, and several houses. There were also showers and flush toilets. A swimming pool was added later, fed with the water that tumbles from the spring in the cliffs behind the camp.

Driving up to the site today, it looks like it could still be inhabited. Bright yellow buildings poke out behind tamarisks and the overgrowth from the spring. This is a fun place to explore; the spring, the camp, and the mine works are easily visible in the surrounding hills. Between the camp and the road, **Gold Hill Mill** is a historic gold processing plant, with a stone *arrastre* (used for grinding gold-bearing rocks into dust) and myriad wheels and pulleys. In the hills on the north side of the road, the **Pink Elephant Mine** inspires the imagination with its psychedelic moniker and the aerial tramway visible from the camp.

Recreation

HIKING
Golden Canyon to Red Cathedral

Distance: 2.5 miles round-trip
Duration: 1 hour
Elevation gain: 530 feet
Effort: Easy
Access: Passenger vehicles
Trailhead: Badwater Basin Road at the Golden Canyon turnoff, 2 miles south of the Badwater Road junction. Take the signed, graded dirt road on the east (left) side of the road to the parking area. Follow the marked trail sign to Golden Canyon (see map p. 41).

This canyon has gentle grades that lead to sheer stone red walls with majestic creases, earning its name. The mouth of the canyon begins along a gravel wash through short narrows with sedimentary and volcanic rocks on the passage walls. The hike can be crowded, but it clears up a bit the farther into the canyon you go. Numbered markers along the way indicate interpretive sights, and a pamphlet is available at the Visitors Center or at the trailhead. When the canyon opens up it is to a gold corridor of badlands, both bright and desolate. The trail ends at a fork about 1 mile in; to reach the **Red Cathedral,** continue hiking another 0.25 mile.

★ Gower Gulch and Golden Canyon via Zabriskie Point

Distance: 6 miles round-trip
Duration: 4-5 hours
Elevation gain: 875 feet
Effort: Moderate
Access: Passenger vehicles

Furnace Creek Hikes

a rock outcropping along Hanaupah Canyon Road

Trail	Effort	Distance	Duration
Natural Bridge	Easy	0.7-1.4 mi rt	30 min-1 hr
Hanaupah Canyon	Easy	2 mi rt	1 hr
Golden Canyon to Red Cathedral	Easy	2.5 mi rt	1 hr
Desolation Canyon	Easy	3.6 mi rt	1.5 hr
Gower Gulch and Golden Canyon via Zabriskie Point	Moderate	6 mi rt	4-5 hr
Hungry Bill's Ranch	Difficult	3.3 mi rt	2-3 hr
Ashford Canyon	Difficult	4.2 mi rt	3-4 hr

Trailhead: Badwater Basin Road at the Golden Canyon turnoff, 2 miles south of the Badwater Road junction. Take the signed, graded dirt road on the east (left) side of the road to the parking area. Follow the marked trail sign to Golden Canyon (see map p. 41). This hike is a Death Valley classic that leads through eroded badlands, old mining claims, shifting canyon scenery, and the spectacular views from Zabriskie Point. The loop starts in Golden Canyon, visits Zabriskie Point, and returns via Gower Gulch, south of Golden Canyon. The trail is very popular and can be crowded near the trailhead and along the first mile.

Begin the hike on the interpretive trail in Golden Canyon. Pamphlets, available at the trailhead, draw your attention to the canyon's geologic features. The **Golden Canyon Trail** leads up a gravel wash for about 1 mile toward the huge **Red Cathedral** formation. Look for the signed junction for Red Cathedral or **Zabriskie Point.**

Golden Canyon

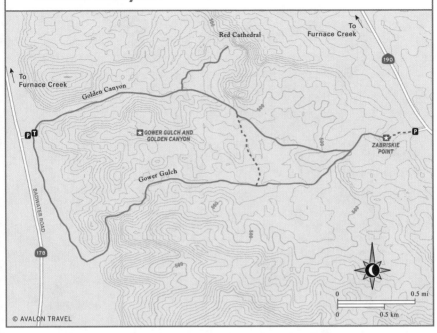

© AVALON TRAVEL

The trail to Zabriskie Point continues up Golden Canyon for another 1.7 miles. Just before 2 miles, the trail comes to a junction in the wash, which is sometimes marked with a sign. For Zabriskie Point, turn left and head east up to reach Zabriskie Point in about 0.8 mile. (Reaching Zabriskie Point might be a proud moment—or you might wonder why you didn't just drive here, as visitors roll up to the famous vista for some photo ops.)

To return from Zabriskie Point via Gower Gulch, retrace your steps for about 0.4 mile to a signed intersection to Golden Canyon or Gower Gulch. Head left into **Gower Gulch** and follow the wash for 2.7 miles back to the parking area. As the canyon walls narrow, look for colorful mineral deposits. You'll also pass some old **borax mines;** signs warn to stay away for fear of being crushed or poisoned. One you emerge from the gulch (5.2 miles into the hike), you're on the home stretch back to the Golden Canyon trailhead.

Another 0.8 mile west across exposed desert will bring you back to the trailhead.

Desolation Canyon

Distance: 3.6 miles round-trip
Duration: 1.5 hours
Elevation gain: 755 feet
Effort: Easy
Access: Passenger vehicles
Trailhead: Desolation Canyon Road is an unmarked 0.5-mile graded road off Badwater Road, 3.7 miles south of Highway 190 (south of Golden Canyon and before Artist's Drive). The road leads to a small parking lot and the start of the trail (see map p. 42).

This is a colorful and less-crowded alternative to Golden Canyon. Desolation Canyon shares the sedimentary rocks of the Artists Formation and the volcanic minerals that gave this area its splashes of muted color. It is also clearly a child of the Black Mountains, with its eroded badlands, also found in Golden Canyon and Gower Gulch slightly north.

Desolation Canyon

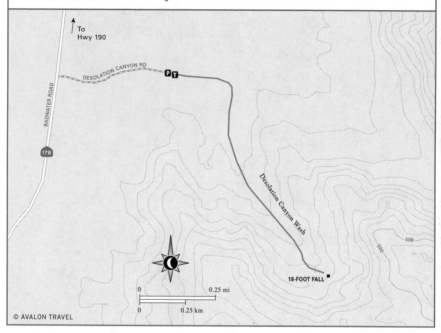

The result is a pleasant walk though colorful mud hills. Note that these hills are very fragile; stay in the canyon wash and do not walk on the hills.

From the parking area, head east toward the wide canyon to enter **Desolation Canyon** wash. The trail follows the mostly hard-packed wash through narrows and badlands. The trail **forks** at 1.2 and 1.5 miles; stay right to remain in the main canyon. The trail continues over a few polished **falls** that you will need to scramble over, and then effectively ends at an **18-foot fall** in about 1.8 miles.

Natural Bridge

Distance: 0.7-1.4 miles round-trip
Duration: 30-45 minutes
Elevation gain: 180-470 feet
Effort: Easy
Access: Passenger vehicles
Trailhead: Badwater Road, 13.1 miles south of

Highway 190. Take the signed and graded dirt road east for 1.8 miles to a small parking lot (see map p. 43).
Natural Bridge is one of the few natural bridges in the park, and it's definitely the biggest. This easy hike is popular, so be prepared to share it. Just 0.7 mile in from the trailhead, **Natural Bridge** spans a red-wall canyon that contrasts with the bright sky above. Look back toward Badwater Basin to see Telescope Peak in the distance.

Most people turn around at the bridge, but the canyon continues another 0.7 mile. Shortly past the arch, check out the polished conglomerate **falls** on the right and look for mud formations that resemble candle drippings high up on the canyon walls. There are two places where you will have to scramble up a few small rock falls, but nothing that is a hike-stopper. The trail effectively ends at a vertical **15-foot fall** another 0.7 mile in. Turn around and retrace your steps to the trailhead.

Natural Bridge

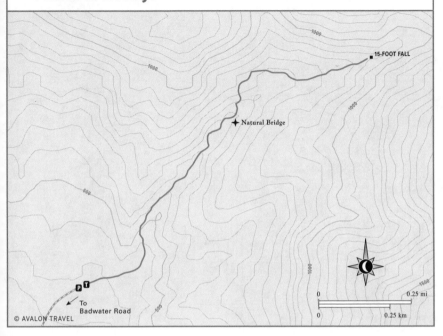

15-FOOT FALL

Natural Bridge

P T

To
Badwater Road

© AVALON TRAVEL

0   0.25 mi

0   0.25 km

Hanaupah Canyon

Distance: 2 miles round-trip
Duration: 1 hour
Elevation gain: 640 feet
Effort: Easy
Access: High-clearance/4WD
Trailhead: From Badwater Basin Road, drive south 10.7 miles on the West Side Road to the signed Hanaupah Canyon Road and turn west. The rough ends in about 8 miles, just short of Hanaupah Spring. A clearly marked trail with a trail marker begins at the end of the road (see map p. 44).

This short, pleasant hike through lower Hanaupah Canyon leads to Shorty Borden's camp and a pretty bubbling creek. From the end of **Hanaupah Canyon Road**, the trailhead is signed with a marker. Head west into the scenic canyon, which starts with deep red walls and eventually opens up. The trail is well defined and easy to follow along a rocky wash for the first mile, but avoid hiking directly in the rocky wash, if you can. You will come to

Shorty Borden's camp and mine in about 1 mile. There's not a whole lot left of the camp, which once had a cabin and a shower house. A picturesque wood-framed mine tunnel that doubled as a workroom sits perched up a steep side trail on the south side of the canyon.

Just past the camp, the stream surfaces, fed by **Hanaupah Spring** as well as rain and snow from the Panamint Mountains. In some years it's an energetic creek with plenty of water; at other times it's a small and charming stream. Here the canyon widens and splits. Stay to the left and enjoy the creek. At this point, I would call it time well spent and return the way you came.

However, this trail does continue, and if you're really lucky, you'll see the creek at full volume. Vegetation is very thick, but it's easy to bypass this section by using the **old mining road** on the north side of the camp at 1 mile. The road swings around a hill and then drops back down to the creek. When it does

Hanaupah Canyon

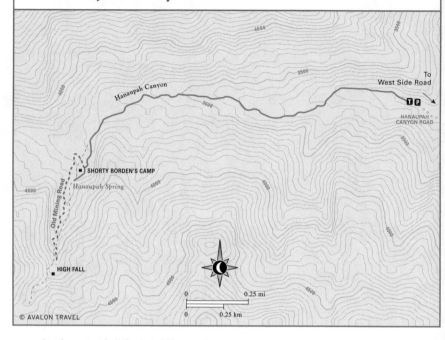

go creek-side again, it's difficult to follow, and you may end up fighting your way through more vegetation. The trail is unmarked and difficult to follow for the rest of the hike. If the creek is running full force, you will have nice views of the narrows at points. If not, it's vegetation city with the occasional teasing sound of running water. The trail finally comes out with a view of a high fall at about 1.5 miles. In some years, water will be streaming out of a hole in the cliff; you may also just be looking at an impressive rock wall with watermarks. Don't say I didn't warn you.

★ Hungry Bill's Ranch
Distance: 3.3 miles round-trip
Duration: 2-3 hours
Elevation gain: 1,514 feet
Effort: Difficult
Access: High-clearance/4WD
Trailhead: From Badwater Basin Road, take West Side Road south for 21.7 miles. Turn west onto the

marked Johnson Canyon Road and drive 10 rough miles west to the road's end at Wilson Spring. The well-worn trail starts from the end of the road and heads into the canyon (see map p. 45).

This is a hike that just keeps giving. One of the most well-watered canyons in Death Valley, gorgeous canyon views, mysteriously constructed stone walls, a historic ranch tied to one of the biggest silver rushes in the area, and the site of a Native American village make this well worth the effort.

Getting here is half the fun, with the proper vehicle. **High clearance** is definitely necessary and **4WD** is required starting at mile 5. Johnson Canyon Road is rough, with rocky washouts that will rattle you across the alluvial fan as you climb toward the canyon mouth. Just past the midway point, around the 5-mile mark, look for a picturesque rock wall and rusted car with a lovely desert patina. The trail begins at the end of the road, just before Wilson Spring, which you can spot

Hungry Bill's Ranch

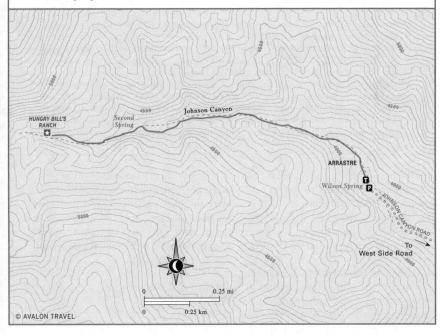

from its small cluster of Willow trees. Park and leave the road clear.

In 1873 a frenzied silver strike occurred just over the Panamint Mountains from Johnson Canyon. To capitalize on the rush, William Johnson, for whom the canyon is named, built a ranch over the mountain pass to feed unruly groups of fortune seekers on their way to Panamint City. The Shoshone people were already living seasonally in the canyon, but Johnson set up camp anyway, creating terraced, irrigated gardens for beans, squash, melons, and corn along with fruit and nut orchards. When a flood nearly wiped out Panamint City, the rush was over and Johnson moved on, leaving trees that hadn't even had a chance to bear fruit. Hungry Bill, a Shoshone man known for his insatiable appetite, took over the ranch with his family and cultivated vegetables and apple, pear, fig, and walnut trees. The site was an ancestral Shoshone village,

so it makes sense that he would establish his ranch here.

The hike to Hungry Bill's Ranch doesn't look long on a map, but the intense elevation gain necessary to bypass the springs and creeks throughout the hike makes it fairly strenuous. **Wilson Spring** lies just beyond the road's end, marked by telltale willows. The other springs at 1.2 and 2.1 miles (past Hungry Bill's Ranch) are unnamed. Note that almost all of the elevation gain on the hike to Hungry Bills occurs over the course of approximately 1.7 miles.

The trail starts out well-defined at the end of the **Johnson Canyon Road** and leads up-canyon, following the stream formed by the intermittent springs; the stream disappears underground at points. Look for an old stone *arrastre* on the left side of the trail in about 0.1 mile. To the untrained eye, this may look like a stone fire pit, but it was actually a simple mill used to pulverize precious ores (like gold)

46

FURNACE CREEK
RECREATION

Shorty Borden

Shorty Borden went far in Death Valley history on the strength of his personality, earning his reputation by being friendly and hospitable. A U.S. Cavalry soldier during World War I, Borden came to Death Valley in the 1920s to prospect. He thought he had found rich silver-lead outcroppings in **Hanaupah Canyon** and set about developing it, singlehandedly digging out the present nine-mile road from the valley floor to his camp with only a pick, a crowbar, a shovel, a little dynamite, and a burro (which might also tell you a little about the road). Apparently this wasn't enough, so he also dug out the well off the **West Side Road** that is now named after him. Shorty did all of this at the age of 66. After the park began attracting visitors in the 1930s, he got by again on his natural friendliness, sharing his meager diet of coffee and beans in exchange for better provisions with any unsuspecting visitor who, against all odds, stumbled on his place.

in order to extract the metals. There are two more *arrastres* on the same side of the creek in another 0.5 mile and 1 mile, but they are not as well preserved and are harder to spot.

About 0.3 mile into the hike, the canyon walls begin to narrow and rise dramatically as the first surface water starts to appear. A **bubbling creek** with small pools causes the canyon wash to become too choked with vegetation to continue as a main route. Stay on the south side of the creek and follow the trail as it climbs steeply to bypass the creek from the top of the canyon walls. Pay attention to follow the trail and find the path of least resistance. The elevation gain is especially tough over the next mile, but it offers beautiful views of the canyon walls. Look down to see **stone walls,** which are part of the charm and historical significance of the canyon. No one knows who made the walls or exactly what they were for, but they're beautifully constructed and it's intriguing to see them snake along the steep canyon sides.

At 1.2 miles, the canyon makes a sharp turn around the **second spring;** cross the creek twice in succession. **Hungry Bill's Ranch** will be evident by its green cleared fields and stone walls. The area farther up canyon with a larger field was thought to be the site of Johnson's ranch. For most people this is an excellent place to end the hike and retrace your steps.

For a **backcountry campsite,** look at the midway point along Johnson Canyon Road,

near the rusted car; it's sheltered and clear that others have used it. In spring, wildflowers will make this little corner extra special. There are other good spots for backcountry camping near the road's end and Wilson Spring. Though this is a popular spot, there's a good chance you will have the place to yourself.

Ashford Canyon

Distance: 4.2 miles
Duration: 3-4 hours
Elevation gain: more than 1,000 feet
Effort: Difficult
Access: High-clearance/4WD preferable, but not necessary
Trailhead: Access the trail via an unmarked dirt road across from Ashford Mill. The road requires a high-clearance vehicle and has a few rough patches. The trailhead begins at the end of the parking lot (see map p. 47).

This is a beautiful, colorful canyon hike with a well-preserved and well-hidden mining camp at the end. The hike follows relics of the old mining road up to Ashford Mine camp, steadily gaining elevation.

The trail starts at a wilderness marker at the end of a small parking area and follows the first canyon's wash for about 0.3 mile until an **old mining road** becomes visible on the left (north); look for a flat place running along the hill. If you pass the mining road, don't worry. This first canyon is lovely, ending at a **high fall** with rock-climbing possibilities. Just backtrack and look again for the old mining

Ashford Canyon

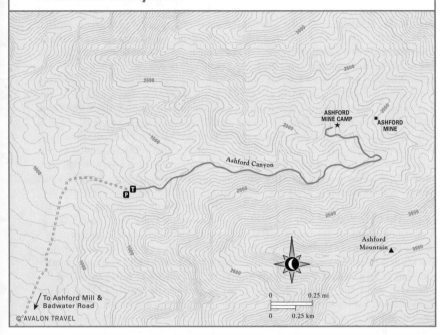

© AVALON TRAVEL

road. Once you've found it, you'll see pieces of the old pavement poking through. Follow the old mining road for about 0.3 mile until it drops back into the main canyon again.

As you hike, look for intersecting side canyons. The **first side canyon** intersects at about 1.2 miles. After the **second side canyon**, at 1.6 miles, look for signs of the old road on your left heading up into the hills to the **Ashford Mine Camp.** The road appears at about 1.8 miles. From here it's only another 0.3 mile to the camp. Follow the old road as it leads up and over the canyon wall, and you will soon be looking down at the camp.

The Ashford Mine Camp is a strangely moving sight, perched in its forgotten ring of hills exposed to the wind and relentless sun. Continue to follow the old road to explore the old cabins and dugouts, partially furnished, telling of life in a lonely mining camp.

BIKING

Mountain bike rentals are available through the **Furnace Creek Ranch General Store**

(760/786-3371, www.furnacecreekresort.com, 7am-10pm daily). The bike rental shop offers mountain bikes with hourly ($15), half-day ($34), and full-day ($49) rates (rates for children's bikes are $5 per hour). Pick-up and drop off is at the Furnace Creek Service Station 7am-4:30pm; late drop-offs can be arranged through the General Store. There are a few easy routes within riding distance of Furnace Creek.

More difficult rides include the hilly nine-mile paved loop of **Artist's Drive** (9 miles one-way) and the exposed gravel loop of the **West Side Road** (up to 40 miles) running along the valley floor.

Furnace Creek Bicycle Path

Starting from the Furnace Creek Visitors Center, the easy **Furnace Creek Bicycle Path** goes along a flat, paved bicycle route for one mile to the historic site of the Harmony Borax Works. It continues along open desert, past white-crusted borax mining fields, and then takes a short and scenic 1.5-mile detour through Mustard Canyon's gravel road. The total distance from Furnace Creek is 3.5 miles.

20-Mule Team Canyon

The short, graded road through **20-Mule Team Canyon** takes you 2.7 miles on a one-way loop through a mudstone canyon past badlands and the site of historic mining prospects. The loop begins about five miles south of Furnace Creek on Highway 190 and exits back onto Highway 190 about eight miles south of Furnace Creek. Complete the loop in about 5.5 miles. From Furnace Creek, the total distance is about 16 miles.

Hole-in-the-Wall Road

A moderate route includes the gravel **Hole-in-the-Wall Road** (3.6 miles one-way). This low-key gravel road cuts through a 400-foot rock wall and is a pleasant detour for drives, bike rides, and hikes. The road begins 1.9 miles south of Zabriskie Point on Highway 190. Watch for a small road sign and a gravel road to the left.

The route heads east through a broad wash with colorful mud hills that pop up occasionally. You'll pass through Hole-in-the-Wall at about 3.6 miles out and you might notice, like other people have, that it's really more of a big gap. Past here the gravel gets deeper and the road gets more difficult until it ends completely at about six miles. A good goal is to make it to Hole-in-the-Wall.

Glancing at a map of the area, you might see a place-name for the enticing-sounding Red Amphitheater a few miles past Hole-in-the-Wall. There is little consensus as to what this actually refers to. If you're feeling ambitious and want to continue up the road, do so, but not with visions of a grand stone formation awaiting you.

Trail Canyon

As a bike route, the main selling points of **Trail Canyon** (5.6 miles one-way) are its low level of use, opportunities for canyon exploration, and picturesque mining ruins. Trail Canyon is accessed via a signed canyon off the West Side Road, 5.3 miles south of Badwater Road. The road is a fairly difficult mountain biking route. It crosses a rocky alluvial fan for about 4.4 miles, steadily climbing uphill into the canyon.

From the canyon mouth, the road drops into a wash and becomes rougher. The destination for most people is the **Broken Pick Mill Site.** A short access road on the left leads to the ruins, about 0.3 mile past the confluence (approximately 5.6 miles in). It is a scenic camp with ruins dating from many different mining eras. The road effectively ends just past the mill site spur.

If you're still up for exploring, hike into the wilderness area along the old road. (Bicycles are not allowed in wilderness areas or on hiking trails.) The wash is wide and steep here, but hiking 1.5 miles will bring you to another group of mines in the main canyon and two side canyons to the west. In addition to mining ruins, the area also has a rich fossil record, which can be seen in some of the side canyons feeding into the main canyon.

Greenwater Valley Road

A lightly traveled road that traverses a large swath of Death Valley, **Greenwater Valley Road** (34.2 miles one-way) is a quiet route across a wide and gentle valley. The road is well graded, and on a bicycle you will notice it runs slightly uphill.

The road begins 7.5 miles south of Highway 190 from a junction with Dante's View Road. It runs straight for 34.2 miles southeast to end at the cheerful town of **Shoshone.** (On some maps and at road entrances, Greenwater Valley Road is marked as Furnace Creek Wash Road.) A few people use the road as a quiet backcountry entrance to the park. Still fewer people use Greenwater Valley Road to connect to a network of 4WD-only roads leading to remote backcountry mining sites and springs.

Beyond this, it is a pleasant ride and overall experience, although with few specific sights to recommend it. However, this is an area of great archaeological significance for the numerous Native American sites that date back thousands of years. Somewhere out there are pictographs, petroglyphs, stone circles, rock walls, and more.

CLIMBING

There is no shortage of rocks in Death Valley, but for some reason it is not as common to see rock climbers as it is in, say, Joshua Tree National Park. Don't let this stop you if rock climbing is your thing. There are hundreds of canyons with dry falls as well as excellent bouldering sites. The Furnace Creek area has a few, although there are more challenging rock climbing opportunities in other areas of the park.

Although it's a remote location, one potential bouldering site is far out on **Warm Spring Canyon Road.** As the road nears the pass into Butte Valley, large granitic boulders dot a field.

Funeral Mountains

Slit Canyon is accessed from Hole-in-the-Wall Road in the southern Funeral Mountains. Hike from the end of Hole-in-the-Wall Road for 1.2 miles northeast across the alluvial fan to where a long, low, yellow-and-tan mudstone hill meets the Funeral Mountains. Slit Canyon has three polished gray dolomite falls within the first two miles of the canyon, not to mention the tall recessed cavern for which the canyon is named.

Black Mountains

Ashford Canyon, on the western side of the Black Mountains, offers a canyon with a steep-walled narrows and four falls. Ashford Canyon can be reached via an unmarked turnoff across from the Ashford Mill on the southern end of Badwater Basin Road. A rough dirt road takes you to a small parking area that ends at the wilderness area.

GOLF

If vacation means golf to you, you're in luck. The **Furnace Creek Golf Course** (Hwy. 190, 760/786-2345, www.furnacecreekresort.com, 6am-6pm daily, greens fees $30-74) claims to be the lowest-elevation golf course in the world. At 214 feet below sea level, it's hard to dispute. This 18-hole golf course doesn't let you forget that it's on an oasis; it's lined with palm and tamarisk trees and dotted with water. Temperatures soar in summer, but the resort takes a tongue-in-cheek approach, hosting the Heatstroke tournament every June.

The Southeast Corner

The lightly visited Southeast Corner of Death Valley makes an excellent **weekend trip.** Sand dunes, mining camps, and lovely springs show off the diversity of Death Valley without the need to brave more formidable expanses. Stay in nearby **Shoshone** or backcountry camp.

The Southeast Corner is located in the southern end of the Black Mountains and remains somewhat disconnected from the Furnace Creek region, since no major park road allows access. To access the Southeastern Corner from Furnace Creek, take Highway 190 east for 30 miles to Highway 127. Take Highway 127 south for 43 miles to the unsigned **Ibex Spring Road** (which requires a high-clearance or 4WD vehicle); Ibex Spring Road connects to the Ibex Spring region. The **Harry Wade Exit Route** (marked with a historical marker) provides access to Saratoga Spring and the Ibex Dunes from Highway 127. It is also possible to drive the Harry Wade Road 25.6 miles south from its intersection with the Badwater Road to the junction with the Saratoga Spring Road. This junction gives access to Saratoga Spring and Ibex Dunes. The Harry Wade Road is an infrequently traveled dirt road that is usually passable with a

The Southeast Corner

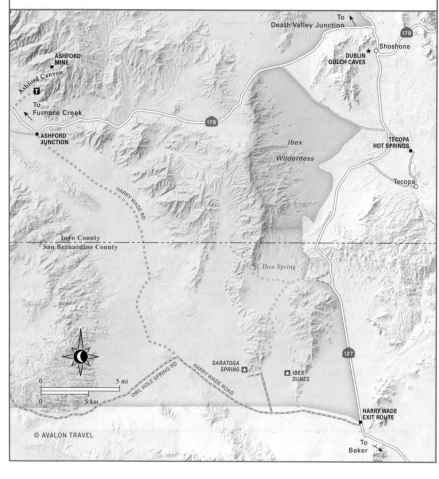

high-clearance vehicle. At times, a 4WD vehicle may be necessary, especially in spring when the Amargosa River may cover portions of the road.

IBEX SPRING

What the **Ibex Spring** mining camp lacks in rip-roaring history—there were no saloon shoot-outs or land swindles—it makes up for in buildings that are still around for us to check out. In the 1940s, when the camp was built, wild speculation had largely been

replaced by a more prosaic approach—mine steadily for what's there instead of the fabled ores that brought prospectors out in droves in the gold rush of 1849. Mining companies in this area went for talc instead of gold (even though "talc fever" doesn't really have the same ring).

The Saratoga Hills, Ibex Dunes, and Black Mountains serve as a backdrop as you make your way across barren desert on the old **Ibex Spring Road** toward the Ibex Spring mining camp. The road has deep washes, but

Ibex Spring

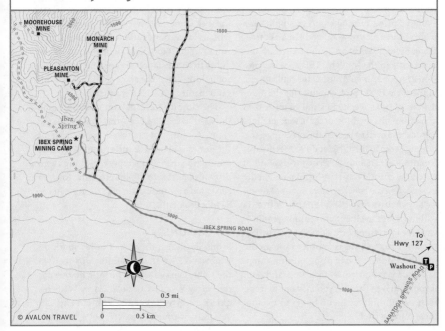

also surviving bits of pavement making for a schizophrenic road condition. It's a decent dirt road, suitable for **high-clearance** vehicles; however, some washes at the start may make a **4WD** vehicle desirable. At 3.2 miles from the highway, there is a major washout, and a 4WD vehicle is necessary to navigate this. Without a high-clearance or 4WD vehicle, this is a good place to park and walk the rest of the way to the site. With the right vehicle, it is possible to drive all the way to the camp.

DIRECTIONS

From Furnace Creek, head east on Highway 190 to the intersection with Highway 127 at Death Valley Junction. From Death Valley Junction, head south 27 miles to the town of Shoshone. From Shoshone, drive south on Highway 127 for 16.3 miles to an unmarked dirt road on the right (west). This is the Ibex Spring Road. The road requires a

high-clearance vehicle and can be sandy or rough at points, but a city SUV should be fine. When the road forks at 2.1 miles, follow the right fork toward the low Ibex Hills in the distance. Park just before the major washout at 3.2 miles.

Hiking

Distance: 5 miles round-trip; 6.2 miles with a side trip to Monarch-Pleasanton Mine

Duration: 2.5-3 hours

Elevation gain: 400 feet

Effort: Moderate

Access: High-clearance vehicle and a short hike, or a 4WD road

Trailhead: Ibex Spring Road washout, 3.2 miles from Hwy. 127

This pleasant walk along the old road gets more interesting as the Ibex Spring mining camp comes into sight. From the washout, follow the well-defined mining road across open desert toward the mining camp, faintly visible tucked against the Saddle Peak Hills. The mining camp comes into clearer view within 2.5 miles.

Ibex Spring mining camp was built on a natural oasis. Cottonwood and tamarisk trees shade a lonely **cabin** and palm trees flash unexpectedly in the sunlight. This area was previously mined for gold during the Bullfrog era, in the early 1900s; look carefully for the foundations of two stone houses and an unmarked grave from this era. Most of the newer buildings were cabins used to house miners during a talc mining boom in the 1930s and 1940s; remnants from this era include a **springhouse** full of water, the chaotic crisscrossing of pipes on the ground, and the concrete-floor shower house.

The **Monarch-Pleasanton Mine** is within view of the Ibex Spring mining camp—its white talc tailings are a dead giveaway. The **Moorehouse Mine** is another mile up the road beyond the Ibex Spring mining camp. The road is rougher past the camp, and even if you've driven this far, you may opt to walk. Plan on 30 minutes to 1.5 hours to explore these mining sites.

★ IBEX DUNES

The **Ibex Dunes** are marked by seclusion and pristine sand-scapes set against the austere cragginess of the Saddle Peak Hills. Although easily accessible, they are very lightly visited due to their remote location. Combine a trip to the Ibex Dunes with a trip to Saratoga Spring, with its lovely ponds and well preserved mine ruins, for an enjoyable day trip. Admiring the dunes from a distance is rewarding, but there's something about the sight of all that smooth sand that inspires us to climb them.

The closest access is about 1.5 miles along the road where there is a tiny pullout on the right. A cross-country walk to the base of the dunes is about **1.2 miles one-way.** The dunes are steep and slippery, making them difficult but fun to climb. From the top you can catch a glimpse of an old talc mine in the Saddle Peak Hills.

DIRECTIONS

From Shoshone, drive 26.2 miles south on Highway 127 to an unassuming dirt road on the right, marked with a historic marker for the Harry Wade Exit Route. Harry Wade requires a **high-clearance vehicle** and can be sandy or rough in places, but a city SUV should be fine. In 5.8 miles, turn right onto Saratoga Spring Road and continue another 2.7 miles to a junction. A left turn leads to Saratoga Spring; turn north (straight right)

a cabin with palm trees at Ibex Spring

toward the Ibex Dunes. Stop within 1 to 1.5 miles, within sight of the dunes.

★ SARATOGA SPRING

Any spring in Death Valley is cause for excitement. While most springs are marked only by a small overgrowth of vegetation, **Saratoga Spring** is a marvelous sight, with a cluster of shining ponds and swishing cane. If you travel to this tucked-away corner in the extreme southeastern end of Death Valley, you have a good chance of having this rare spring to yourself.

From the parking area, a well-marked **trail** (a former mining road) leads past the ponds while providing beautiful views. Tread lightly and be careful not to trample on any of the vegetation around the ponds. Reflecting the desert sky, they are the last thing you might expect to see in the Black Mountains and on this austere valley floor. The trail will quickly take you past the Saratoga Spring in about 0.5 mile. Even this area saw some enterprise; one entrepreneurial man bottled the water, starting the Saratoga Water Company as well as a small resort for a time.

DIRECTIONS

From Furnace Creek, follow Highway 190 east for 30 miles to its junction with Highway 127 at Death Valley Junction. Take Highway 127 south for 27 miles to the town of Shoshone. Continue south on Highway 127 for another 26.2 miles. Turn right (west) on an unassuming dirt road marked with a historic marker for the Harry Wade Exit Route. The road requires a **high-clearance vehicle** and can be sandy or rough in places. In 5.8 miles, turn right onto the Saratoga Spring Road and continue north for 2.7 miles to a junction. The left (west) fork ends at a small parking area for Saratoga Spring.

Hiking

Distance: 2.2 miles round-trip to the first group of mines (south group); 3.4 miles round-trip to second group of mines
Duration: 1.5-2.5 hours

Elevation gain: 270 feet
Effort: Moderate
Access: High-clearance vehicle
Trailhead: The trailhead is clearly marked at the end of the parking area with a sign forbidding vehicles. It is actually the continuance of the mining road, which now serves as the trail.

The shining ponds of Saratoga Spring, peaceful walks along the Ibex Hills, and historic talc mines make this a lovely place to explore. A trail follows what used to be the mining road that served several groups of talc mines. As it winds along the base of the hills, you will see the Saratoga Mines nestled here, a cluster of talc mining sites with well-preserved and picturesque ruins.

Historically, there was a lot of wishful thinking in this area. The first wave of mining exploration began in 1902 when hundreds of people and agencies made a frenzied dash to mine nitrates. Saratoga Spring was pretty inaccessible, however, and niter, used primarily in agriculture, was already cheap. The scheme would never pay off.

A second wave in 1907 had people clinging to tales of gold. The theory was that gold would have washed down to the valley floor through erosion (disregarding the fact that gold traveling downhill breaks up and disperses). Ordinary talc, easily accessible in the Ibex Hills, was eventually settled on, and several mines sprang up in the area.

From the trailhead, look for the faint mining road on the east side of the spring and follow it north past Saratoga Spring. The road passes two **stone buildings,** remains from an earlier mining era (probably gold mining). In 0.9 mile is a faint junction, with a road leading east to the **first group** of mines, picturesque ruins with a tin shack and wooden chute visible from the main trail.

The **second group** of mines await 0.3 mile farther along the main trail. They include a well-preserved headframe, beautifully weathered and standing tall against the backdrop of the hills. The road continues north to the Whitecap (1 mile) and Superior (2.2 miles) Mines. The Pongo Mine requires an additional hike of 0.5 mile along the road, then 2.1 miles east to the mine site; however, with the exception of the Whitecap Mine, the ruins beyond the second group are minimal.

For an easy and rewarding **half-day** hike, visit Saratoga Spring and then hike to the second mine group (3.4 miles round-trip). A visit to the Pongo Mine extends this to about nine miles round-trip—a short full-day hike.

Accommodations

FURNACE CREEK RANCH

The **Furnace Creek Ranch** (Hwy. 190, 760/786-2345, reservations 800/236-7916, www.furnacecreekresort.com, $215-270) was originally built to be the less-formal lodging counterpart to the Furnace Creek Inn, and that tradition continues. From a midday stroll around the grounds, it's evident that some guests never leave the comfortable vicinity of the pool and air-conditioned rooms. There's something wildly luxurious about lounging in the perfect temperature water under the blazing sun and sharp desert mountains in the background.

Casual and family-friendly accommodations are set in a sprawling wood complex of cabins, two-story standard rooms, and deluxe motel-style rooms. **Deluxe rooms** are housed in single-story buildings and usually include two queen beds; private patios feature French doors overlooking a manicured lawn dotted with palm trees leading to the pool. The **wood cabins** are single-story duplexes that give a nod to Furnace Creek's historic status. The cabins, located near the reception area, include either two double beds or one queen. **Standard rooms** are located in four two-story buildings and have two queens (rollaway beds are permitted). All rooms feature French doors with small patios or balconies affording views of the surrounding desert and mountains.

All rooms feature air-conditioning, hair dryers, in-room coffee makers, a mini fridge, TV, and telephones. Standard and Deluxe rooms include full private baths, while cabins include a private bath with a shower but no tub. Restaurants and other amenities are just a few steps away.

INN AT FURNACE CREEK

Death Valley is known for its contrasts, and the **Inn at Furnace Creek** (Hwy. 190, 760/786-2345, reservations 800/236-7916, www.furnacecreekresort.com, mid-Oct.-mid-May, $400-450) provides the ultimate contrast to the austerity of the valley floor with its well-watered grounds and luxury accommodations.

The Pacific Coast Borax Company opened the Inn in 1927. Driving in on Highway 190, you'll see the red tile roofs, palm trees, and classic stucco sculpted into the hillside and set against a backdrop of the Funeral Mountains. Albert C. Martin, a prominent Los Angeles architect, designed the mission-style hotel; its archways and tower are inspired by the Spanish missions on the California coast. Daniel Hull, the landscape architect, created verdant grounds that complement the stark and rocky hillside.

The Inn offers a variety of rooms, as well as one pool bungalow. **Standard rooms** include either a king bed or a double with a twin and have a private bath. Rooms may be located in the main building or on the terrace above the pool and feature views of the gardens, desert, or mountains.

Deluxe rooms are slightly bigger than standard rooms and feature either a king bed or a double with a twin and have a full bath. Most standard rooms connect to a deluxe king room, and all include views. **Luxury Spa rooms** are larger still, with a either king or two doubles, a spa tub, and a terrace with views.

Standard Hillside rooms do not have views but offer an intimate setting with a king bed and a private bath. Suites feature a king and a pullout sofa in an adjoining parlor. The **Pool Bungalow** is a stand-alone building with a queen bed, a full bath, and easy access to the spring-fed pools.

The resort boasts a spring-fed swimming pool, a sauna, luxury spa rooms, a golf course, a tennis court, an exercise room, and an on-site restaurant and lounge. Prices have come a long way from the original $10 per night, which included meals.

CAMPING

There are **four campgrounds** clustered around Furnace Creek, all with their pros and cons. Furnace Creek Campground is the only campground open in summer. Texas Spring and Sunset Campgrounds are open October 15 to May 1. Furnace Creek and Sunset Campgrounds both sit at 196 feet below sea level, making them oppressively hot in summer, and Texas Spring, at sea level, is not much higher or cooler. Site passes for Sunset and Texas Spring are sold at automated kiosks that take major credit cards and cash. Passes are for general overnight admission but do not specify sites.

Summer at Furnace Creek can create its own kind of ghost town due to the excessive heat at lower elevations. If you are planning to camp in Death Valley in summer, you would be wise to camp at higher elevations in other sections of the park.

Tip: All campgrounds can get very windy at night regardless of the time of year or the temperature. If you are tent camping, make sure you have your tent properly staked, and make sure everything that could be blown away is secured (camp chairs love to catch air when you're not watching). If you're relying on RV electric hookups, don't be surprised by electricity surges.

Furnace Creek RV Park and Fiddlers Campground

Located at Furnace Creek Ranch, the privately run **Furnace Creek RV Park and Fiddlers Campground** (760/786-2345 or 800/236-7916, www.furnacecreekresort.com, $18-38) offers 36 RV sites with full hookups and 35 RV or tent sites (no hookups). While not the place for those seeking desert solitude, it does include amenities such as wireless Internet and access to Furnace Creek Ranch's pool, showers, and sports facilities. Communal picnic tables and fire pits are available within the campground but not at individual sites. Sites can be reserved year-round through Furnace Creek Ranch.

Furnace Creek

The **Furnace Creek Campground** (877/444-6777, www.recreation.gov, year-round, $18) is an RV and tent campground with 136 sites. It's the only public campground that takes **reservations** (Oct. 15-Apr. 15) in Death Valley, so for busy weekends in spring or on holidays, or for travelers who like to have a set itinerary, this is a good option. From mid-April to mid-October, sites are first-come, first-served; reservations are not accepted and the fee is reduced to $12. The campground is right next to Furnace Creek Ranch, so while it's easy to walk to dining and amenities, it also means this is not the serene desert escape you might be looking for. The surrounding valley and hills provide a beautiful setting, but the campground itself can be crowded and disorderly. There are some walk-in tent sites, which afford slightly more serenity. **Day passes** ($5) are available for the Furnace Creek Ranch pool and showers. This might be a selling point if you're staying for several days or are visiting in the hotter parts of the year.

Sunset

Sunset Campground (first-come, first-served, Oct.-May, $12) is across the road from Furnace Creek Campground and conveniently located near the services at Furnace Creek Ranch. With 270 sites, it caters mainly to RVs and is peaceful but spare, meaning it is basically a very scenically located parking lot. Amenities include water, flush toilets, and a dump station. It's useful as an overflow if

Furnace Creek Campground is full or to avoid some of the congestion there.

Texas Spring

Texas Spring (first-come, first-served, Oct.-May, $14) shares an entrance with Sunset Campground, but it is a little more scenic, tucked farther into the hills with tamarisks offering shade at a few of the sites. This also means that it is the most popular campground in the area, and its 92 tent and RV sites fill up quickly. Amenities include water, picnic tables, fire pits, flush toilets, and a dump station.

Backcountry Camping

Furnace Creek has the most restrictions on where backcountry camping is allowed. Camping is not allowed on the valley floor from Ashford Mill in the south to two miles north of Stovepipe Wells. Camping is also not allowed directly off the West Side Road, but it is permitted along some of the Panamint Mountain canyon roads that are accessed by the **West Side Road.** To camp off the canyon roads, such as **Johnson and Hanaupah Canyons,** you must drive at least two miles in along any of the canyon roads from the West Side Road. (Pay attention to any posted signs, as the two-mile mark is a general rule of thumb, and some canyon roads may require you to go farther from the West Side Road.)

Backcountry sites are unmarked and have no amenities; look for spots that are flat, have easy turnouts, or look like they have been camped in before. The roads in this area become increasingly rough farther toward the canyon; if you're driving a basic, high-clearance vehicle, such as a city SUV, you might not want to venture much past the two-mile mark. If you do snag one of these canyon spots, they can be austere and quiet with views of Badwater Basin glowing in the distance; however, they can be very windy, especially at night.

Food

Furnace Creek is home to the Furnace Creek Ranch and The Inn at Furnace Creek restaurants. Food can be pricey, so stock up on supplies outside the park. If you get desperate or roll into Death Valley after 9pm when the restaurants close, the **General Store** (Furnace Creek Ranch, Hwy. 190, 7am-10pm daily) has light groceries and even some microwaveable items.

The only other location that offers food on the eastern side of the park is the village of **Stovepipe Wells,** 25 miles northwest. Food is available outside the park at the Longstreet Inn and Casino and the Amargosa Café, both 30 miles east in the Amargosa Valley. There are no other stops for food and water. If you're planning a long day of sightseeing far from the park hub, plan to take a cooler packed with picnic supplies, ice, and drinks.

FURNACE CREEK RANCH

Around dinnertime **Furnace Creek Ranch** (Hwy. 190, 760/786-2345, www.furnacecreekresort.com) buzzes with visitors gathered around the outdoor gas fire rings, sharing a glass of wine, debriefing on the day's sights, or waiting for a table. The restaurants are all fairly casual, and none take reservations. All restaurants are open year-round, but hours may be shorter in summer (mid-May-mid-Oct.). Hours listed are for high-season (mid-Oct.-mid-May). It is best to check with the main office at the Furnace Creek Ranch when you arrive for the most up-to-date hours.

The Wrangler

The Wrangler (6am-9am, 10:30am-2pm, and 5pm-9pm daily, lunch $12-15, dinner $22-38) is a brightly lit steak house with deep booths and minimal decor. A breakfast buffet features classics like sausage biscuits and gravy, French toast, and scrambled eggs and fruit; lunch serves up hot entrées, a salad bar, and desserts. Dinner includes a limited menu with steaks, seafood, pasta, and a salad bar. (For similar dinner prices and loads more atmosphere, visit the restaurant at the Furnace Creek Inn.) On some spring weekends, The Wrangler hosts a popular barbecue cookout dinner.

Corkscrew Saloon

The **Corkscrew Saloon** (hours vary, generally 11am-9pm daily, $7-22) is where people come to duck out of the heat or take a break from their touring schedule. Don't be surprised to find the place moderately jumping at 2pm with people watching a game, basking in the air-conditioning, and sucking down a cold Badwater Ale. The full bar is open until midnight, and the food is better than average, with salads, burgers, and pizzas. Try the Dante's Inferno pizza, with chorizo and jalapeños.

49'er Café

It's hard to imagine a Wild West town without a place called the 49'er. Furnace Creek's **49'er Café** (7am-9pm daily mid-Oct.-mid-May, hours vary in summer, breakfast $4-12, dinner $7-24) serves a basic diner breakfast, ranging from yogurt and omelets to biscuits and gravy, as well as casual dinner fare. You will not be disappointed here.

The 19th Hole

Located just off the golf course, **The 19th Hole** (10:30am-3:30pm daily mid-Oct.-mid-May, $6-12) is open for lunch, serving burgers and sandwiches, and with a full bar and cold beer for golf course takeout.

INN AT FURNACE CREEK

The real star of the show at the **Inn at Furnace Creek Dining Room** (760/786-3385, 7am-10:30am, noon-2:30pm, and 5:30pm-9pm Mon.-Thurs., 7am-10:30am, noon-2:30pm, and 5:30pm-9:30pm Fri.-Sat., 7am-10am and 5:30pm-9pm Sun., mid-Oct.-mid-May, $24-39) may be the view. At sunset, the west-facing bank of windows frames the sun's fiery drop behind the rugged Panamint Mountains. Gilbert Stanley Underwood, the same architect who designed the iconic Ahwahnee Hotel in Yosemite, laid the plans for the Furnace Creek Inn in the 1920s, and the dining room is reflective of classic lodges of the time with its beamed ceiling, exposed brick and adobe fireplace, and an upscale rustic look. An eclectic and seasonally changing menu hits continental, Southwestern, and classic dishes that include steak, fish, and pasta. Stop in at the elegant **bar** (noon-10pm Sun.-Thurs., noon-10:30pm Fri.-Sat.) for a cocktail before dinner.

The Inn caters to lodge guests and those staying at Furnace Creek Ranch; a light dress code (no tank tops or T-shirts) is expected. The dining room and bar are closed during the summer season (mid-May-mid-Oct.), when all services are consolidated at the Ranch.

Beyond the Boundaries

If you plan to enter the park from the east via Highway 190, **Death Valley Junction**, the **Amargosa Valley, Shoshone**, and **Tecopa** are gateways into the park. These towns stretch north to south along Highway 127, which intersects Highway 190 at Death Valley Junction. From Death Valley Junction, Highway 190 heads west for approximately 30 miles to Furnace Creek.

Visitors using the travel hub of **Las Vegas** will follow Nevada State Highway 95 north to Lathrop Wells, before dropping south across the state line via Highway 373/127 to Death Valley Junction. From **Los Angeles,** Highway 15 connects with Highway 127 at its southern terminus.

DEATH VALLEY JUNCTION

Entering the park from the east via **Highway 190** takes you through Death Valley Junction, the small historic outpost at the crossroads of Highway 127 and Highway 190. Lodging and a small seasonal café are available, but there is **no gas or supplies.** The closest gas station is

in Furnace Creek, 31 miles west, or Pahrump, Nevada, 30 miles east. The 30-mile drive west from Death Valley Junction to Furnace Creek takes about half an hour.

Sights

The **Death Valley Junction Historic District** includes the tiny town, hotel, and surrounding property, and it is on the National Register of Historic Places. It's well worth a stop, if not a stay. The hotel staff are friendly and allow curious visitors to wander through the lobby and some of the open hotel rooms. Small donations are appreciated. Staff can also give you a tour of the opera house and its murals, all hand-painted by Marta Becket (minimum $5 per group). The place retains its air of colorful history but has also seen many improvements over the years.

AMARGOSA OPERA HOUSE AND HOTEL

The **Amargosa Opera House and Hotel** (Hwy. 127, Death Valley Junction, 760/852-4441, www.amargosa-opera-house.com,

the Amargosa Opera House

Beyond the Boundaries

7am-10:30pm daily) is a place with a past. This functioning hotel rises like a mirage along the alkali desert floor. Originally constructed by the Pacific Coast Borax Company, the Amargosa Hotel was called Corkhill Hall and had a dormitory for miners, a 23-room hotel, a store, and a dining room. The hotel and the rest of the town fell into decline in the mid-20th century, crumbling and all but forgotten in the desert sun for many years. In the late 1960s Marta Becket, traveling through from New York with her husband, had a flat tire in this desolate place. She ended up staying, painting murals, and breathing life into the old hotel, or maybe kicking up the dust of a life that had never quite expired. The hotel has a reputation for being haunted and has been featured on ghost-hunter TV shows like the Travel Channel's *Ghost Adventures*.

Accommodations and Food

The **Amargosa Opera House and Hotel** (Hwy. 127, Death Valley Junction, 760/852-4441, www.amargosa-opera-house.com, $65-80) is not for the faint of heart; it has a reputation for being haunted. Originally built in 1925 as a company town for miners, the building fell into disrepair until Marta Becket rescued it in the late 1960s to provide entertainment and lodging for desert travelers. The hotel is full of hand-painted murals by Becket, and the opera house offers an entertainment schedule and tours. Located east of the park in the spare Amargosa Desert, it gives you a chance to be part of the local history. Rooms are small and simple, with no extra charge for the character or any mysterious sounds in the night. A small **café** (760/852-4432, 10am-6pm Mon.-Thurs., 8am-8pm Fri.-Sat., 8am-3pm Sun., open seasonally, $8-10) offers basic breakfast, lunch, and dinner.

Getting There

From Furnace Creek, take Highway 190 east for approximately 30 miles to Death Valley Junction. Plan on **30 minutes** for the drive.

AMARGOSA VALLEY

The Amargosa Valley stretches north of Death Valley Junction along **Highway 124** and crosses the state line into Nevada. The Ash Meadows National Wildlife Refuge offers a lovely side trip, while the Longstreet Inn and Casino provides basic **supplies**, accommodations, and Wi-Fi, but **no gas.**

★ Ash Meadows National Wildlife Refuge

Fossil water, melted from the last ice age, supplies this largest remaining oasis in the Mojave Desert and home to nearly 30 endemic plant and animal species. The springs of the **Ash Meadows National Wildlife Refuge** (610 Springs Meadows Rd., Amargosa Valley, NV, 775/372-5435, www.fws.gov, sunrise-sunset daily, free) are clear and warm, reflecting blue against rocky hills and an austere desert backdrop.

However, if things had gone according to plan, you might have been shopping at a select retail space instead of admiring native plants. It's hard to believe, but this was almost a large-scale housing development in the 1980s, complete with shops, 34,000 homes, hotels, airports, and all the comforts of planned living. It was saved from that fate by efforts from the Nature Conservancy and the U.S. Fish and Wildlife Service, which ultimately purchased the land.

Beautiful and serene, a visit to the oasis is an enjoyable hour or two. There are easy interpretive trails, accessible to wheelchairs, and a **visitors center** (9am-4:30pm daily) with exhibits and a bookstore. In addition to clear waters and native flora and fauna, the refuge is known for **Devil's Hole,** managed by Death Valley National Park. Devil's Hole is a geothermal pool surfacing in a limestone cave that goes more than 500 feet deep. Its claims to fame are the rare Devil's Hole Pupfish and the fact that the bottom has never been found. A visit to the site will confirm that it is, indeed, a very deep hole.

Accommodations and Food

The **Longstreet Inn and Casino** (4400 Hwy. 373, Amargosa Valley, 775/372-1777, www.longstreetcasino.com, from $65) is outside California, just far enough into Nevada to make the casino legal. Most people don't come here for the slots, but it is the only option in town if you want a hotel room, a restaurant, and a bar rolled into one. Located just eight miles north of Highway 190, the main eastern route into the park, it's a good

Clear warm springs meander through austere desert at the Ash Meadows National Wildlife Refuge.

lodging alternative to the pricier options in Death Valley.

The rooms are basic budget rooms, but after a day of exploring in the desert, the Longstreet has what you need: Wi-Fi, a laundry room, a convenience store, a bar, and a restaurant. There is also a 51-space **RV Resort.** An outdoor pool is open in summer. The **café** (7am-9pm daily, $9-19) serves basic American food for breakfast, lunch, and dinner. I don't know if there were ever grand visions for the Longstreet, but at this point it has settled into what it is, a basic and friendly lodging and watering hole that attracts an unlikely mix of locals and travelers. Depending on the time of day, expect friendly bartenders, fried food, and old-timers singing karaoke.

Information and Services
There is **no gas** in the Amargosa Valley. The closest gas station is in Furnace Creek, 31 miles west, or Pahrump, Nevada, 30 miles east. The convenience store at the Longstreet Inn and Casino offers basic **groceries** and **supplies.** There is also an ATM, Wi-Fi, and cell phone reception inside the hotel. The closest official park information is inside the park at Furnace Creek, but both the Longstreet and Amargosa hotel staff are friendly and may be able to answer questions about the area.

Getting There
From Death Valley Junction, head north on Highway 127 for 7.5 miles, continuing as it crosses the Nevada state line and turns into Highway 373. The Longstreet Inn and Casino will be on the left just across the state line and marks the beginning of the Amargosa Valley.

To reach the Ash Meadows National Wildlife Refuge, continue north on Highway 373 and turn right (east) onto Spring Meadows Road; drive 5 miles to the refuge entrance. Plan **one hour** for the drive from Furnace Creek.

SHOSHONE
Shoshone functions as the **southern gateway** to Death Valley. The town sits at the

junction of **Highway 127** (from Baker to the south) and **Highway 178** (from Pahrump, Nevada, to the east). Shoshone (www.shoshonevillage.com) is a charming bubble of a town, stuck in a pleasant time warp. It has history as a railroad stop on the Tidewater and Tonopah Railroad but today is now known primarily as a hospitable gateway. The fact that it rests on a hot springs oasis lends a lush and relaxed air to this tiny town, which also conveniently has a post office, **a gas station, a café, a saloon,** and **a convenience store.** It's the last stop before Death Valley and a great place to use as a base camp when exploring the southeastern section of the park.

Sights
DUBLIN GULCH CAVES
The **Dublin Gulch Caves** were hand-dug into the soft hills on the edge of town and used as residences by miners. Wooden doors lead into shadowy rooms that originally held stoves, beds, and all the comforts of home. Most of them are locked, but you can still peer through open windows to see fireplaces and bedsprings in some. They were in use until the 1970s, and the word is that as one occupant died or otherwise moved on, neighbors quickly jumped on the vacancy, upgrading to the more desirable caves. What makes one cave more desirable over another is something to think about as you wander among the hills. Look for roof stovepipes, outhouses, and a can graveyard. This area is for day use only, so camping is not allowed. The caves are located on the south end of town. Park in the dirt parking area and walk past the **Shoshone Cemetery,** where some of the cave residents are buried, along with members of the town's founding family.

SHOSHONE MUSEUM AND VISITORS CENTER
The **Shoshone Museum and Visitors Center** (118 Hwy. 127, 760/852-4524, www.deathvalleychamber.org, 8am-4pm daily, donation) is housed in an old gas station and features exhibits and a well-stocked bookstore

on the area's geology and cultural and natural history. The excavated remains of a prehistoric mammoth are a surprise amid the other exhibits.

Accommodations

Staying at the Shoshone Inn or Shoshone RV Park and Campground will give you access to a hot springs pool at just the right temperature year-round.

The **Shoshone Inn** (Shoshone Village, Hwy. 178, 760/852-4335 or 760/852-4224, $95) greets its visitors with turtle murals and relics from the town's mining days on the site of the old-style motor court motel. Inside, the motel's 17 rooms, five with kitchenettes, are spare and basic but clean. Ask for a key to the inn's private hot springs pool, complete with an artificial waterfall. This is a bright and charming spot, and a great place to set up a base camp for exploring areas in and around the southeastern edge of the park or as a last stop to wash off the dust at the end of your desert vacation.

This is no wild-and-scenic backcountry camping adventure, but instead has some comfy amenities. The **Shoshone RV Park and Campground** (Shoshone Village, Hwy. 178, 760/852-4569, office 1pm-9pm daily,

$20-30) has 25 full-hookup sites, tent camping, very clean flush restrooms and showers, a library, a community room, and a fire pit set around a grassy lawn with palm trees. It's right off the main road, but there is little traffic on this north end of town, so it's relatively peaceful. The best part of the campground is use of the natural warm spring-fed pool. It's big enough to swim laps, and the pool water is at a perfect temperature—it can feel refreshing on a blazing sunny day and warm at cooler times of the year or in the evening. Despite its loveliness and the fact that it's shared with the Shoshone Inn, it's easy to have the pool to yourself.

The place caters mainly to RVs, but the tent sites have grassy spaces and privacy walls that keep out the wind. It's a short walk to the café and saloon in town. If you've been roughing it for a few days, this is a good place to take advantage of the showers or to set up a base camp to explore the southeastern part of the park.

Food

Dig the clean shirt out of your bag and head over to the **Crowbar Café and Saloon** (Shoshone Village, Hwy. 178, 760/852-4224, 8am-9:30pm daily, $8-16) for breakfast, lunch,

The Dublin Gulch Caves had stoves, beds, and iceboxes.

dinner, or drinks. The Crowbar leans a little more heavily toward travelers than locals, but don't hold that against them; there are just more of us. It has been around since the 1930s, and the stripped-down Western atmosphere and well-executed comfort food, from veggie burgers to prime rib, hits the spot in a land of few options. The saloon offers a full bar as well as a few local brews. Shoshone Village is full of nice touches, including strategically placed gas fire rings. The Crowbar doesn't take reservations, and it can get busy for dinner, depending on the season, but you can relax around the warm glow to swap stories from your day's adventures while you wait for a table.

Information and Services

Shoshone has very basic supplies, dining, lodging, tent and RV camping, gas, and propane. There is no cell phone reception in town, but a few places offer Wi-Fi. The **Shoshone Museum and Visitors Center** (Shoshone Village, Hwy. 178, 760/852-4524, www.death-valleychamber.org, 8am-4pm daily) provides free Wi-Fi on-site as well as information about Death Valley. The Shoshone Inn and the Shoshone RV Park and Campground provide free Wi-Fi to guests.

The **Charles Brown General Store** (Shoshone Village, Hwy. 178, 760/852-4224, 7am-8:30pm daily, gas available 24 hours daily) is the last stop for gas and basic supplies before entering Death Valley. The store offers an RV propane station, convenience-store groceries, hot coffee, ice, beer and wine, and gift items such as Native American jewelry. For some reason, buying lottery tickets is also a popular pastime here, and visitors from all over the world on their way into Death Valley line up to contribute to the California economy.

If your **gas** tank isn't full, this is a good place to refuel. Shoshone is relatively isolated, and gas prices reflect this, but prices are still much better than the expensive fuel you will find in the park.

Getting There

The drive west from Shoshone to Furnace Creek takes about **one hour.** Take Highway 127 north to Death Valley Junction, and then continue 30 miles west via Highway 190 to Furnace Creek. It is also possible to take scenic Highway 178, also known as Badwater Basin Road, to Furnace Creek; expect this drive to take about an hour and 45 minutes without stops.

The Shoshone Inn is built over a hot springs oasis.

TECOPA

Once the largest Native American settlements in the area, Tecopa would have likely faded into the history of mining camps and rail stops of the Mojave if it weren't for the natural **hot springs** that bubble to the surface. Visitors to Death Valley usually blow right past the Tecopa turnoff from **Highway 127,** instead stopping in Shoshone 12 miles north. Those who do make the detour come through for a **motel,** a soak, or to explore the Amargosa River Natural Area and China Ranch. Named after Chief Tecopa, a Paiute chief known for his peacemaking, the region also saw brief mining efforts and had a moment as a stop on the Tonopah and Tidewater Railroad.

The motel and café pretty much round out the few services available. There is **no gas.**

Sights
CHINA RANCH DATE FARM

The painted roadside signs for date shakes may lure you in even if you don't know anything about the **China Ranch Date Farm** (China Ranch Rd., 760/852-4415, www.china-ranch.com, 9am-5pm daily, free). Follow the signs from Highway 127 just outside of Tecopa to the ranch. China Ranch Road is a 1.5-lane dirt road that winds through mud hills deep into a scenic canyon to end at the ranch and the Amargosa River Natural Area, a lush riparian environment along the banks of the Amargosa River.

China Ranch has an interesting history that you can learn about at the tiny **museum** housed in an outbuilding on the property. The ranch is open to visitors, and you can stroll through the date trees and picnic at several charming spots with a view of date palms set against the rocky canyon hills. The short interpretive **Creek Trail,** accessed behind the gift shop, follows China Ranch Creek through labeled native vegetation. There are picnic tables along this walk. Bring your own lunch or make an impromptu picnic with salsas, pickles, date nut bread, and other treats from the gift shop.

TECOPA HOT SPRINGS

Natural hot springs in the area have given rise to a small low-key desert community enjoying the sun and solitude. You might wonder how anyone ever ended up here in the first place, but it seems clear that once here, many people have no intention of leaving anytime soon. RVs dot the landscape, and the several sun-beaten resorts in the area cater to this lifestyle.

The Crowbar Café and Saloon serves up breakfast, lunch, and dinner on the way to Death Valley.

Visitors to the area can choose from several developed hot springs to bathe in. Tubs at all resorts are concrete and fed with piped-in natural hot spring water. There are several hot spring resorts, with motel cabins, RV spaces, and tent camping.

Day-use is possible at the **Tecopa Hot Springs Resort** (860 Tecopa Hot Springs Rd., 760/852-4420, $8 per day) with semi-private tubs available. The **Tecopa Hot Springs County Park** (Tecopa Hot Springs Rd., 760/852-4481, $10 per day) offers separate communal clothing-optional tubs for men and women. **Delight's Hot Springs** (368 Hot Springs Rd., 760/852-4343, www. delightshotspringsresort.com, $10 per day) is another option, with private tubs available to adults age 21 and over. Resorts may close in summer; check before visiting.

Hiking

For most of its 185-mile journey through the desert, the Amargosa River disappears underground, but here it swishes along on the surface. If you take one of several trails in the area, you may even have to do some rock hopping. These hikes are accessed from Amargosa River Natural Area, adjoining the China Ranch Date Farm.

The natural area has several different well-marked trails for any ability. Trails lead to the river as well as a slot canyon, through badlands, and past historic remains, including an old saloon and a stop on the Tonopah and Tidewater Railroad. History, water, desert, and natural contrasts abound, but you're never uncomfortably far from fresh baked goodies and a place to rest in the shade.

Keep in mind, this is still desert hiking, and it requires all the same precautions. Carry plenty of water, know your route, use sunscreen and sunglasses, wear proper shoes and clothing, and use common sense. Ask in the gift shop for more information about the trails listed below or other hikes in the area.

Note: The two hikes below can be combined for an extra 0.2 mile and half an hour.

SLOT CANYON TRAIL

Distance: 4 miles round-trip
Duration: 1.5 hours
Elevation gain: 350 feet
Effort: Easy
Trailhead: Behind the gift shop heading south into the canyon
Directions: Access the hike from the China Ranch Date Farm, approximately 5 miles from Tecopa.

If your favorite type of hike is the "everything"

The date shakes at China Ranch are made from a blend of all their varietals.

hike, the Slot Canyon Trail is an excellent way to spend an hour or two. The highlights include an **old stone saloon building** and **assay office**, delicate mud hills, a Tonopah and Tidewater Railroad stop, the Amargosa River, and a lovely slot canyon.

Start the hike behind the China Ranch gift shop and head downcanyon. The beginning of the trail is clear, but there are no name markers. The trail **forks** after about 0.25 mile. Take the right fork and you will eventually pass the picturesque saloon remains. The trail winds through mud hills and then comes out onto a mesa overlooking the remains of **Acme Siding,** an ore-loading site and stop on the Tonopah and Tidewater Railroad from 1905 until 1938. Take the trail off the mesa to the right and continue toward the river. The **slot canyon** will be visible in the distance. Once you cross the river (yes, there's water!), continue up the wash and into the slot canyon with its sandy floor and beautifully eroded igneous rhyolite rock. The canyon is eventually blocked by two vertical dry falls.

WATERFALL TRAIL
Distance: 4 miles round-trip
Duration: 1.5 hours
Elevation gain: 350 feet

Effort: Easy
Trailhead: Behind the gift shop, heading south into the canyon
Directions: Access the hike from the China Ranch Date Farm, approximately 5 miles from Tecopa.

We're not talking Yosemite here, but after an exposed hike along the remains of the Tonopah and Tidewater Railroad rail bed, this tiny pocket of falling water is a sight to behold. This hike follows the same trail directions as the Slot Canyon Trail, starting behind the China Ranch gift shop and heading downcanyon toward the mesa overlook. The trail switchbacks down the left side to the ore-loading site and Tonopah and Tidewater Railroad bed. Follow the rail bed, avoiding washouts, until you get to a **trail** heading left. Take this trail and you'll soon see a **waterfall** sign as the trail continues to a pool on Willow Creek, shortly before it reaches the Amargosa River.

To combine this hike with the **Slot Canyon Trail,** retrace your steps to the Tonopah and Tidewater Railroad bed and follow the tracks. When you get to a fork with a cairn, turn right and follow the trail to the Amargosa River. Cross the river and head up the wash into the slot canyon, which will be visible from the river.

an old assay office and saloon on the Slot Canyon Trail

Accommodations and Food

Keep in mind that the word *resort* covers a wide range of accommodations. The cluster of RVs and cement-block buildings might not immediately suggest it, but **Tecopa Hot Springs Resort** (860 Tecopa Hot Springs Rd., 760/852-4420, www.tecopahotsprings.org, motel rooms $80-105, RV sites $35, tent sites $25-35) falls on the far rustic end of the spectrum. Its cinder-block motel rooms and rail-tie cabins are strewn back from the Tecopa Hot Springs Road, dotted with palm trees and framed by low hills. Some have kitchenettes. The real draw, of course, is the natural mineral hot springs in semiprivate soaking tubs available for resort guests. The springs are also open for **day use** ($8 pp).

The resort offers **RV** and **tent sites,** but motel guests and RVs dominate the scene here, and if you're tent camping, you might be better off backcountry camping on the Bureau of Land Management land off the Furnace Creek Wash Road, or heading to Shoshone. The resort's café, Pastels Bistro, is usually open for weekend dinners in season, but closed in summer; otherwise plan on bringing your own food or eating in Shoshone, eight miles away.

Pastels Bistro (860 Tecopa Hot Springs Rd., 760/852 4420, hours vary, $13-22, cash only) is like having dinner in your bohemian friend's living room. The food is fresh and made with care, and the decor is cozy. Their limited vegetarian-friendly menu is well executed even if it's the last thing you might expect to find out here. Lucky us, since the only other place for a hot meal, or any meal, is in Shoshone, eight miles north. The menu changes often but might include tasty dishes like a chicken panini, vegetable lasagna, beef stew, or black beans and brown rice. Pastels prides itself on organic desserts, made locally.

Located at the Tecopa Hot Springs Resort, it's is something of a local gathering spot and also attracts the RV and hot springs enthusiasts staying in Tecopa, as well folks exploring the southeastern part of Death Valley. The hours are extremely variable, so call before you go, and expect that they will not be open past 9pm.

Information and Services

Free Wi-Fi is available from the parking lot of the **Tecopa Community Center** (400 Tecopa Hot Springs Rd., 760/852-4262). It's worth taking advantage of, since there is little to no cell service available for miles around, even in the town of Shoshone. There are no other services in Tecopa.

Getting There

Tecopa is about 70 miles southeast of Furnace Creek and is accessed via **Tecopa Hot Springs Road,** between Baker and Shoshone. From Tecopa, drive four miles west along Old Spanish Trail Highway to Highway 127. Take Highway 127 north for 35 miles, then turn left (west) on Highway 190 and continue 30 miles to Furnace Creek. Plan about **one hour and 15 minutes** for the drive from Furnace Creek.

Stovepipe Wells and the Nevada Triangle

For such a small slice of Death Valley, the Nevada Triangle holds many attractions.

On a map, the region opens, fanlike, toward northern Death Valley, between the Grapevine and Cottonwood Mountains. Squeezing through the Grapevine Mountains is Titus Canyon Road, which winds more than 27 spectacular backcountry miles down to the valley floor, dense with salt and sand and with little human population. Here, boulder-filled alluvial fans lead to steep mountains and the area's signature wind-sculpted canyons.

Stovepipe Wells, a touring outpost built in 1926, still sits on the toll road (now Hwy. 190) that officially kicked off tourism in Death Valley. The road was originally built to join Stovepipe Wells with Lone Pine in the Sierra Nevada, and now serves as the park hub for this region, with a campground, a hotel, a restaurant, and a gas station.

Black dust clouds have been known to sweep down into Stovepipe Wells seemingly from nowhere. Camping at Stovepipe Wells one spring evening at dinnertime, we noticed a big dark cloud hovering over the Cottonwood Mountains. We had just enough time to look up and wonder if it could possibly be rain on this clear sunny day when the dust storm hit. A downburst of cold air pummeled the campground as we all held on. It swept out as quickly as it came, leaving the campground strewn with equipment—unstaked tents had taken off like kites. Shellshock gave way to awe as a double-rainbow appeared and we realized we had experienced the sheer intensity of the desert.

PLANNING YOUR TIME

The Nevada Triangle sits on the northeastern edge of Death Valley. Navigating this region can be a little tricky and involves some forethought. Some sights, like the ghost town of Chloride City or the spectacular one-way Titus Canyon Road, can only be accessed from outside the park on the Nevada side. **Beatty, Nevada,** offers the closest access to these sights.

Stovepipe Wells is the park hub for this region and is a good place to set up base camp. The village is at 10 feet above sea level and is hot much of the year, and windswept the rest. Using Stovepipe Wells as a base, it's possible to see the highlights and get in one good meaty canyon hike, such as Marble Canyon, in **three days.**

Previous: Goldwell Open Air Museum; Salt Creek. **Above:** hiking the narrows of Fall Canyon

Look for ★ to find recommended sights and activities.

Highlights

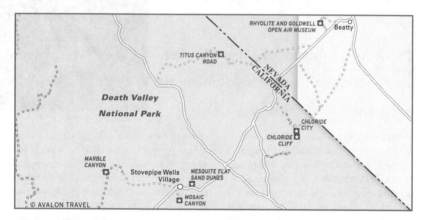

★ **Mesquite Flat Sand Dunes:** These iconic sand dunes are the most popular in the park (page 74).

★ **Titus Canyon Road:** This one-way, 27-mile road winds past rugged rock formations, sweeping canyon views, petroglyphs, and even a ghost town, all eventually leading to the salty and barren Death Valley floor (page 75).

★ **Rhyolite and Goldwell Open Air Museum:** The ghost town of Rhyolite was so rich in its heyday that it was home to an opera house, a school, and a stock exchange. Today, the dirt road through Rhyolite leads past crumbling banks once bursting with gold. Next door, the Goldwell Open Air Museum places a series of public art pieces against the desert backdrop (pages 76 and 77).

★ **Chloride City and Chloride Cliff:** This forgotten silver- and lead-mining district is one of the oldest historical sites in Death Valley. Remains include an old mill, the marked grave of James McKay, and dugout houses scattered around a short loop trail (page 78).

★ **Mosaic Canyon:** Wander through polished marble, colorful mosaic stone, and satisfying narrows on this short and sweet hike (page 82).

★ **Marble Canyon:** A rough but scenic drive into the Cottonwood Mountains pays off in the sculpted narrows and petroglyphs of Marble Canyon (page 83).

Stovepipe Wells and the Nevada Triangle

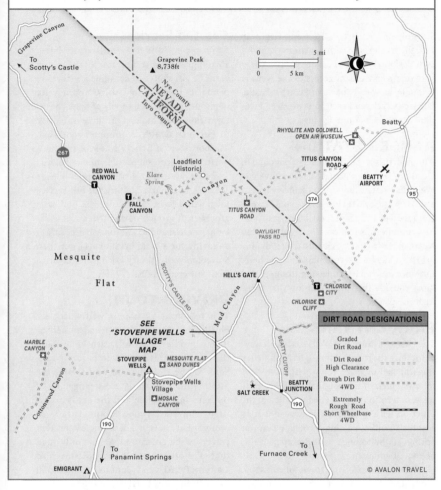

Spend one day near Stovepipe Wells Village, which offers close proximity to the Mesquite Flat sand dunes and several canyon hikes. Visiting Rhyolite or Chloride City, then driving the Titus Canyon Road, will fill a second day. A third day could be spent exploring the Red Wall and Fall Canyons along Highway 190, north of Titus Canyon Road.

Exploring the Park

Stovepipe Wells is located along Highway 190, the main route through the park, about 25 miles northwest of Furnace Creek. A stay here offers convenient access to the Nevada Triangle, as well as parts of Scotty's Castle, Furnace Creek, and even some western locations around Panamint Springs.

RANGER STATION

Although this is the second major park hub in Death Valley, after Furnace Creek, Stovepipe Wells does not have a visitors center. There is a small **Ranger Station** where you can pay entrance fees and get general information and backcountry information. The **Death Valley Natural History Association** (http://dvnha. org) also has books and maps for sale here. Entrance fees can be paid using an automated kiosk outside the ranger station that takes cash and plastic.

PARK ENTRANCES

The village of Stovepipe Wells has been a waypoint since the toll road through Death Valley was finished in 1926. Today, **Highway 190** follows much of the original road. From its western terminus in the Owens Valley, at the junction with U.S. 395, Highway 190 runs east for 45 miles, passing through Panamint Springs and swooping over to Stovepipe Wells, an easy 30 miles away.

The small gateway town of **Beatty, Nevada,** is just beyond the eastern park boundary on **U.S. 95,** about 120 miles northwest of Las Vegas. If you're coming through Las Vegas, it can serve as a good base camp or as a jumping-off point for exploring the park. Beatty is close to the ghost towns of Rhyolite and Chloride City and the scenic Titus Canyon Road. Access to Stovepipe Wells from Beatty is via **Highway 374** (Daylight Pass Rd.), only 34 miles and less than an hour's drive, a snap in Death Valley time.

Gas and Services

Stovepipe Wells has a full-service hotel, a campground, a restaurant, a saloon, and gas. The gift shop and convenience store are primarily invested in T-shirts and novelty items; neither offers a supply of books or information. Your best bet for these is to drive to **Furnace Creek,** 30 minutes southeast. The bookstore at **Scotty's Castle,** one hour north, has a great supply of books and maps.

Beatty, Nevada, just nine miles outside the park boundary, is a tiny but full-service town with hotels, restaurants, gas, and basic groceries. It's rough-hewn main street of saloons, motels, and casinos may better satisfy a craving for a Wild West experience than Stovepipe Wells. Beatty is a 45-minute drive from Stovepipe Wells.

DRIVING TOUR

This region as a whole is well worth exploring. Mining wasn't as prevalent here as it was in other areas of Death Valley, and the main features are the deep, scenic canyons in the Cottonwood and Grapevine Mountains. The region is a strange mix of the very inaccessible and the easily accessible. The Cottonwood Mountains are so remote that there is not a single road that traverses the entire range. The only road that even attempts it is the **Cottonwood Canyon Road,** which runs for 18 miles from its starting point at Highway 190 outside of Stovepipe Wells. It ends beyond the canyon mouth at Cottonwood Springs.

The Grapevine Mountains are relatively accessible compared to the other mountain ranges in the region. The paved **Scotty's Castle Road** runs north-south along the base of the Grapevine Mountains, giving access to scenic canyons such as Fall Canyon and Red Wall Canyon. The Grapevine Mountains can also claim the **Titus Canyon Road,** a scenic popular backcountry drive in the park and the

Driving Distances

From Stovepipe Wells to:	Distance	Duration
Furnace Creek	25 mi	30 min
Panamint Springs	30 mi	30 min
Beatty, NV	35 mi	45 min
Scotty's Castle	44 mi	1 hr
The Racetrack	83 mi	3-4 hr
Eureka Dunes	98 mi	3 hr

only canyon traversed by a road in the southern Grapevine Mountains.

Scenic Four-Wheel Drives
COTTONWOOD CANYON ROAD
Cottonwood Canyon Road is a **primitive 19-mile road** that goes deep into the Cottonwood Mountains. Rough and scenic, it runs through two sets of narrows and past fossils and side canyons to end at lush hidden springs and a series of oases. A hiking trail continues beyond the end of the road to explore **Lower, Middle,** and **Cottonwood Springs**.

To drive the Cottonwood Canyon Road, start from Stovepipe Wells to the left of the campground entrance. You'll know you're in the right place when you see a small airstrip. The road starts off with a bang, spitting through semi-deep sand. The ground eventually becomes more solid, and the road is washboard with some gravel near the end of this stretch. At the 8.6-mile mark, the road enters the Cottonwood Canyon wash and becomes much rougher. At 10.8 miles, the road splits; look for the very faint sign and follow the road to the left toward Cottonwood Canyon.

Because of its scenery and supply of water, a rarity in Death Valley, this is a popular driving, camping, and hiking destination.

Sights

STOVEPIPE WELLS VILLAGE
Stovepipe Wells (Hwy. 190, www.escape-todeathvalley.com) was named for a rusty pipe sticking out of shifting sands that helped travelers, pioneers, and prospectors find the murky well just below the surface. Some enterprising businessperson opened the first services by building a dugout of mud and beer bottles. It was effectively a cellar just below the surface, but it also served to keep travelers cool in the blazing desert sun. Beer, supplied from Tonopah, Nevada, was kept cool in tubs covered with sacks soaked in water. This first incarnation of Stovepipe Wells evolved into a tent outpost and way station as the mining towns of Rhyolite and Skidoo began cranking out their ores in the early 1900s. When the mines closed and the towns faded, so did Stovepipe Wells, returning once again to a humble well amid arid desert.

Windswept, exposed, and sandy, Stovepipe Wells has a certain beauty in its austerity, but it can also feel more like an outpost against the elements than a resort. The toll road was abolished in 1933 when Death Valley became a national monument, but the present Highway 190 follows most of its old route. Stovepipe Wells itself has been remodeled extensively over the years, but it still offers hospitality in this often inhospitable environment.

Stovepipe Wells Village

© AVALON TRAVEL

★ MESQUITE FLAT SAND DUNES

The **Mesquite Flat Sand Dunes** are iconic to Death Valley and are the most popular sight in the park. In order to form, dunes require wind, sand, and a place for the sand to collect. These three things exist in spades in this austere section of the park, just east of the village of Stovepipe Wells. The sculpted dunes are visible from Stovepipe Wells and beyond, rising out of the desert floor to catch the light of the sky in smooth, unbroken crests and lines. Such is the power of the dunes that they seem to draw people from miles around, and you'll find that lots of other people are here to enjoy these vast expanses. The simplicity of the dunes provides a rich experience where you can hike, run in the sand, admire the ripples of the wind, or look for tiny animal tracks.

DIRECTIONS

From Stovepipe Wells, drive two miles east on Highway 190 and look for a signed parking area. From here it's less than 0.5 mile to the base of the dunes. A quieter approach is via the Historic Stovepipe Wells Road, three miles north of Highway 190 off Scotty's Castle Road. A walk to the base of the dunes from here is about one mile. There are several dune fields in the park, but Mesquite Flat is the easiest

to visit—although it's still a long walk across the sand.

DEVIL'S CORNFIELD

What would a field of plants growing in an eternal fiery inferno look like? Very possibly like the **Devil's Cornfield,** just east of Stovepipe Wells. Mounded clumps of these bursting plants stretch in neat rows along the sandy desert floor. The plants are actually the not-so-humble arrowweed plant (the "corn" part of the Devil's Cornfield), in the sunflower family. The salt-tolerant plant has adapted to harsh life in Death Valley and the Sonoran Desert, growing in clumps in order to take root against the shifting sands and incessant desert winds. Native Americans used the plants medicinally, as well as for housing thatch and arrow shafts. The plants themselves make sense, but the effect of the carefully plotted rows of wild plants against the backdrop of the Funeral Mountains is surreal. In the spring the haystacks can blossom, leaving them with blue tops.

DIRECTIONS

From Stovepipe Wells, drive east on Highway 190 for approximately five miles. A brown sign and a few flat paved parking spaces next to the road mark the Devil's Cornfield; however, the area extends on either side of the road for a good part of the drive. Park and wander among the plants, which get bigger a little farther from the road.

SALT CREEK

Salt Creek feels strangely like the East Coast beaches known for salty air, heat, humidity, dunes, and sand grasses—the air smells salty and even feels slightly humid. A weathered, wheelchair-accessible boardwalk follows the miraculous Salt Creek, winding 0.5 mile toward pale, eroded mud hills through an expanse of pickleweed, a salt-resistant desert plant. This place is as desert as it gets, yet here is Salt Creek, valiantly flowing along, supporting a tiny riparian environment, including the endemic **Salt Creek pupfish.** The park is quite proud of this little pupfish, and if you visit Salt Creek, you will understand why. Salt Creek may be a miracle by desert standards, but it's a trickle by forest standards.

Salt Creek is a fragile ecosystem, and your visit can have a swift and negative impact. Respect the desert and other visitors by remaining on the boardwalk.

DIRECTIONS
Salt Creek is about 10 miles east of Stovepipe Wells. Take Highway 190 east for five miles to the intersection with Scotty's Castle Road. Turn south and follow the sign for Salt Creek. Turn right onto the graded dirt road and drive to the parking area at the end.

★ TITUS CANYON ROAD
If you're looking to make a dramatic entrance into Death Valley, drive **Titus Canyon Road.** The **27-mile one-way dirt road** sweeps through rugged rock formations, hangs over canyon views, skirts past **petroglyphs**, and even rolls through a **ghost town**, eventually passing through what is arguably the grand finale: the canyon narrows. The narrows tower overhead, barely letting cars squeeze through before they open wide to reveal the barren Death Valley floor.

Titus Canyon Road has some of the most interesting geology in the park, and it's the most popular backcountry route in Death Valley for a good reason. Aside from taking in the spectacular views that dominate the entire drive, there are some key spots to stop.

DIRECTIONS
The one-way Titus Canyon Road starts from Highway 374 (Daylight Pass Rd.), six miles south of Beatty, Nevada. Plan to spend **three hours** driving Titus Canyon Road to its terminus at Scotty's Castle Road. It's a slow drive on a one-lane dirt road that can be rutted or rocky, and it hugs the canyon wall at points. The National Park Service officially recommends a two-wheel drive **high-clearance** vehicle (an urban SUV is usually fine), but cautions that a 4WD vehicle may be needed in inclement weather.

Early morning and the golden evening hour are lovely times to capture the light, but if you choose to drive this road in the evening, give yourself enough time to reach the valley floor before dark. The National Park Service does not recommend this drive in summer; the area is lightly patrolled, and any breakdown can be dangerous due to the heat.

The straight rows of arrowweed, called "devil's corn," are an uncanny sight in the harsh desert.

Herman William Eichbaum

In Death Valley history, there are always crazed visionaries who try to make the impossible happen. In Stovepipe Wells, this was Herman William Eichbaum. Eichbaum received an engineering degree from the University of Virginia before succumbing to the allure of the West and moving to **Rhyolite**, Nevada, during its boom days. When Rhyolite dried up, Eichbaum spent time in Southern California and on Catalina Island.

He finally returned to Death Valley and built a resort east of the **Mesquite Flat Sand Dunes.** His first step was to build a road to get visitors across the arid valley. He gained approval from the Inyo County Board of Supervisors, submitting a petition signed by several hundred people, including representatives of the borax company and even the colorful Death Valley Scotty. The toll road was completed in March 1926 and Bungalow City was completed in November. Eichbaum's original vision had the resort in the buttes east of the sand dunes overlooking the old Stovepipe Wells. The shifting sands in the area proved to be too much of an obstacle, and the current site of **Stovepipe Wells** (Bungalow City was a short-lived name) was chosen when trucks carrying lumber bogged down in the sand. Eichbaum realized the futility of battling the sands and ordered the trucks to be unloaded and the building to begin there.

Leadville

Folks trying to make a living mining in Death Valley were no strangers to schemes and swindles, but the short-lived town of **Leadville** was built on one of the biggest loads of hype in Death Valley. In 1926, people swarmed to the area, inspired by wanton advertising that greatly exaggerated the potential of ore in the region. A post office lasted less than a year, and the town quickly shut down.

A one-mile **hiking trail** passes through the remains of the town, including several large structures, a dugout, and the remains of the old post office. The **ruins** are disproportionately plentiful compared to the town's short existence in history.

The ruins of Leadville lay scattered on the left side of Titus Canyon Road, 15.7 miles from the start of the drive.

Klare Spring

The **petroglyphs** at **Klare Spring** are among the few petroglyph locations that are publicized in the park. Sadly, this means they've been defaced; people have unfathomably added their own writing on top of these ancient works. Still, the large panel of ancient drawings chipped into rock is a fine one and worth the stop.

Look for Klare Spring on the right, 18.1 miles from the start of the Titus Canyon Road and less than three miles past Leadville.

★ RHYOLITE

Shorty Harris and E. L. Cross sparked the birth of **Rhyolite** (http://rhyolitesite.com) in 1904. While prospecting in the area, they found gold in the Bullfrog Hills, named for their green-spotted rocks. Thousands of people began streaming into the area. The first post office opened in 1905; at its peak in 1907-1908, Rhyolite was probably home to between 3,500 and 5,000 people. The town boasted an ice cream parlor, a school, an ice plant, banks, and a train station. As quickly as Rhyolite sprang up, it started to deflate when the financial panic of 1907 kicked off a rush in the opposite direction. By 1911, the mine had closed, and by 1920, the last holdouts had dwindled to 14 lonely souls.

Today, the main road through the **ghost town** leads past crumbling banks once bursting with gold. Some ruins are two stories tall, towering like era monuments. The beautiful mission-style **train station** remains intact and looks like it could open tomorrow. Side roads lead to the red-light district, **cemetery,** and mine ruins.

Rhyolite might be most famous for its **bottle house,** built by enterprising miner

Tom Kelly out of a plentiful material on hand—beer and liquor bottles. It took over 50,000 bottles to make this structure, which was restored by Paramount Pictures in 1925, as Rhyolite began to be used as a filming location.

★ Goldwell Open Air Museum

The **Goldwell Open Air Museum** (1 Golden St., 702/870-9946, www.goldwellmuseum.org, year-round, free) is a sculpture installation and art park located next to Rhyolite, sharing the land and the desert backdrop. Belgian artists began the museum in the 1980s using the surreal location to showcase larger-than-life sculptures.

The Last Supper, Lady Desert: The Venus of Nevada, and *Tribute to Shorty Harris* are all impossibly big and very haunting. *The Last Supper,* the most prominent piece, features ghostly life-size hollow figures huddled on a wooden platform in an eerie plaster sculpture rendition of Leonardo Da Vinci's famous fresco. *The Venus of Nevada* represents a 3-D woman made of 2-D computer pixels; it stands larger than life, pink and yellow cinder blocks incongruous against the desert

browns and golds. An oversize mosaic couch dwarfs anyone who sits on its riot of bright colors. Other sculptures are a nod to the desert setting. One abstract metal sculpture is intended to be a portrait of Shorty Harris, a desert prospector. A totem-like pole tells the story of Icarus, who flew too close to the sun in Greek mythology, an appropriate statement in the desert. Taken together, the collection is disjointed and surreal against the desert landscape.

A tiny **Visitors Center** (10am-4pm most days) sits centrally located among the sculptures, with T-shirts and museum gifts for sale; there are no services.

DIRECTIONS

Rhyolite is located approximately four miles west of Beatty, Nevada, off of State Highway 374. Take Highway 374 west from Beatty and turn right into the well-marked entrance.

From Stovepipe Wells, Rhyolite is about 30 miles northeast. Head east on Highway 190 to Daylight Pass Road. A well-marked entrance on the left indicates the two-mile road to Rhyolite. Plan to spend an hour or two strolling among the crumbling buildings and art.

The visitor center at the Goldwell Open Air Museum has novelty items and historic pictures of the area.

Stovepipe Wells Hikes

Hikers visit Mosaic Canyon for the polished canyon narrows.

Trail	Effort	Distance	Duration
Chloride City and Chloride Cliff	Easy	1.5-4.5 mi rt	1.5-3 hr
Mosaic Canyon	Easy	2.8 mi rt	1 hr
Marble Canyon	Moderate	3.2 mi rt	2-4 hr
Fall Canyon	Moderate	6.8 mi rt	3 hr
Red Wall Canyon	Moderate	6.4-9.2 mi rt	3-6 hr

Recreation

HIKING
★ Chloride City and Chloride Cliff

Distance: 1.5-4.5 miles round-trip
Duration: 1.5-3 hours
Elevation gain: 230-920 feet
Effort: Easy
Access: High-clearance or passenger vehicle; 4WD not required
Trailhead: From Beatty, drive south on Highway 374 for 8.9 miles. Just outside the park boundary, take Chloride Cliff Road southeast. Drive 6.8 miles to a T junction. Turn right and drive an additional two miles to a fork in the road. Park and walk one mile to the bottom of the hill (see map p. 79).

Chloride Cliff, high up in the Funeral Mountains, offers one of the oldest historical sites in Death Valley along with sweeping views of the valley below.

Chloride Cliff's history is too slow and uneven to call it a boom. In 1871, silver-lead ore was discovered in Chloride Cliff. August Franklin, a civil engineer sent to survey the California-Nevada boundary, staked the first claims and began running a small mining operation. The quality of the ore was good, but the closest town was 180 miles southeast across salt flats, through desolate mountain passes, and without roads or settlements. The mining efforts folded after two years.

Chloride City and Chloride Cliff

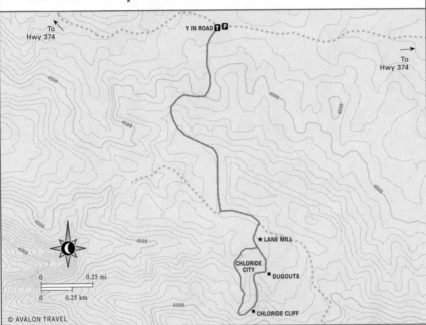

Franklin died in 1904, just missing the next boom in 1905, which spanned the areas below the cliffs and the Bullfrog District around Rhyolite. Chloride City boomed on and off until 1912, and was then intermittently resuscitated by different owners and lessees until the early 1940s. Each time the remoteness was too formidable, even in a region used to being remote.

Today, the town of Chloride City is strewn across a bowl in the steep hills of the Funeral Mountains, rusting quietly in windswept desolation. Even though services can now be found less than an hour away, the site still has the power to evoke the isolation that must have been pervasive here.

After parking, head to the left up the hill for one mile. The top of the hill provides a panoramic view of **Chloride City.** It's an exciting prospect to stand on the edge of the town and see the ruins. An **old road** rings the site and forms the basis for the hike. A

1.5-mile loop through Chloride City will take you past the 1916 Lane Mill, several dugouts, and the original mines and mill. Start at the **water tower** and walk clockwise from north to south past the flattened buildings of Chloride City. Follow the loop to **Lane Mill** (0.4 mile), the miner's hillside **dugout dwellings** (0.8 mile), and pick up a trail to see the immense views of Death Valley from **Chloride Cliff** (on the southern end).

Chloride City is only about 20 miles (less than an hour's drive) from the ghost town of **Rhyolite.** Combine a trip to these two sites to get a sense of this region, which has been connected by mining efforts for more than 100 years. From either Beatty or Stovepipe Wells, allow at least four hours to get to the site and explore.

Fall Canyon
Distance: 6.8 miles round-trip to 18-foot fall
Duration: 3 hours

Fall Canyon

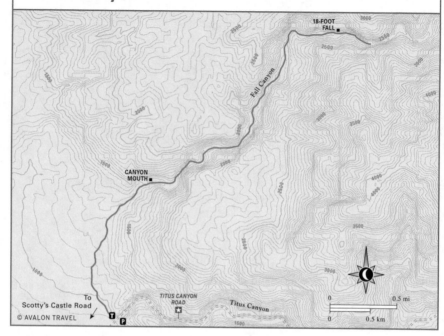

Elevation gain: 1,330 feet

Effort: Moderate

Access: Passenger vehicle from graded dirt road

Trailhead: From Stovepipe Wells, drive east on Highway 190 for 7 miles. Turn left onto Scotty's Castle Road and drive 14.9 miles north to Titus Canyon Road. Turn right onto Titus Canyon Road and drive 2.6 miles to where the two-way section ends. Park in the small parking area near the restrooms (see map p. 80).

Fall Canyon is presumably named for the sleek 18-foot fall that interrupts the first narrows, but it could just as likely have been named for its colors. Yellow, tan, brown, and red hues shift along the towering canyon walls, lovely in the late afternoon. Fall Canyon is a great balance of easy access, spectacular canyon, and moderate hiking. It is the first canyon north of Titus Canyon.

The well-beaten trail starts on the **north side of the parking area.** This exposed trail follows the foot of the mountains, drops into a wash, then swings toward the canyon mouth.

This is the type of hike you will do with your neck craned up to look at the soaring canyon walls. The angle of the canyon walls and the very slight, almost imperceptible elevation gain creates its own world of strange angles, and you may not realize that you are slowly gaining elevation. At 0.9 mile the hike enters **Fall Canyon,** and for the next 2.5 miles you will be rewarded with sweeping cliffs and narrows that are finally broken by an **18-foot fall.** This is a great stopping point, however, and like many of the canyons in this area, the best part lies just beyond.

A rock-climbing maneuver on the south or right side of the fall will put you in the final stretch of the **first narrows.** This last 0.3-mile stretch is winding, polished, deep, and the slimmest of the narrows, a spectacular end to the hike.

Red Wall Canyon

Distance: 6.4 miles round-trip to first narrows; 9.2

Red Wall Canyon

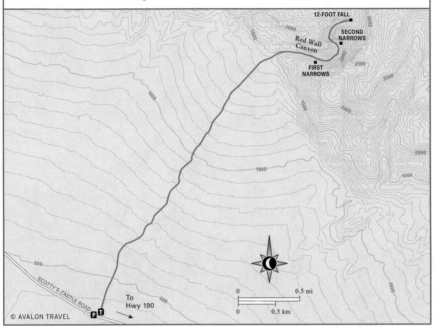

miles round-trip to second narrows
Duration: 3-6 hours
Elevation gain: 1,520-2,420 feet
Effort: Moderate
Access: Passenger vehicle from paved road
Trailhead: Park at mile 19 on Scotty's Castle Road north of where Titus Canyon Road crosses the main highway (see map p. 81).

Red Wall Canyon lives up to its name, boasting lofty red walls and red-walled narrows made of limestone and dolomite stained by oxides. Red Wall Canyon is in the Grapevine Mountains near the spectacular Titus Canyon Road. This whole area is graced with soaring canyon walls and scenically shifting landscapes.

Start hiking **northeast** across the alluvial fan toward the mouth of Red Wall Canyon. There will be several red rock formations in your line of sight, but keep your eyes on the apex of the fan where there is a red and brown gap. This gap is the mouth of Red Wall Canyon. Don't be thrown off by the red rock formations to the left (north).

Crossing the alluvial fan is tough and seemingly endless. Alluvial fans are made when water deposits sediment at the base of a mountain. By nature they are rocky and rise in elevation. If you're wondering why this part of the hike seems so hard, it's because you're slowly gaining elevation, although it's hard to tell without any perspective. You're walking on a tilted world. This section of the hike is also fully exposed, adding to the treadmill feeling. Sweet relief and payoff will be yours once you enter **Red Wall Canyon** at 2.3 miles. There's a good chance you'll have the canyon to yourself.

The **narrows** start 0.5 mile in, winding beneath rich red cliffs. For all the work you've put in to get here, the fun soon comes to an end at less than 0.5 mile farther, when the canyon hits a **25-foot blockage**. If you're a rock climber or an advanced hiker not afraid to

Mosaic Canyon

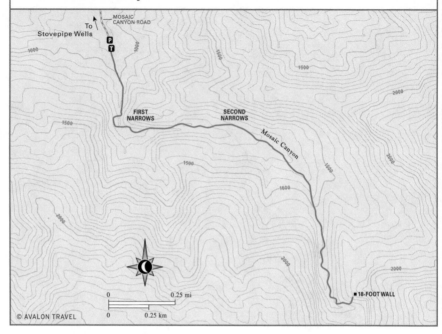

attempt some rock climbing moves, your fun may just be getting started. Climbing shoes are helpful here, as well as some experience.

Of course, the best narrows in the canyon are just beyond this snag. The **first narrows** continue with tortured and folded dolomite for your geological hiking adventure. In another 0.4 mile you will reach the **second narrows,** which last for just under a mile, broken once by a **12-foot fall;** again, a minimal amount of rock climbing comes in handy. Even if you're not rock climbing, the canyon holds a lot of beauty and solitude. Pick the route that suits you, and turn around when you need to.

★ Mosaic Canyon

Distance: 2.8 miles round-trip (through second narrows)
Duration: 1 hour
Elevation gain: 730 feet
Effort: Easy

Access: Passenger vehicles
Trailhead: Mosaic Canyon Road on the western edge of Stovepipe Wells Village (on the same side of the road as Stovepipe Wells Hotel). Turn left (south) onto Mosaic Canyon Road and drive 2.4 miles along a graded dirt road to a small parking area and restrooms at the end (see map p. 82).

Mosaic Canyon is a great introduction to the Cottonwood Mountain canyons. It's accessible but lovely, with a chance to wander through polished marble, colorful mosaic stone, and satisfying narrows. It's an easy drive to the trailhead just outside Stovepipe Wells, and the hike is short and sweet, making this one of the most popular hiking destinations in the Nevada Triangle.

The hike begins at the signed **trailhead** in the parking area and immediately enters a **broad wash,** which is the mouth of the canyon. The straightforward trail continues **south** into the canyon; ignore any side trails. The **first narrows**—pretty but

Marble Canyon

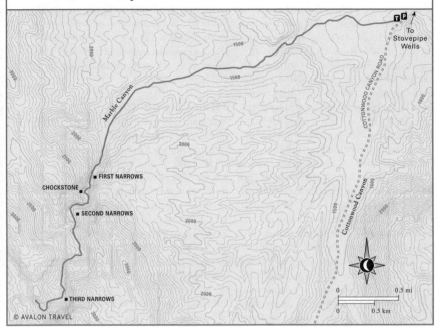

shallow—begin almost immediately and wind between walls of polished marble and mosaics. These are a preview of the **second narrows**, which start behind a boulder jam at 1.1 miles. Bypass the boulders with an easy scramble and follow the trail on the left. The scenic second narrows twist through polished bedrock and rich mosaics, earning the canyon its name. The second narrows end too soon in 0.3 mile at an **18-foot wall.**

The hike can generally be made by anyone as it follows the gravel canyon floor. It does require a few easy rock scrambles over polished bedrock along the way.

★ Marble Canyon
Distance: 3.2 miles round-trip
Duration: 2-4 hours
Elevation gain: 445 feet
Effort: Moderate
Access: High-clearance and 4WD vehicles

Trailhead: At the mouth of Marble Canyon, 13 miles along Cottonwood Canyon Road. The first 8.6 miles have some tricky sections, but are doable with a high-clearance vehicle. A 4WD vehicle may be necessary for the remaining 4.4 miles, or you can hike this section (see map p. 83).

A rough, scenic drive into the Cottonwood Mountains pays off in the sculpted narrows and hidden petroglyphs of Marble Canyon. The petroglyphs are plentiful but faint, inspiring full attention to your surroundings. The real highlights here are the canyon narrows, twisting in colorful corridors that shoot up to frame small pieces of the sky.

The drive to the canyon is half the fun, or half the battle, depending on your vehicle. Cottonwood Canyon Road is a dirt road that starts from Highway 190 in Stovepipe Wells, east of the campground entrance; look for a small airstrip. The road starts off with a bang, spitting through sand. Eventually the ground becomes more solid, but the road is washboard with some gravel near the end of this stretch.

At the 8.6-mile mark, the road enters the Cottonwood Canyon wash and becomes much rougher. A **4WD vehicle** is recommended past this point. If you continue driving, there are many places to turn around if needed. At 10.8 miles, the road splits off toward Cottonwood Canyon; stay right to continue to Marble Canyon. The road is marked with a very faint sign that is easy to miss. At 13 miles, the road ends at the canyon mouth.

The trail is immediately rewarding as it enters the sheer and colorful **narrows**; look for limestone beds with black chert nodules. This first section of the trail ends at a **chockstone** wedged between the canyon walls. Some people turn around here, but a **second set of narrows**—the most spectacular on this hike—lie just beyond this easily passable barrier. Bypass the chockstone with a trail on the right to head into the second narrows. They are deep, twisting, polished, and impressive. The sculpted high walls keep the passage cool and dim even in the heat of the day. The **third narrows** start in another 2.4 miles, after a walk through the mid-canyon. They're less impressive than the first two, but they have walls of polished black and white marble.

If you drove to the canyon mouth, a hike through the second narrows is easy and will take an hour or two; it's an easy day hike. Add another two hours of hiking if you parked before the wash.

BIKING

In the Stovepipe Wells region, smooth highways sail through iconic desert landscape, and rugged backcountry roads meander through scenic canyons. Consider cycling the bell curve of **Highway 190** through Stovepipe Wells to Furnace Creek, 25 miles southeast. You might have to share the road with some cars, Jeeps towing campers, and RVs towing Jeeps, but there are services at either end to regroup and refresh with a cold beverage and snacks.

Riding **Scotty's Castle Road** from Stovepipe Wells to Scotty's Castle (44 miles one-way) will take you past the sprawling Grapevine Mountains to the east and Death Valley salt flats with the remote Cottonwoods as a backdrop to the west. At Scotty's Castle, you can look forward to cold drinks from the gift shop, shade on the castle's grassy lawn, and restrooms.

Titus Canyon Road

Mountain biking the **Titus Canyon Road** offers spectacular views through the canyon, towering rock formations, petroglyphs, a ghost town, and the impressive canyon narrows. The graded gravel road is **27 miles one-way**, starting off Highway 374 in Nevada, about 2.7 miles east of the park boundary, and running east to the mouth of Titus Canyon at Scotty's Castle Road. Grades can be steep on Titus Canyon; fortunately they're usually working in your favor as they head downhill, losing elevation all the way to the salt flats of the valley floor. There are a few cliff-huggers, and the route is the most popular backcountry driving road in the park, so you'll need to watch out for oncoming vehicles. Pull over if you want to stare in wonder and awe, which will be often.

Cottonwood Canyon

The road through **Cottonwood Canyon** has the distinction of being the only road into the remote and lightly visited Cottonwood Mountains. It's a rugged backcountry road, sandy at the beginning and rocky in the canyon. The grade stays fairly even, and the payoff is a scenic canyon and the green Cottonwood Springs. The road is **18 miles one-way** from its intersection with Highway 190 at Stovepipe Wells to the road's end at the first spring in Cottonwood Canyon.

Rhyolite

Crossover riders can make the short trip from Beatty, Nevada, to the ghost town of **Rhyolite,** about **6 miles one-way** to the east. Close-up views of the open desert along Daylight Pass Road lead to the impressive ruins of the old ghost town. Once you arrive, your bicycle will continue to be an asset. The town of Rhyolite has graded dirt tracks crisscrossing its exposed acres leading to the cemetery, the red light district, and the mine ruins.

CLIMBING

The area around Stovepipe Wells is a jackpot for rock climbers. The Grapevine Mountains, with their scenic and twisting gorges, and the Funeral Mountains, filled with unusual geologic formations and chaotic landscapes, offer myriad climbing opportunities.

Grapevine Mountains

Fall Canyon and Red Wall Canyon are in the **Grapevine Mountains,** north of Titus Canyon. Both stand out for soaring canyon walls and lovely colors. While rewarding destinations for hikers, rock climbing here will take these hikes to the next level.

The first stretch in **Fall Canyon** is accessible by hiking, but the canyon walls also offer rock-climbing opportunities. At 2.5 miles, the canyon hits its first major obstacle at an 18-foot fall, a barrier for hikers and a boon for rock climbers. Polished narrows, the tightest in the canyon, lie just beyond.

In **Red Wall Canyon,** the canyon narrows start 2.8 miles into the hike and 2.3 miles above the canyon mouth. The narrows wind through beautiful red canyon walls and end way too soon at a 25-foot wall. Climbing this obstruction can give you access to the final section of the narrows; of course, the nicest part is the most difficult to reach.

Funeral Mountains

Monarch Canyon is located in the northern **Funeral Mountains,** which are divided into upper and lower sections. Highlights in

Upper Monarch Canyon include the small but well-preserved remains of the Indian Mine and Monarch Spring. **Lower Monarch Canyon** eventually leads to an unexpected waterfall, a product of Monarch Spring Creek spilling over the 180-foot drop that divides the upper and lower canyons. The lower canyon has the best rock climbing opportunities in the form of carved falls, found in the main side canyon about 2.2 miles in.

Tucki Mountain

Mosaic Canyon, Grotto Canyon, and Stretched-Pebble Canyon are scenic neighbors, located south of Stovepipe Wells in the rock formations of **Tucki Mountain. Mosaic Canyon,** close to Stovepipe Wells, is one of the most popular and easily accessible hiking destinations in the area. Many visitors hike its lower canyon to see the polished mosaics and marble that form the undulating canyon walls. The first and second narrows offer opportunities for rock climbing fun, while the third narrows provide access to a deep and twisting gorge.

Grotto Canyon is something of a sacred place among rock climbers—a web of narrows and falls, some in the deep shadows of Tucki Mountain, while others reach up briefly to the sunlit surface. Rock climbing is a necessity to explore this labyrinth. Grotto Canyon is east of Mosaic Canyon; access it 2.4 miles east of Stovepipe Wells, across from the parking area for the sand dunes.

Stretched-Pebble Canyon gets its name from the smashed boulders of dolomite and quartzite in the canyon walls. The narrow canyon walls wind into Tucki Mountain; rock climbers will encounter falls and chockstones until reaching the canyon mouth overlooking Death Valley. Access is west of Mosaic Canyon, 3.3 miles west of Stovepipe Wells.

Accommodations and Food

Stovepipe Wells has a campground, a hotel, a restaurant, a saloon, a gift shop, a convenience store, and a gas station with the cheapest gas inside the park boundaries.

STOVEPIPE WELLS

All things being relative, **Stovepipe Wells Hotel** (760/786-2387, www.deathvalleyhotels.com, $117-175) is centrally located. The hotel has 83 basic rooms that are substantially cheaper than those at Furnace Creek, making it a good place to set up base camp to explore the Nevada Triangle as well as to make forays into other regions of the park. **Deluxe rooms** include two queen beds or one king and have views of the Mesquite Flat Sand Dunes. **Standard rooms** have either two queens or one king. **Patio rooms** are original to the hotel and can accommodate one or two people (no cribs or roll-aways). All rooms have air-conditioning, TVs, mini-fridges, coffee makers, and private baths with showers, and include access to the swimming pool. Rooms do not have phones; Wi-Fi is available in the hotel lobby.

The **Toll Road Restaurant** (760/786-2387, 7am-10am and 6pm-10pm daily year-round) serves a buffet breakfast ($7-13) and dinner ($12-20). The **Badwater Saloon** (11:30am-10pm daily year-round) serves lunch (11:30am-2pm daily, $8-15), snacks (2pm-10pm daily), and of course, drinks.

The on-site **Nugget Gift Shop** (7am-9pm daily year-round) stocks Native American crafts and souvenir items. The invitingly named **General Store** (7am-10pm daily year-round) is actually a glorified convenience store and gift shop. They sell souvenir items like specialty candy, T-shirts, and a few basics like cold sodas, beer, ice, coffee, aspirin, and sunscreen, but don't expect to find any next-level camping supplies.

CAMPING

The campground at **Stovepipe Wells** (190 sites, first-come, first-served, Sept. 15-early May, $12) has tent sites and RV sites with hookups. This is a central location for exploring a big swath of Death Valley. Beyond the prime location, the campground mostly resembles a parking lot, although the surrounding desert and Cottonwood Mountains are lovely in their austerity. The campground sits right at sea level, and the sites are completely exposed, which means it can be blazingly hot, and there is no privacy. Prepare to become friends with your neighbors. Amenities include picnic tables, potable water, and flush toilets. There is access to the Stovepipe Wells Hotel pool and showers ($4 per day).

Stovepipe Wells RV Park (14 sites, year-round, $32.75) shares space with the Stovepipe Wells campground; sites are located next to the General Store. RV fees include access to the swimming pool and to Wi-Fi in the hotel lobby.

Backcountry Camping

If you're adventurous and prepared, backcountry camping might be a better and certainly more scenic option than the developed campground at Stovepipe Wells.

Backcountry camping is not allowed off Titus Canyon Road, Mosaic Canyon Road, Grotto Canyon Road, the first eight miles of Cottonwood Canyon Road, or on the valley floor from two miles north of Stovepipe Wells down to Ashford Mill in the Furnace Creek region. This list limits your options since it covers most of the roads that enter the region's mountains and scenic bypasses.

Cottonwood Canyon makes a fine camp, as long as you camp beyond the first eight miles; it is scenic and has a water source. **Chloride City,** in the Nevada Triangle area, offers backcountry options in a scoured landscape with the Funeral Mountains as the backdrop. You'll have no problem finding a place all to yourself out here.

Beyond the Boundaries

Beatty, Nevada is a frontier town and eastern gateway to Death Valley. It's located across the state line on **Highway 374,** about eight miles east of the park boundary and a 45-minute drive northeast of Stovepipe Wells. Beatty is a good place to stop for **accommodations, food,** and **gas.**

Pahrump, Nevada is not a travel destination, but it is the closest place to get **travel essentials** and **services** if you're in a pinch. Pahrump is located 74 miles (one hour) southeast of Beatty via U.S. 95 and Highway 160; it's about 100 miles (two hours) southeast of Stovepipe Wells. Consider it a place to stop for **gas** on the way to or from Las Vegas, but not much else.

BEATTY, NEVADA

Beatty (www.beattynevada.ord) started as a rail and supply stop when the nearby town of **Rhyolite** and the Bullfrog Mining District were booming in the early 1900s. Even as gold ran out and towns in the area collapsed, Beatty remained a railroad hub until 1942, when the tracks were pulled up to contribute to the World War II effort. Since then, Beatty has shifted its focus to tourism.

Beatty still has a frontier-town feel. The town's main street is lined with a row of Western-facade saloons and restaurants, and you're likely to see wild burros roaming the hillsides. Beatty is a great place to set up base camp for exploring Death Valley. It has restaurants, hotels, gas stations with cheap gas, a hardware store, a bank, and a small grocery store. In addition to using the town's services, you can learn more about the history and ghost towns in the area at the **Beatty Museum and Historical Society** (417 Main St., 775/553-2303, www.beattymuseum.org, 10am-3pm daily, donation).

Accommodations

Beatty has a lot of lodging options, from budget motels with charming signs to a casino hotel complex. The **Atomic Inn** (350 S. 1st St., 775/553-2250, www.beattynevada. org, from $57) has converted 1980s military housing into a lightly themed budget motel

Refurbished military housing provides budget motel rooms in the Atomic Inn.

that taps into the Area 51 alien mystique of the Nevada desert. The hotel's 54 rooms have fridges and free Wi-Fi. The **El Portal Motel** (Hwy. 374, 775/553-2912, www.elportalmotel.com, from $66) offers 25 budget motel-style rooms, a seasonal pool, free Wi-Fi, and in-room fridges.

For a whole lot of amenities, try the **Stagecoach Hotel and Casino** (900 E. U.S. 95 N., 775/553-9099, www.bestdeathvalleyhotels.com, from $71). What it lacks in charm and subtlety, it makes up for with an 80-room complex that includes a 24-hour casino, a bar, a Denny's diner, a pool, a hot tub, Wi-Fi, and satellite TV. The **Death Valley Inn and RV Park** (651 U.S. 95 S., 775/553-9702, www.bestdeathvalleyhotels.com, $38-80) offers RV accommodations with 39 pull-through sites with 50-amp hookups, restrooms, a dump station, laundry, showers, and a swimming pool.

Food

The name of the **Happy Burro Chili and Beer** (100 W. Main St., 775/553-9099, 10am-10pm daily, $4-6) says it all. The service is consistently friendly and the chili is delicious, made from tender pieces of steak and the perfect amount of seasoning. Plus, they bring out an arsenal of hot sauces and chili peppers to go with it. The patio can be filled with an eclectic desert mix of cowboys, old-timers, locals, bikers, European travelers, and other passers-through, recently escaped from Vegas. The hot dogs, burgers and, of course, chili are all cheap eats—a sign that you're outside the park boundaries. Pair that with an icy pitcher of beer and you can spend under $20.

To expand your menu options, **KC's Outpost Eatery and Saloon** (100 E. Main St., 775/553-9175, 10am-10pm Sun.-Thurs., 10am-11pm Fri.-Sat., $8-12) has better food than you might expect judging by its unassuming exterior. A range of sandwiches, from meatloaf to turkey to veggie, are served on light and freshly baked bread; specials come with a slice of cake. You can still order food

The Happy Burro Chili and Beer serves great chili on an eclectic patio.

on the saloon side, but the smoky atmosphere might surprise you (Nevada's smoking laws exempts bars, casinos, brothels, and taverns that serve food and alcohol). To dine in fresh air, sit on the eatery side or the patio.

Getting There

Beatty is right on U.S. 95, about an hour south of Tonopah and 120 miles northwest of Las Vegas. From Stovepipe Wells, drive seven miles east on Highway 190 to the junction with Scotty's Castle. Turn left and then right after 0.6 mile onto Daylight Pass Road. Continue east for another 26 miles to Beatty.

PAHRUMP, NEVADA

Pahrump has hotels, RV parks, restaurants, gas, and places to buy a new tire, replace camping equipment, fill prescriptions, or restock groceries and travel supplies. All services, including a Walmart and other big-box stores, are located along Highway 160, which slices through the center of town. Hotels like the **Pahrump Nugget Hotel**

KC's serves delicious sandwiches on homemade bread.

Casino (681 S. Hwy. 160, 866/751-6500, www.pahrumpnugget.com, from $70) are open 24 hours if travel plans in Death Valley go awry. There is also cell phone reception in Pahrump.

Getting There

Pahrump, Nevada is located 74 miles southeast of Beatty via U.S. 95, and 28 miles northeast of Shoshone at the junction of Highways 160 and 372.

Scotty's Castle and the Eureka Valley

Somehow the words *remote* and *vast* don't quite do justice to the Eureka Valley.

These words are often used to describe Death Valley, but the Eureka Valley takes them to the next level. In this northernmost valley, the only existing modern building is the tiny pit toilet at the Eureka Dunes. The trade-off for all this remoteness is the lofty and pristine Eureka Sand Dunes; the alien dry lake bed of "The Racetrack," where rocks move and leave tracks; the shining and desolate views of the Saline Valley from Ubehebe Peak, the highest peak in the Last Chance Range; and the copper mining camps, forgotten and few.

The one bastion of modern civilization, Scotty's Castle, exists thanks to Death Valley Scotty, an infamous swindler who convinced his benefactors to build this Spanish colonial-style mansion in the middle of the desert. The castle stands high and incongruous in the rocky twists of the Grapevine Mountains. Crowds wander its lush green grounds and tour the period-furnished house. Except for restrooms and water, there are no services here. Campgrounds are few and primitive, and there are no gas stations, restaurants, or lodging.

The Last Chance Range divides this area, and its name alludes to the fact that it's the least accessible range in the least accessible region of the park. The sprawling and rugged Eureka Valley is studded with hidden gems. Come prepared for long drives on teeth-rattling roads and take the time to find them. The effort you spend planning to become self-sufficient will pay off with the quiet dazzle of pristine desert, gleaming sand dunes, and starry nights.

PLANNING YOUR TIME

Scotty's Castle and the Eureka Valley are the **least accessible** regions in the park. There is one developed campground and two primitive campgrounds; there are no other accommodations in the region, no services or food, and water is only available at Scotty's Castle and Mesquite Campground. Plan on roughing it and develop a strategy for exploring the area, especially if you want to spend most of your visit here. However, it is also possible to visit a destination or two in this region from one of the park hubs.

There are **three focal points** in this

Previous: the ghost town of Gold Point; the abandoned Lippincott Mine. **Above:** Ubehebe Mine

Look for ★ to find recommended
sights and activities.

Highlights

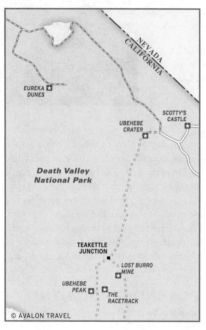

★ **Scotty's Castle:** This Spanish colonial-style mansion lies in the rocky twists of the Grapevine Mountains. It's a popular spot, with well-watered and shady grounds as well as fascinating architecture (page 96).

★ **Ubehebe Crater:** A powerful volcanic explosion created this crater, 600 feet deep and a half a mile across. An easy hike allows you to peer into its colorful depths (page 98).

★ **Eureka Dunes:** The Eureka Dunes are the northernmost destination in the park, so getting to them requires a special trip. Camp in the primitive campground at their base and enjoy sunset from their shining slopes (page 99).

★ **Lost Burro Mine:** There's something about the weathered camp and hand-painted sign that makes the Lost Burro Mine especially picturesque (page 100).

★ **The Racetrack:** This dry lake bed has long attracted visitors because of its strangely moving rocks, which glide across its surface leaving trails (page 101).

★ **Ubehebe Peak:** This wild and rocky peak towers over the Racetrack with sweeping views of the Saline Valley (page 103).

Scotty's Castle and the Eureka Valley

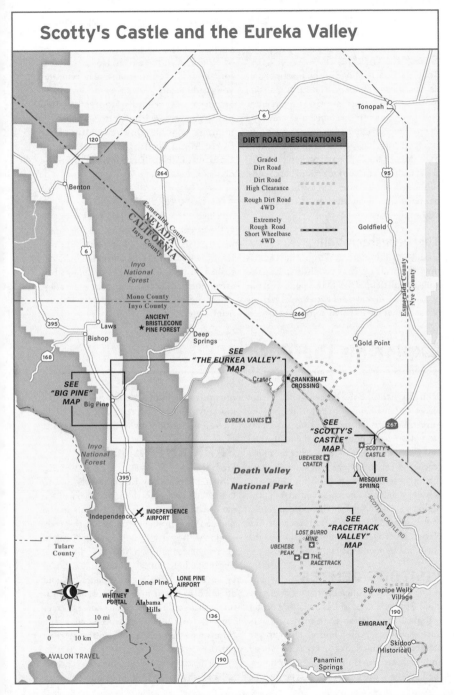

DIRT ROAD DESIGNATIONS

Graded Dirt Road	
Dirt Road High Clearance	
Rough Dirt Road 4WD	
Extremely Rough Road Short Wheelbase 4WD	

© AVALON TRAVEL

region: Scotty's Castle, the Racetrack Valley, and the Eureka Valley.

Scotty's Castle

Scotty's Castle is one of the most popular destinations in the park. The 1920s mansion is on the itinerary of many first-time visitors, and it's common to see tour buses crowding the parking area and folks lining up for tour tickets. Scotty's Castle is within easy reach of both Furnace Creek and Stovepipe Wells, about an hour's drive along paved park roads. While at Scotty's Castle, it's easy to add an interpretive hike along **Ubehebe Crater,** about a 20-minute drive west.

The Racetrack Valley

Despite its remoteness, **The Racetrack** is the biggest draw. Many visitors make the long and difficult drive to this eerie expanse of dry lake bed scattered with the faint trails of rocks that have skated across its surface.

Access is via Racetrack Valley Road, 26 miles of rutted, rocky washboard. Many people stay in Furnace Creek or Stovepipe Wells and turn the adventurous, three- to four-hour drive into a long day trip, but you could easily spend several days here. Set up camp at primitive **Homestake Dry Camp** and explore **Ubehebe Peak,** hidden mining camps like **Ubehebe Mine, Lost Burro Mine, Lippincott Mine,** and the **Goldbelt Mining District,** and even the occasional canyon.

The Eureka Valley

To explore the Eureka Valley, start your trip at the **Eureka Dunes** before heading south into the park. Consider camping at the primitive **Eureka Dunes Dry Camp** so you're not rushed for time. Big Pine-Death Valley Road offers northern access to the Eureka Valley. Otherwise, it's a drive of 50 miles (two hours) from Scotty's Castle.

Exploring the Park

Scotty's Castle and the Eureka Valley are not places you just happen to pass through. The Eureka Valley is located in the northwest region of the park, bounded by the Saline and Last Chance Ranges. To the east are the upper reaches of Death Valley itself, where it turns into a sunbaked wash running along the Nevada state line. The lower boundary of the region partly comprises the eastern flanks of the isolated Cottonwood Mountains. In a place where ruggedness and isolation are the norm, the Eureka Valley outdoes itself.

VISITORS CENTER

While there is no official park hub in this region, **Scotty's Castle** has a visitors center with park information and a ranger on duty during visitors center hours. The **ranger station** at the junction of Scotty's Castle Road and Highway 267 is unstaffed. After hours, the closest place to buy a park pass is from the

Mesquite Spring Campground automated kiosk, which accepts credit cards and cash. There are no park maps available at the kiosk.

PARK ENTRANCES

From the town of Big Pine on U.S. 395, **Big Pine-Death Valley Road** travels east to loosely follow the northern boundary of the park. The road reaches the turnoff to the Eureka Dunes in about 40 miles and the intersection with Scotty's Castle Road in 75 miles; plan on more than **two hours** for this drive. The road is long, but paved and easily accessed by any vehicle, including RVs and trailers, and offers a direct route to the remote and beautiful Eureka Sand Dunes. If you choose to enter the park from Big Pine, be prepared, as the closest park services are 126 miles away in Furnace Creek.

Northeast from Nevada, the easiest access is via **Highway 267.** From its junction with

Driving Distances

From Scotty's Castle to:	Distance	Duration
Stovepipe Wells	44 mi	1 hr
Furnace Creek	55 mi	1 hr
Beatty, NV	62 mi	1.5 hr
Panamint Springs	74 mi	1.5 hr
The Racetrack	35 mi	2 hr
Eureka Dunes	50 mi	2 hr
Gold Point, NV	57 mi	1 hr 15 min
Goldfield, NV	58 mi	1 hr 10 min
Tonopah, NV	82 mi	1 hr 30 min
Big Pine	75 mi	2-3 hr

U.S. 95, one of the main highways through Nevada, it is 26 miles west to Scotty's Castle. The closest towns are Beatty, Nevada, which is 62 miles from Scotty's Castle, and the old mining town of Tonopah, Nevada, 85 miles north along U.S. 95. Either town can be used as a final stop for supplies before entering the park.

Gas and Services

Big Pine offers the closest services to the Eureka Dunes. The town has gas, accommodations, and food. If you are traveling a great distance, it is a good place to spend the night and regroup before entering the park. Otherwise, the closest visitors center is at Scotty's Castle, almost 80 miles east and more than three hours from Big Pine.

Tonopah, Nevada offers basic services, including accommodations, a grocery store, and gas. Although it is a small town, it is the closest service center to the Eureka Valley, 85 miles north of Scotty's Castle. The closest services to Scotty's Castle are in **Beatty, Nevada,** 62 miles southeast.

DRIVING TOUR

Three main roads explore this region: Big Pine-Death Valley Road, South Eureka Road, and The Racetrack Valley Road. Of these, only Big Pine-Death Valley Road is entirely paved, safely allows access to other parts of

the park, and can serve as an entrance or exit route from the park.

Big Pine-Death Valley Road

When Highway 190, the main paved road through the park, ends at Ubehebe Crater, **Big Pine-Death Valley Road** takes over the north-south traverse. It runs along the northeastern side of the park to the northern park boundary. From there it turns west and provides access to **Eureka Dunes Road.** It continues to wander west through the Inyo Mountains, finally intersecting with U.S. 395 and the town of Big Pine on the western side of the park in 75 miles.

South Eureka Road

The paved part of **South Eureka Road** is less than 10 miles long. It starts from Big Pine-Death Valley Road, and the friendly paved road ends at the Eureka Dunes. An extremely rugged road for 4WD vehicles, **Steel Pass Road** continues 29 miles all the way to **Saline Valley Road** on the west side. The harrowing climb through the narrow, sharp dry falls of Dedeckera Canyon makes it suitable only for expert 4WD drivers with the right vehicle, extra gas and water, tools, and a detailed map.

Racetrack Valley Road

Racetrack Valley Road may be an adventure

if you're not used to driving on backcountry roads, or even if you are, depending on the time of year and the condition of the road. From the end of paved Highway 190 at Ubehebe Crater, it drops 26 rocky miles down to the Racetrack Valley in the eastern Cottonwood Mountains. The most popular spot is the Racetrack itself, but Racetrack Valley Road also leads to several other hikes and sites in the area. It officially ends at the **Homestake Dry Camp,** the primitive campground at the southern end of the Racetrack.

From here, an incredibly rough Jeep road takes over to eventually connect with the Saline Valley Road.

Lippincott Mine Road has the dubious distinction of being the roughest road in Death Valley. Although it is just under six miles, it has a reputation for being steep and narrow with cliff-edge washouts. Like Steel Pass Road from the Eureka Dunes, this road is only for expert 4WD drivers with the right vehicle, extra gas and water, tools, and a detailed map.

Sights

★ Scotty's Castle

The history of **Scotty's Castle** (123 Scottys Castle Rd., 760/786-2392, www.nps.gov/deva, grounds 8:30am-4:15pm daily, tours $15-25) is as unlikely as the sight of the turreted castle against the rocky hills. Walter Edward Scott, better known as **Death Valley Scotty,** was an infamous Death Valley swindler. Beginning in 1902 he convinced would-be investor after investor that he had found a rich gold deposit somewhere in Death Valley. To keep investors interested, he produced good-quality ore from other mines, but delayed actual visits to the mine with wild tales of armed gangs, ambushes, and the inferno-like environment and rough terrain of Death Valley. Ultimately his character proved to be the real investment.

What started as his usual swindle of Chicago millionaires Albert and Bessie Johnson turned into a lifelong friendship. Despite Albert Johnson's initial anger when he found out the claims were fraudulent, Scotty's colorful personality won him over. Scotty convinced his rich benefactors to build this Spanish colonial-style mansion, featuring stucco walls, a Spanish tile roof, and tiled walkways. Building began in 1922 and originally encompassed 1,600 acres. When the stock market crashed in 1929, the Johnsons lost money and slowed construction on the house. Some sections, including a large swimming pool, were never fully finished.

A walk around the manicured grounds reveals an elaborate complex with a main **two-story house,** an annex, and a **chiming clock tower.** The interior is fully furnished with the Johnson's original possessions, including 1920s period furnishings, rich tapestries, mosaic tile work, arched doorways, and a spiral staircase. Underground tours reveal the inner workings of the house and thousands of tiles intended for the never completed pool.

Although Death Valley Scotty always claimed that the property was his, he lived in a humble cabin nearby. He is buried on a hill on the property, and his grave can be reached by a short hike.

Visitors Center

The **Visitors Center** (8:30am-4:45pm daily winter; 9:45am-3:45pm daily summer) is located in the castle complex to the right of the main entrance and is staffed with park rangers who can answer questions about Scotty's Castle and other locations in Death Valley. It also houses a Death Valley Natural History Association **bookstore,** a well-stocked retail space that includes Death Valley guidebooks, regional history books, maps, and souvenirs.

Scotty's Castle

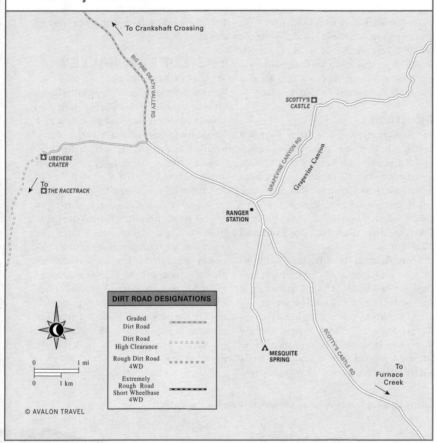

The visitors center also sells limited drinks and snacks and offers a self-guided tour booklet of the grounds.

Tours

This popular spot is open for self-guided tours of the well-watered and shady grounds, and guided tours of the inside of the house with its fascinating architecture and period furnishings. There are two types of guided tours: **House Tours** (daily year-round, hourly daily Nov.-mid-Apr., $15) visit both floors of Scotty's Castle; **Underground Tours** (3-4 times daily Nov.-Apr., $15) visit the basement

and tunnels underneath Scotty's Castle. The tours last about 50 minutes and house tours are offered year-round, though fewer tours are offered in summer. A combined tour ($25) is also available. Same-day tickets are available at the visitors center; however, both tours are incredibly popular, and getting tickets can require waits of up to two hours. To cut down on wait times, make a **tour reservation** (877/444-6777, www.recreation.gov) up to 24 hours in advance.

Tours of the **Lower Vine Ranch,** (2 miles round-trip, 2.5 hours, 1-2 times weekly Jan.-Apr., 877/444-6777, www.recreation.gov, $20), known as Scotty's cabin residence, are available by reservation only.

Scotty's Castle is a fascinating location, but the crowds can easily take away from the history and setting. Book ahead, choose the earlier or later tour times, or visit in the off-season. If getting into a tour seems like too much work, an early-morning visit is a nice way to see the grounds without the chaos.

Directions
To reach Scotty's Castle **from Furnace Creek**, take Highway 190 north for 17 miles to the junction with Scotty's Castle Road. Turn right and continue north for 33.4 miles to the fork at the Grapevine Ranger Station. Follow the right fork for three miles to Scotty's Castle, which is on the left. From Furnace Creek, the drive takes about **one hour and 10 minutes.**

From Beatty, Nevada, head south for 26 miles on Highway 374, which turns into Daylight Pass Road. At 26 miles, turn right onto Scotty's Castle Road and continue north for 33.4 miles to the fork at the Grapevine Ranger Station. Follow the right fork for three miles to Scotty's Castle, which is on the left, for a drive of about 1.5 hours. A faster but less scenic route takes U.S. 95 north from

Beatty for 35 miles. Turn left onto Scotty's Castle Road (Hwy. 267) and continue another 26 miles to Scotty's Castle, on the right. This drive takes about **one hour and 15 minutes.**

THE EUREKA VALLEY
★ Ubehebe Crater
Perhaps 300 years ago, a powerful volcanic explosion created this colorful crater that measures 600 feet deep and 0.5 mile across. **Ubehebe Crater** is actually part of a cluster of volcanic craters that include the **Little Hebe Crater,** a smaller and younger crater just to the west.

An easy 1.5-mile round-trip **hike** around the edge of Ubehebe Crater allows you to peer down into the colorful depths of Ubehebe Crater, Little Hebe Crater, and other smaller craters. Known as maar volcanoes, the craters at Ubehebe were created through steam and gas explosions, formed when hot magma reached ground water. Looking into their depths will give you a sense of the force of the explosion. It may be tempting to hike down to the bottom of the craters, and some people do, but it's harder to get back out.

You can see the Ubehebe Crater from the

Colorful Ubehebe Crater reminds visitors of Death Valley's volcanic past.

The Eureka Valley

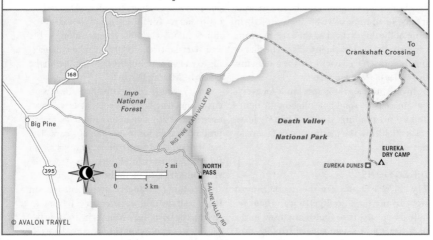

© AVALON TRAVEL

parking area, but the hike will give you better views of the cluster of craters and the striated peaks of the Last Chance Range. As you scan over the vista, especially to the north and east where you drove in, notice the cinder fields—dark layers of volcanic ash covering the landscape. The cinders came from Ubehebe Crater and will remind you again of the force of the explosion.

DIRECTIONS

From Furnace Creek, head north on Highway 190 for 17 miles to the junction with Scotty's Castle Road. Turn right and continue north for 33.4 miles to the fork at the Grapevine Ranger Station. At the fork, continue left on Highway 190 for 5.4 miles to the signed parking area for Ubehebe Crater. The drive takes about **one hour and 20 minutes.**

From Scotty's Castle, drive southwest on Scotty's Castle Road toward the intersection with Highway 190. At the intersection near the Grapevine Ranger Station, turn right onto Highway 190 and drive 5.4 miles to the signed parking area for Ubehebe Crater. From Scotty's Castle, this is only a **20-minute drive.**

★ Eureka Dunes

Isolated, beautiful, and pristine, the **Eureka Dunes** rise from the Eureka Valley floor, a gleaming mountain of sand framed by the rugged dark mountains of the Last Chance Range. The Eureka Dunes cover an area three miles wide and one mile long; they are the tallest sand dunes in California, towering more than 680 feet from the enclosed valley floor. At the Eureka Dunes, everything seems to be broken down to the most basic yet somehow most majestic elements.

It's hard to resist climbing the dunes—give in to this temptation. From the **Eureka Dunes Dry Camp** at the base of the dunes, a **hike** into the dunes may cover 0.5 to 2.5 miles, depending on how far you walk. The climb up is hard, one step forward and then a slide back. You may be climbing 300 to 600 feet, depending on which ridge you tackle. When you reach the ridgeline, you will be rewarded with more sculpted dunes and sweeping views of the valley.

In all this quiet sand and desert, it's possible that a slight rumbling sound may break the stillness. The Eureka Dunes are singing dunes, and small avalanches of sand sometimes resonate with a deep booming sound.

And then there's the possibility that fighter planes from Nellis Air Force Base, to the east, may be out showing off. On one trip we were treated to an impressive air show directly in front of the dunes that had the early morning campers stopped in their tracks. The planes finally corkscrewed back over the mountains in a series of flashy moves.

In order to keep the Dunes lovely for everyone, there is no sand boarding on the dunes and no off-roading; the sand boards leave tracks that ruin the pristine views for everyone else.

DIRECTIONS

The Eureka Dunes are the northernmost sight in the park, and getting to them requires a special trip—but if anything in the park deserves its own special trip, it's this. Fortunately, you can easily spend a night or two to soak in this special place. The **Eureka Dunes Dry Camp,** at the base of the dunes, has primitive camping spots with fire pits, picnic tables, and one pit toilet.

From Scotty's Castle, the dunes are nearly 50 miles, or **two hours** away. Take Scotty's Castle Road southwest for three miles to its intersection with Highway 190. Turn left onto Highway 190 and drive north for 2.8 miles to the intersection with Big Pine-Death Valley Road. Turn right and continue 21.8 miles to Crankshaft Crossing, marked by a sign and rusted crankshafts. Turn left to stay on Big Pine-Death Valley Road and continue 12.2 miles to South Eureka Road. Turn left to reach the dunes in 9.6 miles.

From Stovepipe Wells, the drive is 87 miles, and **from Furnace Creek,** it's 97 miles; both drives are just under **three hours.**

RACETRACK VALLEY
★ Lost Burro Mine

There's something about the small weathered cabin, stone dugout, and hand-painted sign that make the **Lost Burro Mine** especially picturesque despite the austere setting. Tucked away in a hidden corner of the

Racetrack Valley, this old gold-mining camp offers an easy stroll through a time capsule. A prospector who came across it while rounding up his burros filed the original claims for the mine in 1907. The mine chugged along in fits and starts until the 1970s, somehow managing to end up as one of the richest mines in the Ubehebe Mining District.

Today you'll see a site that's heavy on charm, but it's a humble spot that doesn't necessarily give any sign of its good track record producing gold for more than 60 years. The well-preserved **stamp mill** is easily visible on the hillside just behind the camp; its weathered timbers and metal inner workings are still standing. Strangely, no records remain to tell us if the mill was ever used. Beyond its charm, the Lost Burro Mine is interesting because it was a gold camp in a region where talc and copper were the backbone of the mining efforts.

DIRECTIONS

Lost Burro Mine is accessed from **Racetrack Valley Road.** From Scotty's Castle, drive southwest on Scotty's Castle Road to its intersection with Highway 190. At the intersection near the Grapevine Ranger Station, turn right onto Highway 190 and drive 5.4 miles to the signed parking area for Ubehebe Crater. Racetrack Valley Road splits off (a right turn) before the parking area and continues south into the Racetrack Valley. Follow the Racetrack Valley Road 19.4 miles south to the signed Teakettle Junction. Turn left at Teakettle Junction toward Hunter Mountain, and in 3.2 miles you will reach a four-way junction. The right spur ends at the Lost Burro Mine in 1.1 miles.

Racetrack Valley Road is a **maintained gravel road** up to the four-way junction, but the 1.1-mile spur is for **4WD** vehicles. You might be able to do it with a high-clearance vehicle, but there is nowhere to turn around once you're committed. Without a 4WD vehicle, park at the four-way junction instead and walk 1.1 miles along the right spur to the camp. It's a pleasant walk, and will give you

Racetrack Valley

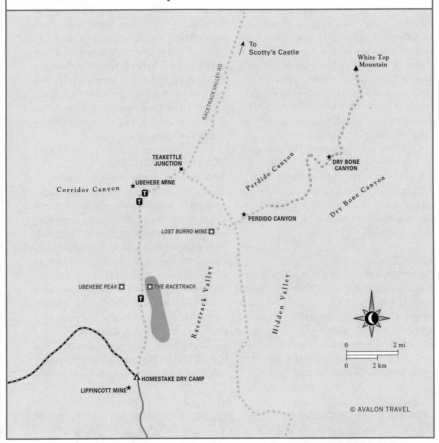

To Scotty's Castle

White Top Mountain

RACETRACK VALLEY RD

TEAKETTLE JUNCTION

UBEHEBE MINE

Corridor Canyon

Perdido Canyon

DRY BONE CANYON

Dry Bone Canyon

PERDIDO CANYON

LOST BURRO MINE

UBEHEBE PEAK

THE RACETRACK

Racetrack Valley

Hidden Valley

0   2 mi
0   2 km

HOMESTAKE DRY CAMP

LIPPINCOTT MINE

© AVALON TRAVEL

views of scattered artifacts and windblown Joshua trees.

★ The Racetrack

Maybe it's the long white-knuckle road to **The Racetrack** that rattles you into a sort-of delirium, but the place holds a special draw—the white expanse of dry lake bed, the dark rock formation called **The Grandstand,** the extreme stillness, and the faint tracks left by moving rocks all work together to create a surreal experience.

The dry lake bed that is the Racetrack has long attracted visitors to this extreme location

because of its strangely **moving rocks,** which glide across its surface and leave trails. Until very recently no one had ever seen the rocks move. The evidence was the faint tracks on the expanse (known as the playa) left by the rocks themselves, which range from baseball- to boulder-size. Aliens, wind, water, and ice were popular theories. The code was recently cracked when researchers actually saw the rocks move. Thin ice sheets acted as sails in a light wind, enough to propel the rocks across the surface and create the mysterious tracks. But just because the mystery was solved, it doesn't make this place any less mystical.

An adventurous drive takes you to this special spot deep in the Racetrack Valley. From the start of Racetrack Valley Road, west of Ubehebe Crater, it's a long but scenic haul; take the time to pull over to appreciate the Joshua trees and soak in the desert air. You'll know you're getting close when you pass **Teakettle Junction** at 19.4 miles. A high-clearance vehicle is usually adequate along the length of Racetrack Valley Road, but a 4WD vehicle may be preferable or necessary at times due to flooding and washouts.

Count on a full day to visit the Racetrack. You may also be able to fit in a stop to the Ubehebe Crater and the Lost Burro Mine. If you plan to do any of the hikes in the area, get an even earlier start or camp at the primitive **Homestake Dry Camp** at the southern end of the Racetrack.

DIRECTIONS

Racetrack Valley Road is 26 miles of very rough washboard road. A **high-clearance vehicle** is necessary, but you probably won't need a 4WD vehicle, depending on rains, washouts, and how recently the road has been graded. Access Racetrack Valley Road just west of Ubehebe Crater, about **20 minutes from Scotty's Castle.**

At the intersection near the Grapevine Ranger Station, turn right onto Highway 190 and drive 5.4 miles to the signed parking area for Ubehebe Crater. Racetrack Valley Road splits off (a right turn) before the parking area and continues south into the Racetrack Valley. Take Racetrack Valley Road 19.4 miles south to the signed Teakettle Junction and continue south for another six miles to the Racetrack.

From Furnace Creek or **Stovepipe Wells**, the drive takes more than **three hours each way.**

TEAKETTLE JUNCTION

Adorned with an impressive array of colorful teakettles, the wooden sign that marks **Teakettle Junction** sits along Racetrack Valley Road 19.4 miles from its beginning and marks the crossroads between **Racetrack Valley** and **Hidden Valley.** The signed junction points the way to Hunter Mountain (at the southern end of Hidden Valley), the Racetrack, and the Grapevine Station near Scotty's Castle. From here, it's only **6 miles to the Racetrack.** After the long road, it's a great place for a break and a photo op.

No one really knows how the tradition started, but this famous landmark is so regularly loaded with old teakettles left by visitors

The Racetrack

that the National Park Service has to clear them out periodically.

THE GRANDSTAND

From Teakettle Junction, Racetrack Valley Road continues south for six miles to the first parking area, which is the turnout for **The Grandstand** (you can't miss it). It's hard to tear your eyes away from the dark mass of rocks rising incongruously from the center of the Racetrack's pale, smooth expanse. It's the only tall rock outcropping in the blinding

flatness of the Racetrack, and it's hard to resist wanting to climb it.

To see the famous **moving rocks** in the area near the Grandstand, the best view is farther south. Continue south along Racetrack Valley Road for two more miles and park in the small parking area at the southern end of the playa. Look carefully for the smooth, faint trails on the cracked playa surface (but avoid walking on the playa after a rain). You'll see rocks of varying size resting at the ends of these tracks.

Recreation

HIKING
★ Ubehebe Peak

Distance: 6 miles round-trip
Duration: 2-5 hours
Elevation gain: 2,000 feet
Effort: Difficult
Access: High-clearance vehicle
Trailhead: The Racetrack via Racetrack Valley Road. Begin the trail from the Grandstand turnout, the first parking area you come to at the Racetrack. You will see the rock-lined trail heading up the mountain from the parking lot (see map p. 105).

This wild and rocky peak is the highest summit towering over the Racetrack in the Last Chance Range. It's a difficult climb, but you'll have sweeping views of the Racetrack the whole way up.

This hike looks intimidating from the trailhead—and it is. It's steep nearly the whole way. Unlike many Death Valley hikes, however, there is actually a trail, built by miners as a mule trail to haul out copper ore. The trail's wide start might momentarily lull you into thinking you can breeze through the hike, but a glance up at the summit will bring you to your senses. The elevation gain—nearly 2,000 feet from the trailhead to the summit—starts quickly and never relents.

From the trailhead, a series of **switchbacks** climb the eastern face of the mountain to the **divide** in 1.9 miles. At the

mountain divide, the hike really pays off with views of the Saline Valley on one side and the Racetrack Valley on the other. From here you can continue up to the summit, or call it a day and head back down for a 3.8-mile round-trip hike in about two hours. The good news is that even if you only make it to the divide, you'll still have great views and bragging rights.

At the divide there is a **junction**. To continue to the summit, take the **left trail** to stay on the main trail; it is more worn and obvious than a fainter trail that veers to the right, which leads down to copper mines and the Saline Valley. Past the divide, the trail gets even steeper and cuts through sheer mountain walls. After traversing a **lower summit**, you reach the **saddle**, the end of the trail, in 0.6 mile. From here, you must navigate a rocky ridge for 0.3 mile to the windswept **summit** of Ubehebe Peak to the south. If you just make it to the lower summit, don't feel too bad—the views from here are spectacular as well.

Ubehebe Mine

Distance: 0.7 mile one-way
Duration: 1 hour
Elevation gain: Negligible
Effort: Easy
Access: High-clearance vehicle
Trailhead: On Racetrack Valley Road, drive 19.4 miles south to the signed Teakettle Junction. Continue south

Scotty's Castle Hikes

Old mining equipment from the Lippincott Mine contrasts with beautiful views of the Cottonwood Mountains.

Trail	Effort	Distance	Duration
Ubehebe Mine	Easy	0.7 mi one-way	1 hr
Lippincott Mine	Easy	1.1 mi one-way	1 hr
Corridor Canyon	Moderate	2.9-4.5 mi one-way	4-5 hr
Ubehebe Peak	Difficult	6 mi rt	2-5 hr

on Racetrack Valley Road past Teakettle Junction for 2.2 miles. The road to the Ubehebe Mine is a spur on the right (west) side of the road. Depending on how tough your vehicle is, you might be able to drive to the camp, but the best idea is to park (see map p. 101).

Like many Death Valley mining camps, the Ubehebe Mine tells a story of isolation and perseverance. History and weather have made the camp picturesque, but the daily grind here was probably not quite so charming. The Ubehebe Mine started as a copper mine, but lead quickly became the focus. The mine chugged along from 1906 to 1968, until its tunnels were stripped clean. Blink and you'll miss the turnoff to this far-flung lead mining camp in the Last Chance Mountains.

From **Racetrack Valley Road**, walk 0.7 mile west following the worn-out **old spur mining road**. At the **camp**, you'll find a

well-preserved headframe, the remains of one cabin, and other mining artifacts, including an old cook stove, metal storage drums, and railroad tracks to nowhere. It's a beautiful, quiet spot and an easy walk.

Visiting the old mine makes a great side trip on your way out to the Racetrack. The long drive will give you a sense of the massive effort it took to get materials, vehicles, and people out here, even though they might have had it comparatively easy; Racetrack Valley Road was newly completed when the mine was starting up and conveniently passed within a mile.

Corridor Canyon
Distance: 2.9-3.8 miles one-way
Duration: 4-5 hours
Elevation gain: 880-1,050 feet

Ubehebe Peak

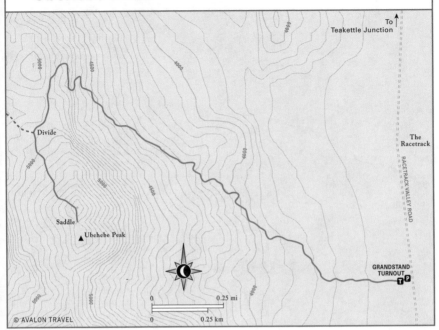

Divide

The
Racetrack

RACETRACK VALLEY ROAD

To
Teakettle Junction

Saddle

▲ Ubehebe Peak

GRANDSTAND
TURNOUT

0   0.25 mi

0   0.25 km

© AVALON TRAVEL

Effort: Moderate

Access: High-clearance vehicle

Trailhead: Take Racetrack Valley Road 19.4 miles south to the signed Teakettle Junction. Continue south past Teakettle Junction for 2.2 miles. The hike starts at the Ubehebe Mine Camp, a spur on the right 0.7 mile from Racetrack Valley Road. The trail starts in the wash to the west of the Ubehebe Mine (see map p. 106).

Corridor Canyon is part of a network of canyons. This quiet hike passes through two sets of narrows, a slot canyon, and walls of fossils before entering its namesake corridor, sliced straight and smooth for the better part of a mile. Corridor Canyon is a local name that you won't find on maps, but you can find your way to it by starting at the Ubehebe Mine.

From **Ubehebe Mine Camp,** continue west into the wash and past the camp; you will reach the smooth, gray walls of the **first narrows** in 1.5 miles. After only 0.2 mile, the narrows open to a wash in the wide main canyon. This broad landscape continues for about

one mile. Make sure to orient yourself where you've walked out of the narrows; don't mistakenly follow the broad wash trending north instead of reentering the first narrows to the east on your return.

At 2.9 miles, the **second set of narrows** begins. Shortly after, these are interrupted by a polished **10-foot limestone fall.** There are handholds to climb it, but it may stop some hikers. You can turn around here for a 5.8-mile round-trip hike from the Ubehebe Mine camp, or 7.2 miles round-trip from Racetrack Valley Road.

Beyond the fall, the **second narrows** continue, leading to a deep **slot canyon** in 0.2 mile. Just beyond the slot, **Corridor Canyon** intersects at a right angle—the highlight of this hike. You can explore in either direction, but the long straight Corridor runs to the left (south); not only is it impressive, there are fewer falls and impediments along this stretch. The lower Corridor runs for about

Corridor Canyon

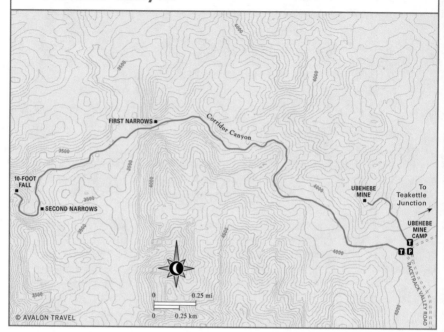

0.7 mile, ending where the canyon makes a nearly 180-degree turn. Turning right leads to a network of canyons that end at the Saline Valley Road in nine miles, but navigation here requires preparation, a topo map, and excellent backcountry skills. To make the return hike from the lower end of the Corridor, retrace your steps 0.7 mile to the slot canyon and follow your original path east to the Ubehebe Mine Camp in 3.1 miles.

Lippincott Mine

Distance: 1.1 miles one-way
Duration: 1 hour
Elevation gain: 90 feet
Effort: Easy
Access: High-clearance vehicle
Trailhead: Take Racetrack Valley Road 19.4 miles south to Teakettle Junction. Continue south on Racetrack Valley Road for another eight miles to the southern end of the Racetrack playa. Continue another two miles south beyond the playa for a total of 29.4

miles from Highway 190. A small campground sign and a few graded spaces mark Homestake Dry Camp (see map p. 101).

Despite its extreme remoteness and lack of good access to water, the Lippincott Mine was the most active mine in the Racetrack area, producing lead, silver, and zinc in its nearly 50-year run. Evidence of this history is scattered all around the site. Old foundations, equipment, and beautifully weathered timbers are set against gorgeous views of the Racetrack Valley.

From **Homestake Dry Camp**, walk south for 0.4 mile along **Racetrack Valley Road;** look for the mine's yellow water truck visible in the distance. Cabin foundations, old cook stoves, and other evidence of mine life lie scattered along the trail. The road **forks** at the water truck. The main road, **Lippincott Mine Road,** heads west up a ridge, arriving at the Lippincott Mine and great views of the Saline Valley in another 0.7 mile.

The Corridor Canyon hike passes through stratified rock formations.

to the Racetrack—an ambitious goal for this ride. Even if you don't make it the whole way, Racetrack Valley Road is still scenic and rewarding. Depending on the time of year or day of the week, you may have the place to yourself, or you may watch a steady stream of Jeeps parade past you on their way to the Racetrack. There is no shoulder on this rocky road, but you'll be able to see and hear cars coming easily in time to pull off to the side.

Hidden Valley Road

At Teakettle Junction, turn left (southeast) to head south into Hidden Valley. **Hidden Valley Road** is quiet, scenic, and mostly flat, with little traffic. The road runs through several historic mining areas to the base of Hunter Mountain. (A side trip to the Lost Burro Mine is accessible via a 1.1-mile right spur, 3.2 miles south of Teakettle Junction.) At **13 miles one-way,** the route ends at the **Goldbelt Spring Mining District**, which lies north of Hunter Mountain. The Goldbelt Camp has some cabin remains and an old truck. Beyond the camp, the road becomes rougher, for 4WD vehicles, and climbs steeply over Hunter Mountain.

Big Pine-Death Valley Road

Big Pine-Death Valley Road runs **25 miles one-way** from the Mesquite Spring Campground area north toward Crankshaft Crossing and will give you the classic sweeping expanses of upper Death Valley. From the intersection of Mesquite Spring Campground with Highway 190, the road is paved for 3.4 miles before continuing as a graded dirt road for 21.8 miles north to Crankshaft Crossing. Crankshaft Crossing, named for an old crankshaft that was left as a landmark, is just a jog in the road as it heads up toward the junction with Eureka Dunes Road, but it's as good a destination as any. This is exposed and lies at a low elevation, so set a good endpoint or turn around when you feel like it.

CLIMBING

The Cottonwood Mountains offer some fine climbing, with long, secluded canyons and

The Lippincott Mine Road has the dubious distinction of being one of the scariest roads in Death Valley. A road map of Death Valley shows a black-and-red color scheme, meaning you're likely to get stuck or break your vehicle. Fortunately, you don't actually have to drive this road to see the Lippincott Mine.

BIKING

You have to be a real go-getter, rewarded by a serious physical challenge, to cycle in this region. Road biking is tough due to the lack of paved roads, and the glass-smooth highways that slice through the park's other regions are mostly absent. That said, there are a few options.

Racetrack Valley Road

Joshua trees and the hills of the Cottonwood and Last Chance Mountains make for a shifting and scenic backdrop along the fairly flat **Racetrack Valley Road**. It's also incredibly long: **26 miles one-way** from where it leaves the pavement at Ubehebe Crater all the way good narrows. Dry Bone Canyon, Bighorn Gorge, and Perdido Canyon offer passages laced with fossils and polished falls. All are located in the White Top Mountain area of the Cottonwood Mountains at elevations over 6,000 feet, which means that the temperatures are cooler than at any of the valley floors.

Cottonwood Mountains

Just past the mouth of **Perdido Canyon,** dark canyon walls line a wash sprinkled with Joshua trees, providing good opportunities for climbing. Beyond this, fossil hunting is the best game here.

The leaning walls and Joshua trees of **Dry Bone Canyon** eventually lead to three sets of narrows with some polished falls for climbing. There is a formidable slot canyon after the first narrows that you will have to work your way into via a bypass and climb down from a ridge if you want to enter its depths. There are also petroglyphs in Dry Bone Canyon, a reward for carefully picking your way through this remote spot.

Bighorn Gorge has colorful high walls, polished narrows, and falls and chockstones. The falls dividing the canyon's three sets of narrows provide climbing opportunities. There are also side canyons to explore. If you're lucky, you'll see the canyon's namesake animal.

DIRECTIONS

All three canyons can be accessed via Racetrack Valley Road. From Highway 190 at Ubehebe Crater, take Racetrack Valley Road 19.7 miles to Teakettle Junction. At Teakettle Junction, turn left toward Hunter Mountain.

Drive 3.2 miles and turn left at White Top Mountain Road, just past Lost Burro Gap.

For **Perdido Canyon,** drive an additional 0.8 mile and park. Perdido Canyon is 0.5 mile north of the road behind the low hills at the end of the alluvial fan. For **Dry Bone Canyon,** drive 7.4 miles to the wash of Dry Bone Canyon and park. For **Bighorn Gorge,** drive 10 miles to a fork in the road and a divide overlooking Bighorn Gorge. Take the right spur and park at the turnout on the right. Bighorn Gorge is a wide forested opening to the north. Beyond the wash of Dry Bone Canyon, the road gets considerably worse. When visiting Bighorn Gorge it is also possible to park at the Dry Bone Canyon wash and hike 2.7 miles to the mouth of Bighorn Gorge.

Like many sites in the vicinity of the Racetrack, getting here is half the battle. Be sure to budget at least **1.5 hours for the drive** from Ubehebe Crater. It's also a good idea to camp near the canyon mouth the night before to get an early start.

Corridor Canyon

You can visit an old mining camp as well as get in a lovely canyon hike and some good climbing with a visit to **Corridor Canyon,** which starts from the Ubehebe Mine Camp. To get here, take Racetrack Valley Road 19.7 miles to Teakettle Junction then continue for 2.2 miles. The 0.7-mile spur to the Ubehebe Mine is on the right. It's an old rutted road, and it may be better to park and walk from here. Corridor Canyon has polished falls, narrows, a slot canyon, and the strangely special Corridor with its soaring smooth walls. Hiking upcanyon toward Round Valley gives you short narrows and falls.

Accommodations and Food

There are **no services** in the Eureka Valley region—no hotels, restaurants, or gas. The park hubs of Stovepipe Wells and Furnace Creek are one to three hours' drive south, and the closest services are in Big Pine, about 50 miles (two hours) west. **Scotty's Castle** offers some bottled drinks and premade sandwiches, but hours are limited, and there are no other supplies. Bring your own food and water, make sure you have enough gas, and be prepared to camp.

CAMPING
Mesquite Spring
Mesquite Spring (30 sites, first-come, first-served, year-round, $12) is the only developed campground in the region. It's a pretty campground, dotted with mesquite bushes and set along low hills less than five miles west from Scotty's Castle. At an elevation of 1,800 feet, the temperature is bearable most of the year, except summer. Sites are exposed, but spaced far enough apart that you get some privacy. Though reservations aren't accepted, it's very likely you'll get a spot, even in the busy spring

season. Stop to reserve a spot first thing in the morning; pay via an automated kiosk, which takes credit cards and cash, and put your receipt on the site marker. Amenities include picnic tables, fire pits, and access to flush toilets and water; there are no RV hookups, but there is a dump station.

DIRECTIONS
The turnoff to Mesquite Spring is located 0.6 mile south of the intersection of Scotty's Castle Road and Highway 190; from the turnoff, continue 1.9 miles south to the campground.

Eureka Dunes Dry Camp
Eureka Dunes Dry Camp (first-come, first-served, free) is a small, primitive maintained campground. A stay here puts you within easy distance of the remote Eureka Dunes. Sites have fire pits and sturdy cement picnic tables; there is no water and no electric hookups, but there is a pit toilet. If all the sites are full, there are backcountry camping spaces just beyond the campground off Eureka Road. The only

Campsites at Mesquite Spring campground are tucked along low hills.

thing that distinguishes them from the official campsites is their lack of a picnic table and a fire pit.

DIRECTIONS

To get here from the intersection of Scotty's Castle Road and Highway 190, head north for 2.8 miles and continue on Big Pine-Death Valley Road for 21.8 miles. At Crankshaft Crossing, marked by a sign and rusted crankshafts, turn left (southwest) to stay on Big Pine-Death Valley Road. The turnoff to Eureka Dry Camp is 12.2 miles farther. Turn left onto the South Eureka Road and drive 9.6 miles to the campground at the base of the dunes. Big Pine-Death Valley Road, as well as Eureka Dunes Road, are graded dirt roads usually suitable for passenger cars and good enough to bring a camper or RV to this spot.

Homestake Dry Camp

In Racetrack Valley, your best bet is **Homestake Dry Camp** (first-come, first-served, free), a primitive maintained campground. Four camp spaces have been graded so that you can comfortably park and pitch a tent. In the highly unlikely event that these sites are full, simply set up camp nearby. The only amenity is one decrepit pit toilet, and there are no fire pits provided, so fires are not permitted. Bring your own water. Despite the lack of amenities, the campground serves as a good base to explore the surrounding area—Ubehebe Peak, the Racetrack, Lippincott Mine, Ubehebe Lead Mine, and Corridor Canyon.

DIRECTIONS

To reach Homestake Dry Camp, access the Racetrack Valley Road from where it leaves paved Highway 190 and drive 19.4 miles south to Teakettle Junction. Continue south on the Racetrack Valley Road for eight miles to the southern end of the Racetrack playa. Continue two miles south beyond the playa, a total of 29.4 miles from Highway 190, to a small campground sign and the graded camping spaces that mark Homestake Dry Camp.

Backcountry Camping

Only a few roads traverse this region, so it's important to know where backcountry car camping is allowed. The main dirt road, Racetrack Valley Road, is tempting, but there is no camping between Teakettle Junction and Homestake Dry Camp.

Instead, consider turning left at Teakettle Junction and heading south along Hidden

Primitive campsites at the Homestake Dry Camp offer cleared places to set up for the night.

Valley Road toward **Hunter Mountain.** The road is passable in a high-clearance vehicle for 13 miles to the area around Goldbelt Spring, at the base of Hunter Mountain. Beyond Goldbelt Spring, the road becomes 4WD-only as it climbs Hunter Mountain.

If you plan to rock-climb or explore the Cottonwood Mountain Canyons, camp in the vicinity of **White Top Mountain.** White Top Mountain Road is located off Hidden Valley Road; take the left turn at the junction 3.2 miles south of Teakettle Junction. The road begins as passable for high-clearance vehicles, then requires a 4WD vehicle after about five miles. There is no camping allowed at the Ubehebe Mine or the Lost Burro Mine.

Beyond the Boundaries

Like many of the areas around the Death Valley National Park's boundaries, the northern side has beautiful mountain passes, desert expanses, and old mining towns worthy of exploration.

The town of **Big Pine,** west on U.S. 395, provides **supplies, gas,** and two access points for exploration. Heading east on **Highway 168,** a right turn leads to **Big Pine-Death Valley Road,** which stretches 75 miles southeast, passing the North Pass of the Saline Valley Road and the Eureka Dunes before dropping down to meet the northern terminus of Scotty's Castle Road.

Follow Highway 168 northeast and you will reach a junction with **Highway 266** in 35 miles. A drive east on Highway 266 brings you to the ghost town of **Gold Point,** Nevada before eventually meeting up with U.S. 95 in another 16 miles. The towns of **Goldfield** and **Tonopah** lie further north on U.S. 95, though only Tonopah offers **gas** or supplies.

BIG PINE

Big Pine provides the northernmost and remotest access to the park via either the **North Pass of Saline Valley Road** or **Big Pine-Death Valley Road.** The town offers gas, lodging, food, and outdoor supplies. It also provides a refueling stop for people heading into or out of the Sierra Nevada Mountains to the west or Death Valley to the east.

Accommodations
A string of no-frills motels include the **Starlight Motel** (511 S. Main St., 760/938-2011, from $75), **Big Pine Motel** (370 S. Main St., 760/938-2282, from $65), and the **Bristlecone Motel** (101 N. Main St., 760/938-2067, http://bristleconemotel.webs.com, from $69), which has a relatively well-stocked general store with groceries, a hardware section, and camping and fishing supplies. There are also laundry and showers on-site.

Eight miles north of Big Pine, RV sites, tent cabins, and hot springs can be found at **Keough's Hot Springs Resort** (800 Keough Hot Springs Rd., Bishop, 760/872-4670, www.keoughshotsprings.com, RV sites $23-38, tent cabins $75-90, modular trailers $115-135).

Food
There are a few restaurants in town. The **Copper Top BBQ** (310 N. Main St., http://coppertopbbq.com, 11am-6pm Wed.-Sun., $8-23) has good take-out portions as well as outdoor tables for families and picnics. **Rossi's Place** (142 S. Main St., 5pm-9pm Thurs.-Mon., $6-18) is a small café with pizza, sandwiches, and salads as well as beer, wine, and cocktails. The **Country Kitchen** (181 S. Main St., 760/938-2402, 6:30am-8:30pm daily, $6-12) is a casual diner with breakfast, sandwiches, salads, burgers, dinner plates, beer, and wine.

Getting There
Big Pine is located on U.S. 395, about 43 miles north of Lone Pine and 15 miles south of Bishop.

Big Pine

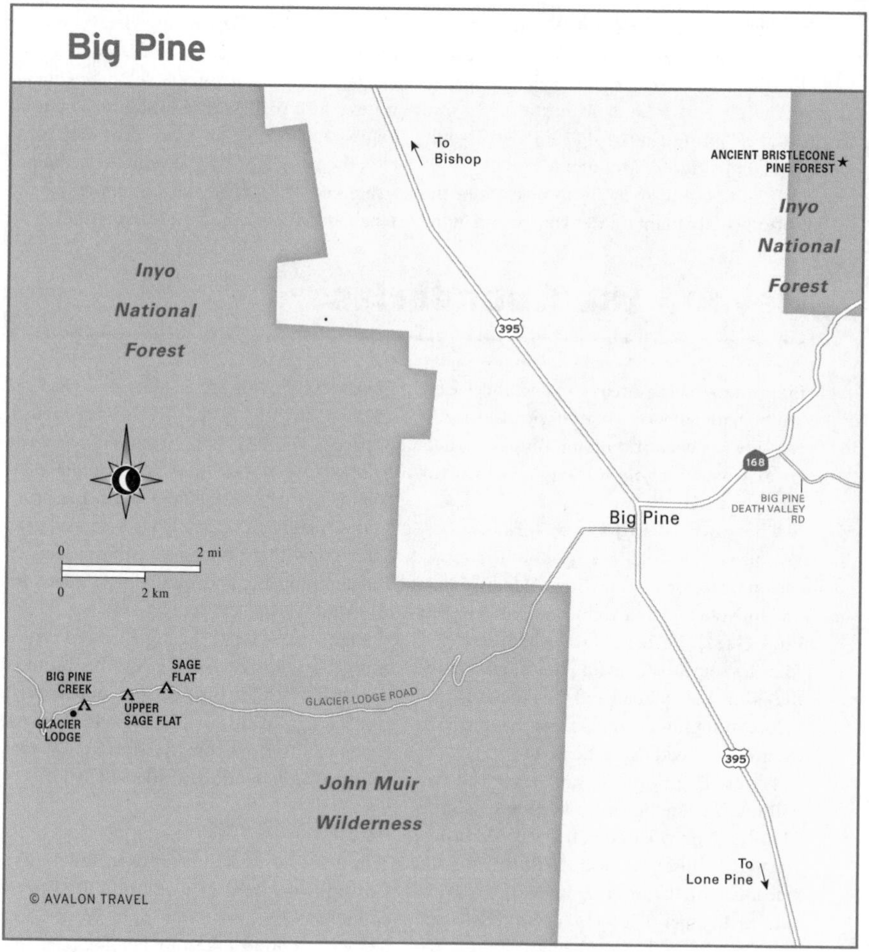

To Bishop

ANCIENT BRISTLECONE
PINE FOREST ★

Inyo

National

Forest

Inyo

National

Forest

395

168

BIG PINE
DEATH VALLEY
RD

Big Pine

0   2 mi

0   2 km

BIG PINE
CREEK

SAGE
FLAT

GLACIER LODGE ROAD

UPPER
SAGE FLAT

GLACIER
LODGE

John Muir

Wilderness

395

To
Lone Pine

© AVALON TRAVEL

John Muir Wilderness

The classic alpine terrain of the **John Muir Wilderness** (www.fs.usda.gov) is not an aside—it's a destination with jewel-like turquoise glacial lakes, craggy snow-covered peaks, glaciers, and meadows. The area has miles of trails to take you through the dazzling wilderness for day hikes and backpacking trips. It is also home to the Palisades Glacier, the southernmost glacier in the United States. The area is best visited from **late spring** to **early fall** due to the high elevation and possibility of snow and ice.

ACCOMMODATIONS AND CAMPING

Spend the night at historic **Glacier Lodge** (Glacier Lodge Rd., 11 miles west of U.S. 395, 760/938-2837, www.jewelofthesierra.com, Apr.-Nov., tent or RV sites $25-50, cabins $110-150) located along Glacier Lodge Road, which heads west into mountain wilderness and U.S. Forest Service lands. Glacier Lodge is a historic mountain retreat built in 1917. The lodge itself burned down in 1998, but it still offers rustic cabins as well as RV and tent camping.

U.S. Forest Service **campgrounds** (877/444-6777, www.recreation.gov, $22) in this area include **Sage Flat** (28 sites, first-come first-served, mid-Apr.-mid-Nov.), **Upper Sage Flat,** (21 sites, May-mid-Oct.), and **Big Pine Creek** (30 sites, May-mid-Oct.). All are pretty, shaded canyon campgrounds with water and toilets. The campgrounds are located just off Glacier Lodge Road, and are visible from the road.

GETTING THERE
The North Fork of Big Pine Canyon and the John Muir Wilderness area are reached by heading west from Crocker Avenue, in the center of Big Pine, and continuing 10 miles west on Glacier Lodge Road. The road leads to campgrounds, Glacier Lodge, and spectacular alpine hikes.

Ancient Bristlecone Pine Forest
The **Ancient Bristlecone Pine Forest** (760/873-2500, www.fs.usda.gov, 6am-10pm daily mid-May-Nov., visitors center 10am-4pm Fri.-Mon., $6 per vehicle), in the White Mountains east of Big Pine, has some of the oldest trees in the world, including the Methuselah Tree, dated at 4,750 years old.

White Mountain Road winds into the mountains and provides breathtaking views of the Sierra Nevada Mountains and Owens Valley. Stop in at the **Schulman Grove Visitors Center** (760/873-2500 or 760/873-2400) and have a look at the **Schulman Grove,** accessible from the visitors center parking lot.

Three interpretive **hiking trails** (1-5 miles) traverse the Schulman Grove, offering close-up views of bristlecone pines, historic mining cabins, and the Methuselah Tree. It's a surreal experience to wander through the ancient trees and think about the changes the world has seen as they stood quietly growing into their gnarled shapes above a landscape that was once covered by glaciers. The **Patriarch Grove** lies 12 miles north of the Schulman Grove on a graded dirt road and is home to the world's largest bristlecone pine.

Allow at least **three hours** for a round-trip

visit from Big Pine, although you could easily spend a whole day hiking and visiting both groves. The campgrounds along the Glacier Lodge Road are a good overnight option.

GETTING THERE
From Big Pine, follow Highway 168 east for 13 miles to White Mountain Road. Turn left (north) and drive 10 miles to the Schulman Grove Visitors Center. For road closures and conditions, call 760/873-2500 or contact the Inyo National Forest Ranger Station (760/873-2400). Plan **one hour** for the drive from Big Pine.

SYLVANIA MOUNTAINS AND HIGHWAY 266
From the town of Big Pine, you can take a scenic drive east through the Sylvania Mountains along lonely Highway 266. The scenery changes from mountain passes dotted with pinyon pines to austere, blinding desert. The ghost towns of **Palmetto** and **Lida** are sprawling ruins near the highway. Both were silver-mining towns founded in the 1860s, and the old stone foundations date from this time. Palmetto had its last run in 1920 and is now completely abandoned. Lida had several booms before the post office closed for good in 1918. Today, it's a picturesque place with cabins and other ruins. A few of the cabins are still inhabited, so please respect any private property.

Gold Point
The pièce de résistance along Highway 266 is the ghost town of **Gold Point, Nevada** (http://goldpointghosttown.com). Gold Point was a mining camp in the 1860s, but it didn't become a town until 1908. It was originally called Hornsilver, but the name was eventually changed. The town had the usual story of boom and bust, although it was never completely abandoned. In the early 1980s, two friends began buying up the mostly abandoned property and stabilizing the cabins and town buildings. Today, the result is a Wild West gem—gritty, isolated, and

authentic, open to travelers with a fascination for these kinds of tucked-away pieces of history.

Owner Herb Robbins and his business partner, Walt, are usually on the premises, willing to open the saloon and share a beer and stories. You can wander the town to your heart's content and take pictures, but please keep in mind that this is private property with several year-round residents, so be respectful.

For anyone who has ever fantasized about owning an old town, this place resonates. There is no charge to visit the town, but donations are appreciated to keep restoration efforts going. A word to the wise: the good folks of Gold Point, Nevada value their fierce independence and have made every effort to establish an autonomous community—avoid talking politics.

GETTING THERE

From Big Pine, it is 76 miles east (2 hours) to Gold Point via Highways 168 and 266. From Highway 266, the paved Highway 774 heads south to Gold Point in eight miles.

From Scotty's Castle within the park, turn right (northwest) on Scotty's Castle Road (Hwy. 267) and drive 26 miles to the junction with U.S. 95. Turn left onto U.S. 95 and drive north for 16 miles. At the signed Lida Junction, turn left onto Highway 266 and continue 7.2 miles. Turn left onto paved Highway 774, signed with a historical marker for Gold Point, and continue eight miles. The drive from Scotty's Castle will take about 1 hour and 15 minutes.

U.S. 95

Heading beyond the boundaries into Nevada, it's easy to lose yourself on the open highway, following highway signs that lure you farther and farther north to **Goldfield,** then **Tonopah,** time capsules of the American West. From Gold Point, it is 15 miles east to U.S. 95 at the Lida Junction (Hwy. 266 and U.S. 95), then another 15 miles north to Goldfield (plan 30 minutes for the drive).

Goldfield has a saloon (which doubles as a motel), one restaurant, and basic **supplies,** but no gas. The closest **gas** is in Tonopah, 27 miles north, a drive of about 30 minutes.

Goldfield

It's hard to know what to expect from the town of **Goldfield, Nevada** (http://goldfieldnevada.org). Various reports contradict each other, reporting it to be a ghost

restored cabins along Gold Point's main street

town, dead and boarded up, a haunted relic, or an active place with quaint businesses. I can't say that Goldfield is alive and well, but it's not entirely dead either. More than 200 people call the town home, and it has plenty to recommend it, including early 1900s architecture, well-preserved buildings from the gold-mining era, a main street with trading posts and shops open for business, and one of the oldest continuously operating saloons in the state. Goldfield had its boom between 1905 and 1910, and for a brief time it was the largest city in Nevada. Evidence of the boom remains, especially the reputedly haunted **Goldfield Hotel** (Euclid Ave.). The hotel is impressive in its brick grandeur, proud and sadly abandoned. Many people have made plans to restore the hotel over the years, but somehow it's never worked out.

ACCOMMODATIONS AND FOOD

The **Santa Fe Saloon** (925 N. 5th Ave., 775/485-3431, 2pm-8pm daily) is a great place to quench your thirst and meet the locals. The rail yard of the Bullfrog and Goldfield Railroad is across from the bar, an interesting place to explore.

Goldfield has one working restaurant—the **Dinky Diner** (323 Crook Ave., 775/485-3231, 7am-7pm Mon.-Sat., 7am-2pm Sun., $6-10). The **Santa Fe Saloon** (925 N. 5th Ave., 775/485-3431, call for reservations 2pm-8pm daily, from $55) offers limited lodging in its adjacent eight-room motel. **The General Store** (777 Crook Ave., 775/485-3477, 8am-8pm daily) stocks basic groceries and hardware supplies.

Tonopah

The small town of **Tonopah, Nevada** (www.tonophanevada.com), 27 miles north of Goldfield on U.S. 95, is an interesting mix of old and new. The **Tonopah Historic Mining Park** (110 Burro Ave., 775/482-9274, http://tonopahhistoricminingpark.com, 9am-5pm daily, $5 adults, $4 children) features a tour of mining tunnels, mine buildings, and artifacts.

ACCOMMODATIONS AND FOOD

The reportedly haunted **Mizpah Hotel** (100 N. Main St., 775/482-3030, www.mizpahhotel.net, $99-139) was built in 1907. It eventually fell into decline, but was given an impressive makeover in 2011. The hotel is decorated in period furnishings, deep reds, and carved wood. A fully stocked and staffed

The historic Mizpah Hotel has been restored to its former glory.

bar (11am-midnight daily) runs along a wall of leaded glass windows. Marble tables and plush seating dot the lobby, and a **café** (6am-10pm daily) provides food and drinks at cozy tables. The Mizpah is by far the best game in town for lodging and refreshments, filled with locals and travelers alike.

Getting There

It is possible to reach the towns of Goldfield and Tonopa, Nevada from Scotty's Castle via Highway 267 to U.S. 95, 26 miles east. From the junction with U.S. 95, turn north to reach Goldfield in 30 miles and Tonopah in 58 miles.

Panamint Springs and the Saline Valley

Look for ★ to find recommended
sights and activities.

Highlights

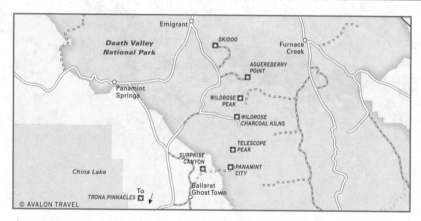

★ **Wildrose Charcoal Kilns:** Once used to make charcoal for the mining efforts in the area, these kilns now stand as works of hand-engineered beauty (page 125).

★ **Aguereberry Point:** Pete Aguereberry, a hermit miner, built the road to Aguereberry Point. His legacy is most certainly the spectacular views of the valley that he gave us (page 125).

★ **Skidoo:** Even though this former mining town is wiped clean off the map, it's still worth a visit. Push on past the barren town site to find the rare and well-preserved stamp mill (page 126).

★ **Surprise Canyon:** Cool pools, lush greenery, and beautifully sculpted white canyon walls make this a great place to escape the heat of the valley floor and soak in the beauty of the canyon (page 137).

★ **Panamint City:** The hike to the silver-boom ghost town of Panamint City follows the scenic but strenuous Surprise Canyon. Crawl over waterfalls, trudge through creek beds, and scramble over rocks—all the while wondering how a road was ever built through here (page 138).

★ **Telescope Peak:** The 13-mile hike to reach this highest peak in the park is well worth every switchback, affording sweeping views of Death Valley to the east and Panamint Valley to the west (page 140).

★ **Wildrose Peak:** Gnarled bristlecone pines mark the way through the tight switchbacks that lead to this windswept summit with panoramic views of the valley (page 141).

★ **Trona Pinnacles:** Limestone tufa formations rise from an ancient lake bed to create a place that is haunting and powerful (page 154).

P
art of the joy of visiting Death Valley is feeling like you've come to the ends of the earth, or even that you've landed on another planet entirely as you gaze over the cracked and alien landscape.

In the western Panamint Mountains, the relatively high number of creeks and springs, historical sites, and network of old roads that just won't die create a different kind of planet—one more akin to *Indiana Jones and the Temple of Doom* than *Star Wars*.

Old cabins and ghost camps are scattered through the wrinkled folds of the Panamints; some are forgotten, rotting into trickling springs, while others remain well visited by those still caught by the camp's mystique. Tales of silver spread through the mountains and caused towns like Panamint City to swell and burst. Today, some time and effort can take you to these hulks of history to marvel at the sheer determination that got people and equipment up to these remote and rugged locations. The western Panamint canyons are wet by comparison to the rest of Death Valley, and it's not unheard of for a flood to wipe out everything in its path, scouring a canyon down to the bare rock, marooning trucks and

equipment. Of course, there's the marvel of seeing water in the desert, plummeting down a canyon to form waterfalls and pools or gurgling along the surface, all making for a wet and wild hiking experience.

Joshua tree forests, a salt lake, and one washboard road make the Saline Valley a time capsule of tourism—Death Valley before Death Valley was a destination. In the Saline Valley, you give up your civilized right to a cell phone for a quiet and beautifully varied landscape. Driving Saline Valley Road will take you past rarely visited sand dunes and give you access to quiet ghost camps and scenic canyons.

Death Valley is known for its contrasts, and the Panamint Springs area is no exception. The drop from Telescope Peak, the highest mountain in the park, down to the valley floor is a dizzying 11,331 feet, higher than the South Rim of the Grand Canyon. Enter Surprise Canyon from the blazing-hot ghost

---

Previous: Aguereberry Camp; the ghost town of Skidoo. **Above:** Panamint City

Panamint Springs and The Saline Valley

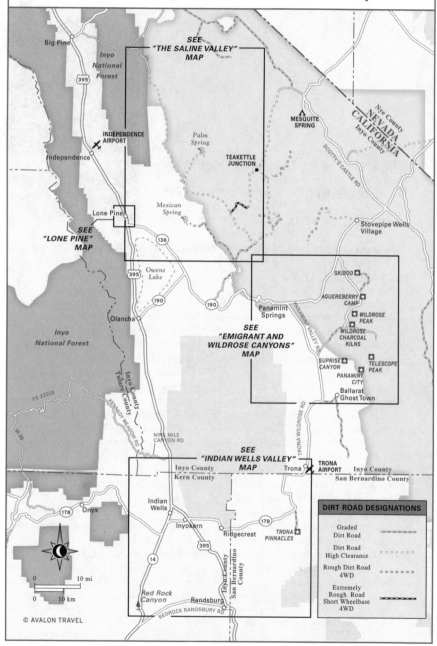

SEE "THE SALINE VALLEY" MAP

Big Pine

Inyo National Forest

395

Palm Spring

MESQUITE SPRING

Nye County NEVADA
CALIFORNIA Inyo County

INDEPENDENCE AIRPORT

TEAKETTLE JUNCTION

SCOTTY'S CASTLE RD

Independence

Mexican Spring

Stovepipe Wells Village

Lone Pine

SEE "LONE PINE" MAP

136

SKIDOO

395

Owens Lake

190

AGUEREBERRY CAMP

190

Panamint Springs

WILDROSE PEAK

WILDROSE CHARCOAL KILNS

Olancha

SEE "EMIGRANT AND WILDROSE CANYONS" MAP

SUPRISE CANYON

PANAMINT CITY

TELESCOPE PEAK

PANAMINT VALLEY RD

Inyo National Forest

Ballarat Ghost Town

FS 22S05

Inyo County
Tulare County

KENNEDY MEADOW RD

NINE MILE CANYON RD

TRONA WILDROSE RD

M 95

SEE "INDIAN WELLS VALLEY" MAP

Inyo County
Kern County

TRONA AIRPORT

Trona

Inyo County
San Bernardino County

178

Onyx

Indian Wells

Inyokern

178

Ridgecrest

TRONA PINNACLES

395

14

Red Rock Canyon

Randsburg

Inyo County
San Bernardino County

REDROCK RANDSBURY RD

0   10 mi
0   10 km

© AVALON TRAVEL

DIRT ROAD DESIGNATIONS

Graded Dirt Road

Dirt Road High Clearance

Rough Dirt Road 4WD

Extremely Rough Road Short Wheelbase 4WD

town of Ballarat only to have to fight your way through dense greenery, scrambling over waterfalls and past sculpted white canyon narrows. Winter brings snow and ice at the higher elevations; summer brings scorching sun. All year long brings the possibility of wind that has no scruples about scooping up your camping equipment to sacrifice to the desert gods. This western side of Death Valley will grab you with the stinging silence of the Saline Valley and rope you in with the untamed canyons of the Panamint Mountains. People come back year after year and season after season—it's different every time.

PLANNING YOUR TIME

This wild and diverse region is a favorite of the 4WD crowd as well as desert history buffs—4WD trails and historic sites dominate the landscape. But developing a plan of attack is key. The jutting elevation, long and lonely roads, twisting canyons, and adventurous hikes guarantee that you won't be able to do everything in one driving tour. Pick your sights, pick your drives, pick your hikes, and explore this region with a full tank of gas and everything else you need to survive, including water.

Concentrate your exploration on **three areas:** the Emigrant and Wildrose Canyon Area, the western Panamint canyons, and the Saline Valley.

Emigrant and Wildrose Canyon Area

The Emigrant Canyon and Wildrose Canyon area is the **most accessible** in this region. Setting up a nice base camp at the **Wildrose Campground** allows easy access to notable hikes as well as fragments of mining history around the Harrisburg Flats region. Plan **three days**: one day to hike Telescope Peak, one to hike Wildrose Peak and visit the Charcoal Kilns, and one day to see everything else.

The high mountain elevations in this region mean that it might be possible to extend the Death Valley season and escape the summer heat. Telescope Peak, the highest point in the park, has snow most of the year, and most of the campgrounds in nearby Wildrose Canyon are only open **March to November,** the opposite of the schedule in the rest of the park. The upper-elevation hikes are best during early summer.

Western Panamint Canyons

Ballarat, on the eastern edge of the Panamint Valley against the western Panamint Mountains, is a good jumping-off point for exploring the Panamint Canyons with a **4WD vehicle** or **backpacking.** All canyon roads require a 4WD vehicle, but it is still possible to explore some wonderful canyon hikes with a regular SUV. Even a passenger car can access a few special places.

The Saline Valley

All areas of the Panamint Springs region are remote, but the Saline Valley might win a competition for which gets the least visitors. **Saline Valley Road** traverses the region, beginning in the north near the town of Big Pine and intersecting with Highway 190 farther south, west of Panamint Springs. To drive Saline Valley Road takes the better part of a day without stops, no matter where you're coming from. You will probably need a **high-clearance vehicle,** but a 4WD vehicle is usually not necessary, except when rain and snow have created hazardous driving conditions.

Plan at least **three days** to explore this area, and consider camping at primitive Warm Springs Camp, with a central location in the Saline Valley. The best times to visit are **spring** and **fall.** Summer sees blazing temperatures; in winter, rain and snow can render the Saline Valley Road impassable.

Exploring the Park

The Panamint Springs region is a vast and geographically diverse area located on the western side of the park. At its upper end, the isolated Saline Valley lies tucked between the Inyo and Cottonwood Mountains, traversed only by the rough Saline Valley Road.

The lower section of this region is dominated by the western Panamint Mountains, the term referring to the western slope of these rugged mountains. The Panamint Mountains form the western edge of the park boundary and essentially create a barrier between the Panamint Valley to the west and Death Valley to the east. The barrier is highly effective and dictates the way you visit the park.

Choose a side: will it be the western or eastern canyons? The eastern canyons feed into Death Valley itself. The Death Valley National Park boundary is somewhere in the middle of the Panamint Mountains. Only one road goes all the way through to the other side—Goler Canyon via Mengel Pass—but this is not a viable route for casual sightseeing.

VISITORS CENTER

There are **no visitors centers** or entrance stations in this region of the park. The only services are located in Panamint Springs, the main hub and the only place that offers food and lodging. If you're not here, you're camping. It is possible to use Panamint Springs Resort as a base camp for day trips, but longer drives and hikes might cut it close to get back here by dinnertime.

PARK ENTRANCES

Highway 190 is the main route into the park from the west side. The paved road bisects the region, entering the park at the Panamint Springs Resort. From here, it is a drive of 30 miles east to Stovepipe Wells, the closest official park entrance station, and 56 miles east to Furnace Creek, the two park hubs.

Three roads feed into the park from **U.S.**

395. From the west, **Highway 190** splits from U.S. 395 at Olancha. From Olancha, it is 45 miles east to Panamint Springs, the park hub. From the north and west, **Highway 136** leaves U.S. 395 south of Lone Pine (24 miles north of Olancha) to head east, intersecting with Highway 190 in 18 miles. Highway 190 then continues 30 miles east to Panamint Springs. The total distance from Lone Pine to Panamint Springs is about 50 miles.

From the south, **Highway 178** splits east from U.S. 395 at Inyokern. Highway 178 then heads 34 miles east through Ridgecrest before swinging north through the mining town of Trona, where it becomes **Trona Wildrose Road.** Just south of the park boundary, Trona Wildrose Road splits. Panamint Valley Road leads 14 miles north to Highway 190, just east of Panamint Springs, while Wildrose Canyon Road heads directly west to the Wildrose Canyon and Emigrant Canyon areas.

Trona Wildrose Road is subject to washouts, especially the section south from the Panamint Valley Road split with Ballarat Road, 22 miles north of Trona. Check road conditions ahead of time. If the road is closed, use the paved Nadeau Street, 18 miles north of Trona and 3.8 miles south of Ballarat. From Trona, turn left onto Nadeau Street to continue heading north for 8.1 miles. Turn right onto graded and unpaved Slate Range Road. Slate Range Road intersects with Panamint Valley Road in 4.9 miles. Follow Panamint Valley Road north to Highway 190, then drop back down into the Wildrose Canyon area via Emigrant Canyon Road.

Gas and Services

Big Pine is located on U.S. 395, about 43 miles north of Lone Pine. The town provides the northernmost access to the park via either the North Pass of Saline Valley Road or Big Pine-Death Valley Road. Big Pine offers gas, lodging, food, and outdoor supplies. It also

Driving Distances

From Panamint Springs:	Distance	Duration
Stovepipe Wells	30 mi	30 min
Furnace Creek	55 mi	1 hr
Scotty's Castle	74 mi	1.5 hr
The Racetrack	100 mi	3.5 hr
Eureka Dunes	120 mi	3.5 hr
Olancha	45 mi	45 min
Lone Pine	50 mi	1 hr
Big Pine	93 mi	1.5 hr
Ridgecrest	70 mi (via Trona Wildrose Rd.) or 100 mi (via U.S. 395)	1.5 hr
Trona	48 mi (via Trona Wildrose Rd.)	1 hr

provides a refueling stop for people heading into or out of the Sierra Nevada Mountains to the west or Death Valley to the east.

Lone Pine, south on U.S. 395, is a busy little town filled with hikers, climbers, and travelers on their way to northern lakes and ski resorts. Services include motels, restaurants, groceries, outdoor supplies, and gas. If you have had a long drive to the area and want to make a fresh entrance to Death Valley the next day, this is an excellent place to stop, regroup, and venture on.

If you blink, you'll miss **Olancha**—and you'll also miss your last chance to fill up on gas before turning east off U.S. 395 toward Panamint Springs, 45 miles away. Stopping here, just south of Lone Pine, can save you the sticker shock of Panamint Springs. The small roadside **Ranch House Café** (760/764-2363, 7am-8pm daily, $5-15) serves big portions of homespun food—burgers, sandwiches, and salads. The cute atmosphere and good service make it a pleasant stop into or out of Death Valley. Other services include a convenience store and a motel.

In the Indian Wells Valley, **Inyokern, Ridgecrest,** and **Trona** offer southern access to the park; all have gas stations and convenience stores. Trona is the last stop for gas before the park, but gas stations may not be open after business hours. Play it safe and fill up in Ridgecrest, a good-size town with

grocery stores, hotels, and most of the common chain stores. If you forgot something or need supplies, you can probably find it here. For a charming place to stay near the park boundary, Lone Pine is a better bet.

DRIVING TOUR

The western Panamints start on Bureau of Land Management land and stretch east into Death Valley National Park. The **4WD drives** here are rugged with shifting conditions, and they require technical skill and equipment. Only one road goes through clear to the other side—the Goler Canyon road via Mengel Pass—but to call Mengel Pass a road is a stretch. It's a cliff-hugger and a nail-biter. Do not attempt it unless you have experience and the right equipment. Other canyon drives in the area only flirt with the mountain passes before they head back down to the Panamint Valley. Roads in Jail Canyon and Pleasant Canyon, for example, nose their way toward Death Valley but end without going all the way through.

Saline Valley Road

Saline Valley Road's condition has improved over the years, but it remains long, with more than **50 miles of winding dirt**. Despite its remoteness, many people drive this road in all forms of vehicle—from apocalyptic 4WD desert beasts with military tires to adorable little VW buses with matching curtains. When the road is dry in optimal conditions, it is passable by any manner of vehicle, but the going is not smooth. Rocks, washboard, sand in places, and the sheer length of the road make it an endurance test; getting a flat or two is a distinct possibility. On the bright side, alpine forests, abundant Joshua trees, stellar views, remote sand dunes, bird's-eye views of the Saline Valley, and access to powerfully beautiful canyons make it worth the haul.

Summer brings intense heat and keeps most visitors away. Winter can bring snow, ice, and road closures; carry chains. Be prepared with gas, food, and water.

Scenic Four-Wheel Drives
PLEASANT CANYON
TO ROGERS PASS

The rugged road that winds through **Pleasant Canyon** leads to forested mountains, backcountry cabins, and historic gold mining camps of the western Panamint Mountains. A **4WD vehicle is mandatory** for this drive.

Starting from Ballarat, the canyon springs are one of the highlights of the lower canyon. If you are driving, you will be driving directly in the creek, tunneling through greenery. **Clair Camp,** a ghost town with a ton of charm and history, is six miles inside the canyon. This is doable as a full-day hike. If you are driving, make sure you get out to explore the camp's stone dugouts, cabins, relics of daily life, and mill for processing ore.

The road to the World Beater and Ratcliff Mines branches off to the right a mile past Clare Camp. Between the World Beater and Ratcliff Mine, the road climbs steeply along the canyon walls. The **World Beater mine's** highlights include a rustic cabin and the ruins of a stone stamp mill. The **Ratcliff Mine** has

the remains of two tramways to service its lower tunnels as well as striking views of the Panamint Valley below. The Ratcliff Mine has two side roads, one climbing up on the right and the second that leads down to other prospects. Note that the second junction is the last place you will be able to turn around. This is a good place to park. Visiting these mines is doable as a side trip from the main Pleasant Canyon Road.

Once you return to the main road, you will reach **Upper Pleasant Canyon,** which opens into a valley. Past the World Beater Mine Road you'll come to a spring feeding into a tub. Burros love this spot so all water should be purified, even if it comes from the pipe. Just beyond, a side road on the left leads to another gold mine. The **Porter Mine** is located in upper Happy Canyon. The stone ruins here are the walls of the **Stone Corral,** once the property of Panamint Tom. He is the brother of Hungry Bill, a Shoshone who famously cultivated gardens and orchards in Johnson Canyon and sold the fresh fruit and vegetables to miners over the mountain in the silver boomtown of Panamint City. Panamint Tom was famous in his own right for his horse raids as far as Los Angeles.

Although the road can be driven with a return loop through South Park Canyon, *this is only recommended for expert drivers with experience.* That drive is not covered in this book. The road through South Park Canyon has many dangerous sections, including Chicken Rock, a high, steep canted bit of road that slops directly toward the precipitous mountainside. Rollovers on this section of road are well documented and not uncommon. The Bridge is a dangerously washed out section of road patched with a bridge made of telephone poles and chicken wire. If you are intrigued by South Park Canyon, consider hiking it instead.

Sights

EMIGRANT AND WILDROSE CANYON AREAS

★ Wildrose Charcoal Kilns

Once used to make charcoal for the mining efforts in the area, the **Wildrose Charcoal Kilns** now stand as works of hand-engineered beauty. The kilns are made of cut limestone, quarried locally and cemented with gravel, lime, and sand. They stand approximately 25 feet tall, their walls curving gracefully inward to form a beehive shape. The Modock Consolidated Mining Company built them in 1877 to fuel the smelters of lead-silver mines in the Argus range to the west. The structures were designed to reflect as much interior heat as possible, but who knew that sound waves have similar properties? Open arched doorways lead to the interior of the kilns; stomp around on the floors of each one to capture the hollow echoes. Each kiln stands as a mini cathedral, the echoes swelling to the industry that once rang out across the canyon.

If you hike along the **Wildrose Peak Trail,** which starts at the first charcoal kiln, you'll see tree stumps along the mostly forested trail. The trees were cut down and fed to the kilns to feed the mining operations that were king here. This is an easy trip from Wildrose Campground or on your way to hike Wildrose or Telescope Peak.

DIRECTIONS

From Panamint Springs, drive 16 miles east on Highway 190 to Emigrant Canyon Road. Turn right onto Emigrant Canyon Road and drive 21 miles south to the road's end. The kilns are located seven miles past Wildrose Campground. The road is paved most of the way; the last two miles of gravel are slightly rough, but should be suitable for most cars.

Aguereberry Camp

Pete Aguereberry came to Death Valley in 1905 in search of gold and found it, working what would become the **Eureka Mine** until his death in 1945. The hill where Pete Aguereberry originally filed claims with fellow prospector Shorty Borden attracted a temporary mining camp called Harrisburg. In 1907 Pete had control of the Eureka Mine, and the few hundred people that had set up their tents in the hopes of cashing in eventually left. He nearly singlehandedly built and worked the Eureka Mine for 40 years, carving out a permanent life in the fleeting world of mining.

Today, you can explore the **original camp,** visible from Aguereberry Point Road. One of the three **cabins** was Pete Aguereberry's, built in 1907 and still partially furnished. Remains of the Eureka Mine can be explored just over the hill to the south behind the camp. Wander around to find the mine site, look for flat places where the tent city stood, and keep your eye out for tin cans and other camp artifacts.

DIRECTIONS

From Panamint Springs, drive 16 miles east on Highway 190 to Emigrant Canyon Road. Turn right onto Emigrant Canyon Road and drive 10.3 miles south. Turn left (east) onto Aguereberry Point Road and continue 1.4 miles to Aguereberry Camp.

★ Aguereberry Point

Pete Aguereberry, a miner who took his place in Death Valley history through sheer perseverance, built the road to **Aguereberry Point** to show friends his favorite view. He eked out a living from the Eureka Mine located just off the Aguereberry Point Road long after the area was abandoned in favor of other boom sites. His legacy is most certainly the spectacular views he gave us of Death Valley—across the valley floor southeast to Badwater Basin, the Black Mountains, and the green oasis of Furnace Creek.

Emigrant and Wildrose Canyons

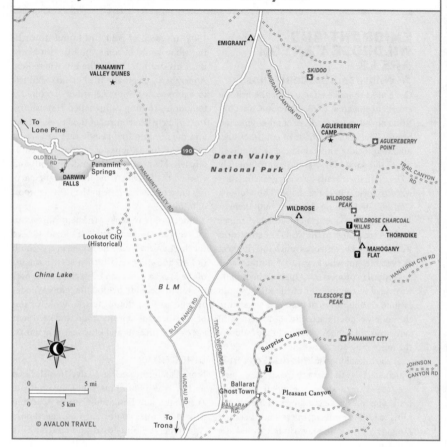

DIRECTIONS

From Panamint Springs, drive 16 miles east on Highway 190 to Emigrant Canyon Road. Turn right onto Emigrant Canyon Road and drive 10.3 miles south. Turn left (east) onto Aguereberry Point Road and continue a little over six miles, past Aguereberry Camp, to the road's end. The road require a **high-clearance vehicle,** especially on the last hill (0.5 mile) until the point where spectacular views await.

★ Skidoo

As far as mining towns go, the town of Skidoo lived to a ripe old age, producing gold from 1906 all the way until 1917. Strangely, none of the town site remains; foundations, businesses, and cabins are all gone, marked only by an interpretive sign and scattered artifacts. It's still worth the visit for the rare and well-preserved **stamp mill,** located beyond the town site. The views of Death Valley are spectacular.

Skidoo may best be known for the grisly lynching that took place here in 1908. Joe Simpson, co-owner of the Gold Seal Saloon, murdered Jim Arnold, a well-respected citizen and businessman. Simpson was then lynched by an angry mob. Pictures of Joe Simpson hanging from a noose are well documented, but how these pictures came to be is not totally clear. Legend has it that his body was dug up and then photographed for the benefit of reporters from Los Angeles who came to check out the story a few days after the lynching. Other versions suggest that a Skidoo mine physician named McDonald exhumed Simpson's body to study the effects of syphilis on the brain. What is clear is that after Simpson was exhumed, the good doctor decapitated him to study his brain. He then preserved the skull by setting it on an anthill to let nature take its course. The skull ended up in a doctor's office in the nearby mining town of Trona, and then into a private collection.

DIRECTIONS

From Highway 190, drive 9.4 miles south to Emigrant Canyon Road and turn left onto the modestly marked, dirt Skidoo Road. The long and slowly winding road is graded and passable by most cars, but a **high-clearance vehicle** is recommended. You'll reach the town site of Skidoo in approximately seven miles.

The stamp mill is about two miles past the town site. To reach the stamp mill, continue past the town site, staying left at the first fork. The road splits again, and any of the paths offer a view of the stamp mill, although the left fork leads most directly to it. The last mile of road is rough, climbing up the hillside with rocky patches with only a small parking area. If you are driving a passenger vehicle, park and walk the last mile.

WESTERN PANAMINTS

The western Panamints are formidable and sheer, with a rich mining history and enough springs and creeks to keep your hiking exciting and fresh.

Ballarat

Ballarat has been teetering on the edge of ghost-town status for more than 100 years, but it can't quite get there. The town looks like a mirage when you approach it, set on the shimmering salt flats of the Panamint Valley floor, dwarfed against the dramatic backdrop of the Panamint Mountains.

Ballarat had its heyday between 1897 and 1905 as a resupply and entertainment center serving the nearby gold and silver mines. At its height, it claimed all the institutions of civilization, including a post office, a school, general stores, a jail, and more than its share of

Aguereberry Point has sweeping views of Death Valley from 6,433 feet.

saloons. The only thing lacking was a church, an oversight that has not gone unnoticed by people who pay attention to this kind of history.

Although the post office closed in 1917, Ballarat continues to be a nerve center of sorts for this remote area and is a must-stop for news about road, camping, and hiking conditions.

The town has a **general store** that serves as a welcome center. While the store does not have regular hours, the caretaker is usually on-site, and it has been open every time I passed through. The only supplies available are icy cold beer and soda dispensed from an antique ice chest. When the temperatures soar to well over 100°F, this may well seem like the momentary answer to your needs.

It's polite to stop in at the general store and say hello to caretaker **Rocky Novak,** the only full-time resident of Ballarat. Rocky once lived at the Chris Wicht Camp in Surprise Canyon and worked in Panamint City for years. Rocky can offer helpful tips and will likely be in tune with any major Death Valley news before the National Park Service can get the word out. He has a wealth of information about the area past and present that he will gladly share. While here, consider making a small donation toward maintaining this historic space.

The semi-ghost town is also worth a stop in its own right. Newer trailers are mixed in among the original adobe structures and wood cabins. The original **jail** has been slightly restored and is open to visitors. You're free to wander around the town, but the buildings behind the store are off-limits. The **cemetery** is just west of town, surrounded by a wrought-iron fence.

Charles Manson's final hideout, the **Barker Ranch,** is located in the vicinity. A truck reputedly owned by the Manson family now sits in front of the general store with other vehicles, quietly rusting against the mountain backdrop.

While there are no services in Ballarat, camping is allowed with permission from the caretaker. The jail also doubles as a no-frills **cabin** open to camping.

DIRECTIONS

From Panamint Springs, take Panamint Valley Road south for 14 miles; continue right for nine miles as it turns into Trona Wildrose Road. A historic marker will direct you to the turnoff for the town via Ballarat Road.

You can also reach Ballarat from the north

the general store in the not-quite-ghost-town of Ballarat

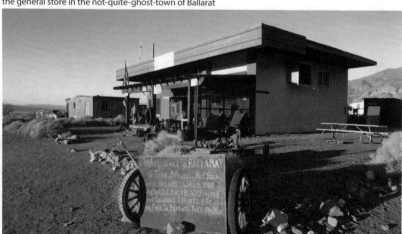

via Indian Ranch Road, 0.4 mile south of Panamint Valley Road. Less than 12 miles on this graded dirt road will take you to the town. All routes are dusty but fairly level, and you should be able to make the trip in any type of vehicle.

THE SALINE VALLEY

In some ways, the Saline Valley is a smaller, more rugged, and more isolated Death Valley. The formidable Inyo Mountains jut toward the sky on the west side, and the Panamint Mountains form a barrier to the east. If you make it all the way out here, you likely have some specific destination in mind. The Saline Valley Road is a highly scenic drive through beautiful desert. Two passes give rise to some dizzying views as well as access to the pristine Saline Valley Dunes, the spiky acres of Joshua trees at Lee Flat, the historic Salt Tramway, and rugged, rewarding canyons with some historic mining ruins.

There are **no services** in the Saline Valley.

Saline Valley Road

Saline Valley Road is the only road with access to the remote Saline Valley. The rough road ranges from graded dirt to high clearance and parallels the western boundary of the park for about 80 miles.

Saline Valley Road is a county road, maintained and graded by Inyo County. During good weather, the road conditions are generally good, with **graded gravel** allowing for moderate speeds of 25 to 35 mph. A **high-clearance vehicle** is preferable, but a 4WD vehicle may be necessary. However, the road is prone to washouts after rain and during snowy conditions in winter, when chains are required. Any inclement weather can turn the road treacherous with deep mud, sand, and washouts. Inyo County closes the road during these times, so always check road conditions before driving and obey any road closures.

Even in optimal conditions, *this drive is not to be undertaken lightly.* If you plan to drive this road **bring extra food, water,** and **tools,** and be prepared for anything. Even

on a good day, it is possible that the washboard road could cause mechanical failure or a flat tire. And a flat tire here could mean being stranded for days. If you get into a true emergency, Saline Valley Warm Springs has a year-round caretaker generally available with a radio and the ability to contact the outside world. During spring and holiday weekends, there may be traffic to the hot springs, but the rest of the year, don't count on seeing another soul.

From end to end, the drive takes **6-7 hours,** depending upon your vehicle and the road conditions. There are two points of entry to the Saline Valley Road. Depending on where you enter the Saline Valley, the road is referred to as driving through the North or South Pass.

NORTH PASS

The north entrance, or North Pass, is a mountain pass that reaches 7,300 feet elevation; it can be snowy in winter. The closest services are at the town of **Big Pine,** a few miles west of where Saline Valley Road emerges onto the pavement at **Big Pine-Death Valley Road.**

SOUTH PASS

The South Pass is another mountain pass that reaches just under 6,000 feet elevation; it can also be snowy in winter. The closest services to the south are at **Panamint Springs,** 13 miles east of where Saline Valley Road emerges onto **Highway 190.** Most people use the South Pass to access sites along the road, especially the remote Saline Valley Warm Springs.

Lee Flat Joshua Tree Forest

Lee Flat is home to the most impressive Joshua tree forest in the park, covering more than 4,000 acres of valley and hillsides. The trees thrive here both in height and sheer quantity, dominating the landscape with their jaunty, spiky presence.

Lee Flat is a high-desert valley, and a drive through the graded roads will skew your idea of what a desert should look like. Mounded green hills keep you snaking along

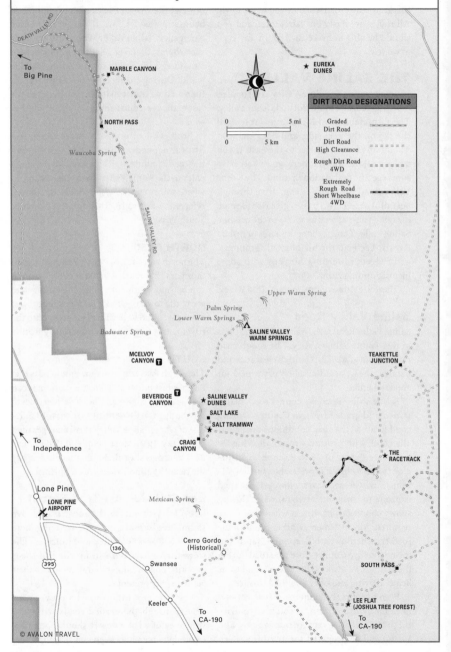

The Saline Valley

DEATH VALLEY RD

To
Big Pine

MARBLE CANYON

NORTH PASS

EUREKA
DUNES

Waucoba Spring

SALINE VALLEY RD

DIRT ROAD DESIGNATIONS

Graded Dirt Road	
Dirt Road High Clearance	
Rough Dirt Road 4WD	
Extremely Rough Road Short Wheelbase 4WD	

0   5 mi
0   5 km

Upper Warm Spring

Palm Spring
Lower Warm Springs

SALINE VALLEY
WARM SPRINGS

Badwater Springs

MCELVOY
CANYON

TEAKETTLE
JUNCTION

BEVERIDGE
CANYON

SALINE VALLEY
DUNES

SALT LAKE

SALT TRAMWAY

CRAIG
CANYON

To
Independence

THE
RACETRACK

Lone Pine

LONE PINE
AIRPORT

Mexican Spring

136

395

Cerro Gordo
(Historical)

Swansea

SOUTH PASS

Keeler

To
CA-190

LEE FLAT
(JOSHUA TREE FOREST)

To
CA-190

© AVALON TRAVEL

The historic Salt Tramway carried salt from the valley floor across the Inyo Mountains.

at an elevation of more than 5,000 feet. The cool air snaps, a relief from the desert floor. In spring, wildflowers pop out at every turn. Pull off the road to wander through this place, which feels bright, spacious, timeless, and secret all at once.

DIRECTIONS

From the **South Pass** near Panamint Springs, set aside **3-4 hours** for the leisurely, scenic drive to Lee Flat. The best access to Lee Flat is via Saline Valley Road. From Highway 190, follow Saline Valley Road north for 8.2 miles to a fork. The left fork leads to Lee Flat Road; the right fork continues along Saline Valley Road. Turn left onto Lee Flat Road to venture deeper into the thick of this special place.

Salt Tramway

Death Valley saw many grand mining dreams go head-to-head with the incredibly rugged landscape. The venture for halite, humble table salt, rivaled the biggest. White Smith was an attorney who came to work for the

local borax mines as a teamster. It was his vision of the halite deposits at the appropriately named Salt Lake that became responsible for the operation.

To mine the salt, an aerial tramway was built in 1912-1913. The tramway consisted of a series of massive wooden towers that climbed 7,700 feet over 13.5 miles. The salt was mined through a system that required flooding the playa and then letting the water evaporate. The revealed salt deposits were then loaded into buggies and transported by wooden cart to the tramway terminal. The tramway carried the salt, bucket by bucket, over the rugged terrain to Owens Valley on the other side of the Inyo Mountains. More than 30,000 tons of salt were transported in its 12 years of operation. Although the mine had some periods of idleness, it closed for good in 1933 at the height of the Great Depression.

In 1974 the **Salt Tramway** was placed on the National Register of Historic Places. You can see part of the tramway as you head north through the South Pass on Saline Valley Road in the area of Salt Lake. Some of the tramway towers are visible south of the road, where they cling to the side of the sheer Inyo Mountains. While they may look tiny, dwarfed by the mountains, the towers' true size is apparent on the valley floor. North of the road, the massive, solidly built timbers extend along an access road toward Salt Lake.

LOWER TRAMWAY

To walk out to the lower tramway, take the short maintenance road that passes three tramway towers to end at Salt Lake. **Salt Lake** is a salt-crusted expanse, sometimes covered with a shallow layer of water after a rain. From Saline Valley Road, the first tram tower is less than 0.5 mile away. The road passes two other towers and ends at the lake's edge. Wooden stakes mark the shallow ponds used for salt evaporation.

UPPER TRAMWAY

An extremely rugged and strenuous **trail** (used to build and maintain the Salt Tramway) leads to the upper tramway towers. Looking at the tiny towers clinging to side of the Inyo Mountains, try to imagine how this feat of engineering was achieved in the harsh terrain, remote location, and unforgiving weather. An insane level of persistence and vision, mind-boggling to contemplate, made this a reality.

The trail travels more than five miles past the first **10 control towers**. However, a walk just to the base of the Inyo Mountains along Salt Tramway Road leads past several towers to end at the biggest tower on the valley floor in less than two miles. Where the maintenance road intersects with Saline Valley Road, take the very faint south fork toward the Inyo Mountains for less 0.5 mile to its end. The trail starts as the continuation of the maintenance road along the valley floor; in less than two miles, it meets the base of the Inyo Mountains. From this point, the trail becomes extremely strenuous—switchbacks up the mountain are very precarious with sheer drop-offs. This section of the trail requires research and preparation.

DIRECTIONS

The tramway crosses Saline Valley Road about 35 miles north of Highway 190 (via the **South Pass**). From the south, the tramway is about five miles south of the Saline Valley Dunes. As the towers come into view, look for the unsigned road that leads directly to them, connecting them along the valley floor.

Saline Valley Dunes

The first time I came out to the sand dunes, I was so busy using them as a landmark to get to Saline Valley Warm Springs that it didn't occur to me to admire them on their own. These sand dunes in the Saline Valley are isolated and pristine, set strikingly against the stark Inyo Mountains. By all means—stop your car, get out, and explore the dunes.

The **Saline Valley Dunes** are wide and shifting, only covering about 2.2 square miles; the highest dunes are about 20 feet tall. They might not look impressive from the road, but it's easy to become immersed in this undulating sea of sand. As the sand ripples toward the

mountains, creating a smooth place to walk, yours might be the only human tracks. When ready, follow your tracks back to your car.

DIRECTIONS

The sand dunes are less than one mile from **Saline Valley Road** and are easily visible from the road. A short-access spur, about 1.5 miles south of Warm Springs Road, heads east toward the foot of the dunes in less than 0.5 mile. The spur is very faint, not much more than a 4WD track; if you can't find it, park and walk the short stretch from Saline Valley Road.

Saline Valley Warm Springs

The **Saline Valley Warm Springs** have been cultivated for decades by people seeking to make an idyllic place to camp and relax in this isolated location. In the 1960s and 1970s, this was a hippie hot spot. The National Park Service took over management of the land in 1994, with a compromise that allows a caretaker and visitors to maintain and regulate the area. The tradition of being free and naked in the great outdoors has continued, and many people treat the springs as clothing-optional.

Although this is an extremely remote spot, many people make the trek to the springs; it can get very busy, especially on long weekends in spring and fall. For your own enjoyment, and to experience the peaceful surroundings, avoid these times if possible. The springs can be accessed via either the **North or South Pass,** depending on your vehicle, current road conditions, and your point of origin.

There are three sets of warm springs. Allow a minimum of **three days** to visit: one day to drive in, one day to soak and relax, and one day to return. Most people stay for several days or weeks, getting into the peaceful groove of soaking and relaxing. The Saline Valley Warm Springs have a year-round caretaker, and over the years many improvements have been made: warm **outdoor showers, restrooms** (pit toilets), and impeccably maintained springs and grounds.

Be prepared for blazing sun in the summer, cold temperatures in the winter, and the possibility of stinging sandstorms year-round (consider bringing goggles). The wind out here is no joke, and it will grab a tent or other belongings in a moment. On one trip, I woke to find my entire camp alcove shelter had blown away without a trace. If you find it in some distant canyon in the Saline Valley, you're welcome to it.

LOWER WARM SPRINGS

The **Lower Warm Springs** are lush and serene, with a shaded rock pool and a cultivated green lawn where people gather, picnic, and relax—this is where most of the action is. There are less than 10 **campsites** tucked away in the mesquite trees nearest the main springs. When full, other campsites spill out into the exposed desert or toward the Palm Spring.

PALM SPRING

Palm Spring, 0.7 mile east on Warm Springs Road, is a little quieter. By contrast, it is austere and exposed to the blinding glare of the desert. It's a surreal experience to be sitting chest-deep in the natural mineral waters, at eye level with the expanse of desert but protected from its cold, heat, and stinging sand. Some people camp here or between Lower Warm Spring and Palm Spring. **Camping** is open desert camping; campsites are not defined.

UPPER WARM SPRINGS

The **Upper Warm Springs** are 2.4 miles northeast on Warm Springs Road, which gets progressively rockier. A **high-clearance vehicle,** and possibly a 4WD vehicle, is necessary. It's also a nice hike from Lower Warm Springs or Palm Spring. The upper spring is a deep-blue pool, the most natural state of the three, and is surrounded by a fence to fend off **wild burros,** which roam freely in the area. It is possible to open-desert camp at Upper Warm Springs, although most people prefer to camp at Lower Warm Springs or Palm Spring, where there are restrooms, outdoor showers, and other campers.

Marble Canyon

Marble Canyon is a scenic **ghost camp** located in the Inyo Mountains on Saline Valley Road via the North Pass. Marble Canyon was first mined around 1882, but the most intensive efforts occurred in the 1930s and continued until the 1960s. Today, the remains of the large gold placer mine include historic cabins and mining headframes scattered around the canyon floor.

Saline Valley Road goes directly through the site. Getting out of the car to explore will reveal several **cabins** of varying ages, along with **mine works**. The oldest cabins with stone foundations are located in the wash of Marble Canyon along a primitive spur, the unmarked Jackass Flats Road.

DIRECTIONS

Marble Canyon is best reached via the **North Pass.** From Big Pine, drive east on Highway 168 for about two miles. Turn right onto Big Pine-Death Valley Road and continue east for about 12 miles. Turn right onto Saline Valley Road to head south. Marble Canyon lies at the bottom of a series of switchbacks, more than six miles from Big Pine-Death Valley Road. The road veers east into Marble Canyon and then curves in a sharp right to follow Opal Canyon to the south; Marble Canyon begins at the curve.

From the curve in Saline Valley Road, Jackass Flats Road continues east into the wash of Marble Canyon for about 1.5 miles, then turns right (south) into Opal Canyon. To explore Marble Canyon, either walk this road or drive and park near the turn. The road is rough; a **high-clearance vehicle,** possibly a 4WD vehicle, is necessary.

The drive can also be done as a day trip from Saline Valley Warm Springs; it's about 1.5-2 hours each way. From the junction of Warm Springs Road and Saline Valley Road, head north for about 26 miles to Marble Canyon.

Recreation

HIKING
Darwin Falls

Distance: 2 miles round-trip
Duration: 1.5 hours
Elevation gain: 220 feet
Effort: Easy
Access: Passenger vehicle
Trailhead: From Panamint Springs, drive one mile west on Highway 190. Turn left onto a graded dirt road and continue to the parking area just past the fork at 2.5 miles. The right fork leads to the falls (see map p. 136).

The marvel of **Darwin Falls** is that they exist at all. The hike to the first falls is an easy and quick detour from Panamint Springs. A short **one-mile walk** along a canyon creek leads you to a sight to behold: actual water streaming over slanted bedrock. This is where most people stop. About 1.5 hours should get you to the falls and back in time for a nice lunch on the Panamint Springs patio.

The hike is not pristine wilderness, however; a pipeline follows the well-used trail. The area is also an active wash, and signs of flooding, churned dirt, and rocks, are everywhere.

Three more waterfalls lie beyond the first falls, but they require climbing and very careful navigation. *Do not attempt this casually.* Any hiking around waterfalls can be extremely dangerous.

Panamint Valley Dunes

Distance: 7 miles round-trip
Duration: 4-5 hours
Elevation gain: 750 feet
Effort: Moderate
Access: Passenger vehicle
Trailhead: From Panamint Springs, drive east for 4.5 miles to Big Four Mine Road (labeled "Lake Hill" on maps). Turn left and drive the graded road for 5.8 miles, to the first sharp right turn, and park (see map p. 126).

These star-shaped dunes are located in the northern reaches of Panamint Valley, accessible only by a **long desert walk across sand.** Dunes have a magnetic pull that draws us close, something that tells us those mountains of sand will be even more fascinating close up. For the **Panamint Valley Dunes,** we can only hope that this pull

The remains of a mining camp are scattered across Marble Canyon along the North Pass of the Saline Valley Road.

Panamint Springs Hikes

The creekbed in McElvoy Canyon creates a green swath against the austere Saline Valley.

Trail	Effort	Distance	Duration
Darwin Falls	Easy	2 mi rt	1.5 hr
McElvoy Canyon	Moderate	1.6 mi rt	2 hr
Surprise Canyon	Moderate	1.6-2.6 mi rt	4 hr
Panamint Valley Dunes	Moderate	7 mi rt	4-5 hr
Wildrose Peak	Moderate	9 mi rt	4-5 hr
Beveridge Canyon	Moderate to strenuous	1-2.4 mi rt	1-5 hr
Panamint City	Strenuous	11 mi rt	10-12 hr
Telescope Peak	Strenuous	13 mi rt	7-8 hr

lasts the **3.5 miles** of hiking over the flat, exposed sand that's required to reach them.

McElvoy Canyon

Distance: 1.6 miles round-trip
Duration: 2 hours
Elevation gain: 530 feet
Effort: Moderate
Access: High-clearance/4WD
Trailhead: From Panamint Springs, drive 13 miles west on Highway 190 to Saline Valley Road. Turn right and drive 34.5 miles north on Saline Valley Road. A faint, unmaintained road leads west toward the Inyo Mountains and the deep cut of McElvoy Canyon. The road is 7.6 miles north of the Salt Tramway Junction (1 mile south of Warm Springs Rd.) and is hard to follow, requiring a high-clearance vehicle and a 4WD vehicle in places. The road continues up a rough alluvial fan just south of McElvoy Canyon to end in one mile (see map p. 130).

A deep canyon, a waterfall, and a bubbling creek create a cool world far removed from the surrounding desert of the Saline Valley. You have to make the journey into **McElvoy Canyon** on faith, since there is no sign of this lively creek and waterfall until you're on top of it.

From end of the road to McElvoy Canyon, walk northwest a few hundred yards toward

Darwin Falls

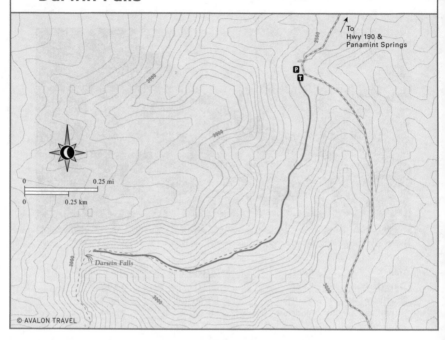

the canyon entrance until you reach the edge of a **deep wash.** Follow the bank for a short distance toward the mountains until you find a break that lets you walk down into the wash. An **unmarked trail** will be visible leading down into the wash and continuing toward the canyon mouth.

Soon the magic begins, and you'll be walking along a **bubbling creek**. Following the creek will take you to the canyon mouth in about 0.5 mile from the edge of the wash. In another 0.3 mile you will reach a **grotto waterfall,** cool with hanging ferns. There is a second waterfall 0.5 mile beyond the first, but it involves a moderate rock-climb over a dry slant to the right of the creek to get you beyond the grotto.

Beveridge Canyon

Distance: 1 mile round-trip
Duration: 1 hour
Elevation gain: 385 feet

Effort: Moderate to strenuous
Access: High-clearance/4WD
Trailhead: Lower Beveridge Canyon is accessed from Saline Valley Road. A faint, primitive road starts less than 32 miles north of Highway 190 via the Saline Valley Road South Pass (4 miles south of Warm Springs Rd.) to climb a fan toward the canyon mouth. Follow the road as far as you can, then park and walk (see map p. 137).

Beveridge Canyon shares a name and canyon with Beveridge, a fabled ghost town deep in the Inyo Mountains, reputed to be the remotest ghost town in the Mojave Desert. The only way to reach the ghost town of Beveridge is via the upper canyon in the Inyo Mountains wilderness. The lower canyon has its own intense beauty and draw, if you can get through even a piece of it.

Depending on where you park, you will reach the abandoned **Trio Mill Site** and camp in about 0.3 mile, walking west along the road toward the canyon mouth. The

Beveridge Canyon

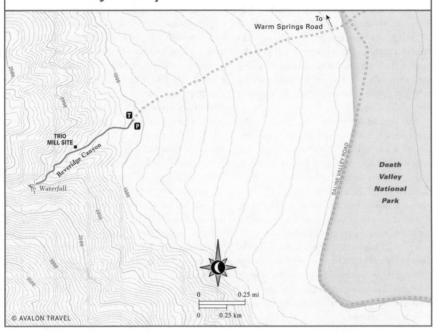

camp is littered with antique equipment, a truck graveyard, and a decaying cabin whose yard is dotted with metal junk sculptures and other deteriorating buildings (this is private property).

The camp is on the edge of a very rocky, boulder-filled wash that leads to the canyon mouth and the first **waterfall** in about 0.2 mile. Sculpted narrows, waterfalls, and intense greenery fill the canyon. Hiking beyond the first waterfall is extremely strenuous and requires rock-climbing skills; however, it is possible to hike to the first waterfall without any special moves. Beveridge Canyon is generally water-filled, but may dry up at the lower elevations during very dry years.

★ Surprise Canyon
Distance: 1.6-2.6 miles round-trip
Duration: 4 hours
Elevation gain: 665 feet
Effort: Moderate

Access: Passenger vehicle; high-clearance recommended

Trailhead: From Ballarat, drive two miles north along Indian Ranch Road to the signed turnoff for Surprise Canyon. At the junction, turn right (west) and drive four miles up the road to the historic Chris Wicht Camp; park in the small parking area. The road is rocky, but it is maintained by Inyo County and may be passable with a passenger car (see map p. 139).

The **Chris Wicht Camp** is named for the superintendent of the Campbird Mine in the mid-1920s. The camp was in use on and off from the 1870s and now serves as the trailhead for Surprise Canyon. At the far (east) end of the parking area, an unsigned but well-established **trail** follows a creek east into the canyon.

The reason for the canyon's name becomes abundantly clear as you encounter the lush greenery and narrows of this lovely place. Surprise Canyon serves as the main hiking thoroughfare to the picturesque ghost town of Panamint City, but is also worth exploring on its own.

Be prepared for an **erratic trail**. It follows the canyon and is difficult to lose, but it crisscrosses the creek to avoid the need to bushwhack through the deep vegetation at the canyon floor. At times the trail and the creek are one and the same. If you just give in to the fact that you're going to get wet, this can be part of the adventure.

Aim for the **narrows**, a highlight of the canyon with their smooth marble walls and mossy waterfalls. The narrows begin 0.8 mile into the hike and last for about 0.5 mile. You'll need to do some rock scrambling to get through here. The hike up through the narrows will only take a few hours, but if it's hot, you might want to allow time for resting by the creek, soaking your feet in the cool pools, and picnicking next to the splashing creek. This is a good place to visit in **late spring,** and you might be satisfied to splash through the canyon, enjoying the contrast of the water with the hot desert air and the slight relief from the elevation.

Beyond the narrows, the trail follows the canyon to the ghost town of Panamint City at 5.5 miles.

★ Panamint City

Distance: 11 miles round-trip
Duration: 10-12 hours
Elevation gain: 3,660 feet
Effort: Strenuous
Access: Passenger vehicle; high-clearance recommended
Trailhead: From Ballarat, drive two miles north along Indian Ranch Road to the signed turnoff for Surprise Canyon. At the junction, turn right (west) and drive four miles up the road to the historic Chris Wicht Camp; park in the small parking area. The road is rocky, but it is maintained by Inyo County and may be passable with a passenger car (see map p. 139).

This is a long, strenuous hike but worth every rocky step. The trail follows Surprise Canyon for the first 1.3 miles. The destination, the silver-boom ghost town of Panamint City, is scenic, well preserved, and forested with junipers

and pinyons. There are cabins, a mill, and artifacts for days. The relatively high elevation of the area (5,000-8,000 feet) means that the canyon and surrounding mines can be cold and snowy in winter, while summer can be broiling. The best time to hike is in **spring**.

Don't be fooled by the five miles to the ghost town. The hike is long and demanding. It zigzags up the scenic but strenuous **Surprise Canyon,** a destination in its own right. There is a beaten path most of the way, but the problem is that there isn't just one path. Spur paths dead-end, and you will definitely do some bushwhacking. Just when you've given up all hope of ever reaching Panamint City, when you've become convinced that you've wandered up a side canyon and lost the trail completely, pause, have a snack, regroup, and trudge on. Panamint City is just around the next corner, or the next. Watch out for rattlesnakes, and don't give up. You'll be fine as long as you're following the canyon. All roads lead to Panamint City.

From **Chris Wicht Camp**, follow the unsigned but well-worn trail east into the canyon. The **narrows** begin at 0.8 mile, and they require some rock scrambling to get through. The trail crosses the creek several times; plan on getting wet. Past the narrows, look for steel poles as the trail bypasses the canyon high on the south side to avoid the creek. What was once a road here is now not much more than a scree-filled trail suitable for goats. A road used to go through Surprise Canyon all the way to Panamint City. Even after the road washed out, it was a favorite pastime of the 4WD set to climb their way up to the town site, winching up the waterfalls and taking all day to get there. The canyon is a great example of the desert reclaiming the land, and it's hard to imagine that a road ever went through here.

After the canyon narrows, you'll pass two springs. **Limekiln Spring,** at 1.8 miles, is signaled by a huge wall of hops, which some people call grapevine; according to the caretaker at Ballarat, they are actually hops. The next spring, 3.1 miles in, is called **Brewery Spring.** The trail through Brewery Spring

Surprise Canyon and Panamint City

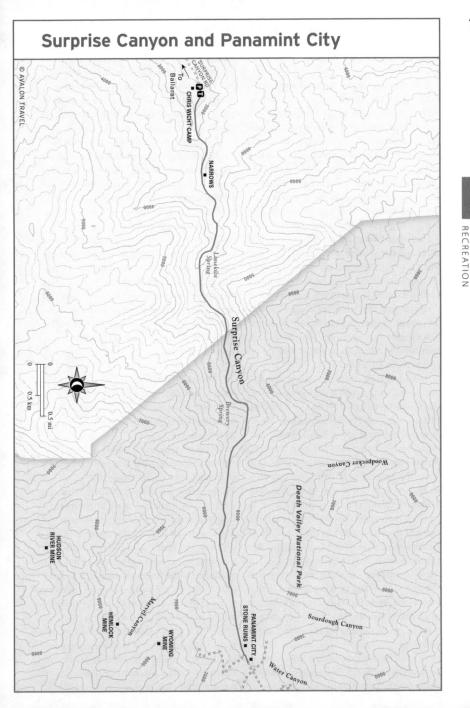

© AVALON TRAVEL

To
Ballarat

SURPRISE
CANYON RD

CHRIS WICHT CAMP

NARROWS

Limekiln
Spring

Surprise Canyon

Brewery
Spring

0
0.5 km

0
0.5 mi

Woodpecker Canyon

Death Valley National Park

HUDSON
RIVER MINE

Marvel Canyon

HEMLOCK
MINE

WYOMING
MINE

PANAMINT CITY
STONE RUINS

Sourdough Canyon

Water Canyon

leads directly through the creek under a tunnel of trees and vines. This is the last water before Panamint City, more than two miles away.

Past Brewery Spring, the canyon jogs to the east, and you're on the home stretch. The final mile is grueling, but with its two tracks, you can tell that this was actually a road at some point. It would take a military-grade vehicle to actually clear the rocky terrain today. You'll know you're almost there when you see the iconic brick smokestack of the mill. Suddenly **stone ruins** begin to spring up by the trail. This was Main Street, and from here, you make your grand entrance into town.

Panamint City was founded in the early 1870s and saw mining efforts until the 1980s, when a series of floods wiped out the road leading to the town. The town had a tough and lawless reputation, so much so that Wells Fargo refused to open a bank here. To solve the problem of not having a bank, 450-pound silver ingots were cast and transported, unguarded, to Los Angeles. There were no reported thefts after this.

The plumbing of the old town site still works, and you might be able to count on tap water from some of the old pumps. Although the trail is blessed with an abundance of water, all water should be treated, even from the pumps at Panamint City. The **Wyoming Mine** and road are visible high up on the mountain. **Sourdough Canyon,** on the left just before you reach the brick smelter, has a mill and camp worth exploring on an easy stroll. **Water Canyon** continues north of town and veers to the left. The old Thompson camp in Water Canyon has a few cabins, just past where the road crosses the creek. If you push on, you'll see the remains of a 1957 Chevy, and in this green space that borders the creek, the remains of an old water tank. It is overgrown, but there's just enough space to squeeze in and soak your feet in the cold water.

The way back is much easier now that you know what to expect. There's icy cold beer waiting in the general store at Ballarat.

BACKPACKING

This is a long and strenuous hike; as a day hike, it is exhausting and doesn't give you time to explore the area. Panamint City is best done as a backpacking trip with one day to hike in, a day to explore and relax, and a day to hike out. Once you've reached the ghost town, set up camp and explore at your leisure.

If you can't make it all the way to Panamint City in one day, signs of **campsites** appear just past Brewery Spring. This is the last water before Panamint City, and if you continue through, you'll be splashing along the trail as you head through a tunnel of vines and trees. This area seems like too much of a snake magnet for my taste, but it's not the worst idea to camp just beyond the spring and make the last leg of the trip without your heavy pack. About one mile past Brewery Spring, where the canyon jogs to the north and then east again, there's a great campsite in the crook of the canyon, elevated from the trail with a wind wall, flat spaces for tents, and lots of nice rocks for sitting.

★ Telescope Peak

Distance: 14 miles round-trip
Duration: 7-9 hours
Elevation gain: 2,929 feet
Effort: Strenuous
Access: High-clearance; 4WD may be necessary
Trailhead: Mahogany Flat Campground, at the end of Wildrose Canyon Road (see map p. 142).

The highest peak in Death Valley, Telescope Peak is snow-covered most of the year. It juts vertically from the valley floor to tower 11,049 feet above Badwater Basin, the lowest point in Death Valley. The 14-mile hike to reach the peak is worth every switchback and is one of the few maintained trails in the park. This hike gives and gives with sweeping views of Death Valley to the east, Panamint Valley to the west, and sometimes both at once. It's a great place to cap off extensive travel in Death Valley. If you've been wandering down in the canyons and valley floors, this is your chance to have a personal travel retrospective.

The straightforward trail starts out in a forest of pinyon, juniper, and mahogany, then swings around **Rogers Peak,** slowly gaining elevation until you reach open, windswept **Arcane Meadows** at 2.4 miles. From here, the Panamint Valley and the Argus Range come into view. You'll see the trail snaking along the ridge toward Telescope Peak, slowly getting closer and in sight the whole hike. The next **two miles** along the ridge are fairly level. To the west are sweeping views toward Tuber and Jail Canyons; to the east, you'll see the three forks of Hanaupah Canyon.

About **four miles** in, the hike starts to climb—the **last mile** is steep switchbacks. The landscape gets increasingly windswept, barren, and rocky as the elevation reaches dizzying heights. Ancient and gnarled Bristlecone pines dot the trail above the tree line. It's not just the amazing views that will take your breath away—the lack of oxygen at this elevation may make the long set of switchbacks to the summit slow going. Soak it all in from the top as you look from the salt flats of Death Valley to the distant Sierra Nevada Mountains.

Late spring, **May or June,** is the best time to do this hike. Most of the rest of the year sees the trail covered in snow and ice. In summer a haze can settle in over the valleys and lessen the views.

★ Wildrose Peak

Distance: 9 miles round-trip
Duration: 4-6 hours
Elevation gain: 2,164 feet
Effort: Moderate
Access: Passenger vehicle
Trailhead: Wildrose Charcoal Kilns (see map p. 143).

This pretty, well-maintained trail lures you on with juniper trees, conifer forests, sparkling ancient schist, and glimpses of the canyons below. Stretches of welcome shade for hiking, coupled with the relatively high elevation, makes this a good choice for **late spring** or **early summer.**

The clearly marked trail begins at the **westernmost charcoal kiln.** The trail starts out fairly level, but this is small comfort because sooner rather than later, you'll have to start climbing. The trail is intermittently steep up to the **saddle,** at 2.1 miles, where you have sweeping views of Death Valley. If you are not set on reaching the summit, this is a rewarding place to stop and turn around.

After climbing again, the trail reaches a **second saddle,** with more views, at 3.1 miles. From here, Wildrose Peak is 1.1 miles

looking across windswept Arcane Meadows to Telescope Peak

Telescope Peak

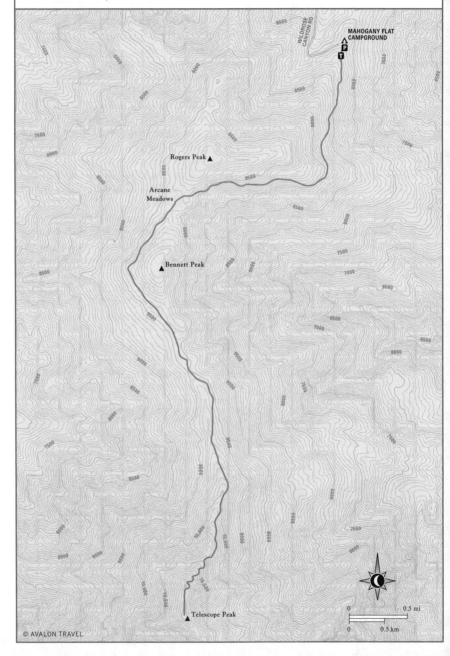

MAHOGANY FLAT
CAMPGROUND

WILDROSE CANYON RD

Rogers Peak ▲

Arcane
Meadows

▲ Bennett Peak

▲ Telescope Peak

© AVALON TRAVEL

0   0.5 mi

0   0.5 km

Wildrose Peak

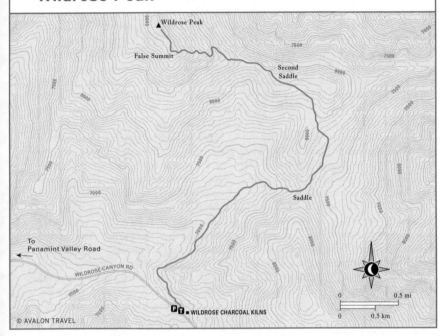

Wildrose Peak
False Summit
Second Saddle
Saddle
To Panamint Valley Road
WILDROSE CANYON RD
WILDROSE CHARCOAL KILNS
© AVALON TRAVEL

0   0.5 mi
0   0.5 km

farther via a **steep trail;** it feels like you're climbing straight up the side of the mountain, and then comes a series of increasingly steep and tight switchbacks. The views become increasingly more impressive as you look down into Death Valley Canyon, Trail Canyon, and Death Valley itself. The scenery becomes as rarified as the air, and you'll begin passing gnarled and ancient bristlecone pines.

Beware a **false summit** 0.2 mile before the actual summit. Just as you're about to start celebrating your ascent, you'll see the trail continues along a ridge to the actual summit. Fortunately, this is an easy, level stroll. You're rewarded for your pain and suffering with panoramic views from the windswept **summit.** The tiny road you see in the distance to the northeast is Aguereberry Point.

BIKING

This region is way too rugged and the distances too great to be suitable for most bike rides. However, the few paved roads that crisscross the western side of the park are tempting—a road cyclist's dream of freedom with miles of pavement set against the sparseness of the rolling hills and carved drama of the mountains. Roads are wide and swooping, and you'll feel like a raven soaring over the desert floor.

Highway 190

Highway 190, past Panamint Springs, winds dramatically into the park. It is **31 miles (one way)** east to Stovepipe Wells and **45 miles (one way)** west to Olancha and U.S. 395. Set your own destination, since there's nothing much on either side of Panamint Springs. You'll be rewarded by views, more views, and smooth road.

Trona Wildrose Road

Biking the road from Trona offers similar hardship and reward. From the mining town of Trona, **Trona Wildrose Road** climbs the length of Panamint Valley, more than **50 miles (one way)** north to Panamint Springs Resort, which will surely seem like heaven on earth after that journey. The road stretches out seemingly endlessly. Though there is minimal traffic, be wary of the lack of shoulder; even the scariest RV towing a Jeep, however, will most likely have room to pass you safely.

CLIMBING

The Panamint Springs region is a wet and wild world of possibility for rock climbing. Many canyons in the region were sculpted by water, creating carved falls and undulating canyon walls, features that may look like a buzz-kill to hikers but signal that the fun is just about to begin for rock climbers. Much of the water that formed the canyons is still present, creating refreshing challenges for those who attempt to hike and climb here. Breaking out your climbing skills and equipment can give you access to the upper reaches of canyons that don't give up their secrets so easily.

Darwin Falls offers a small stroll to a humble waterfall, impressive mostly due to its bone-dry location in the Panamint Valley. However, just beyond the lower waterfall lie three more waterfalls, increasingly tall and slender streams of water dropping into the stone-lined pools below.

Inyo Mountain Wilderness Area

Beveridge Canyon, McElvoy Canyon, and Craig Canyon are a power trio in the Inyo Mountain Wilderness Area, clustered near the Salt Tramway and Warm Springs Road. A trip here brings you to deep gorges and tumbling waterfalls, enticing you to push through to the next round. These three climbs require technical skills, climbing experience, and in some cases, equipment.

The deep narrows at the mouth of **McElvoy Canyon** has a hiking trail that leads first to one waterfall and then another. Beyond the second waterfall, a technical climb bypasses the waterfall and leads to narrows and a third waterfall.

A creek and waterfalls dominate **Beveridge Canyon,** making it both spectacularly beautiful and impossibly rugged at the same time. Climb past the first two waterfalls to reach the wet narrows, high and sweeping polished white marble. Beyond this, three waterfalls lead through the narrows, taking you deeper into the creek and waterfalls only to effectively end at the final waterfall, 60 feet high and topped with a chockstone.

Craig Canyon, by comparison, is refreshingly dry. The goal here is to get to the colorful and winding narrows two miles into the deep canyon, an adventure-filled day that requires getting past nine falls and many boulder jams.

Accommodations and Food

PANAMINT SPRINGS

Panamint Springs Resort (40440 Hwy. 190, 775/482-7680, www.panamintsprings.com, 7am-9:30pm daily year-round) offers the only accommodations, food, supplies, and gas within the park boundaries on the west side of the park. The rustic resort opened in 1937, when the first toll road across the Panamint Valley was built from Stovepipe Wells. Today, it's a welcome and unexpected sight as you cross into Death Valley, rising out of the desert floor and beckoning with a deep veranda and fan palms.

The resort has affordable motel rooms, a cottage, tent cabins, RV spaces, and tent sites. The 14 basic **motel rooms** ($79-169) vary only by bed type: one queen; one king; one queen and one double; or one queen and two doubles. All rooms have evaporative cooling systems with vents in the ceiling and a private bath with a shower. Rooms with three beds include air-conditioning units.

A two-bedroom **cottage** ($149-169), situated behind the resort's restaurant, comes with a queen bed, one bunk bed (double on bottom and single on top), a living area, satellite TV, air-conditioning, and a private bath with a full tub and shower.

There are no phones in any rooms, and Panamint Springs does not have a landline. Cell phones will not work. There is a general store with basic supplies, gas, and an ATM. Wireless Internet is available on request for sending basic messages (no streaming).

The Panamint Springs Resort **restaurant** (7am-9pm daily year-round) features a breakfast buffet (7am-11am daily) and appetizers, burgers, pizzas, and salads. The **bar** serves wine and more than 150 beers. The down side of having all this great stuff in the middle of nowhere is that it can get very busy. Rooms can get fully booked months ahead of time, especially for holiday weekends. Tour buses have been known to pull up and swamp the dining area. Of course, this gives you a chance to sip a cold craft beer on the porch while you wait, but don't be surprised that you're not the only one who knows about this not-so-hidden gem.

CAMPING
Panamint Springs Resort

The **Panamint Springs Resort Campground** (40440 Hwy. 190, 775/482-7680, www.panamintsprings.com, 7am-9:30pm daily year-round, $10-65) has a total of 76 accommodations, including **tent cabins** (1-5 people, $35-65), **RV sites** (30- and 50-amp hookups, $20-35), **tent sites** (1 tent, 1 vehicle, $10), and one group site. All sites have fire pits; most have picnic tables. Amenities include drinking water and flush toilets. Best of all, they have **hot showers** (free with a site, fee for non-guests), a rarity in Death Valley campgrounds (Furnace Creek, the crowded hub on the other side of the park, is the only other campground with showers). The campsites can fill quickly, so make reservations well ahead of time. There is a surcharge of $5 for pets in RV and tent sites.

Emigrant

Emigrant Campground (10 sites, first-come, first-serve, year-round, free) is a tiny tent-only campground located at the junction of Highway 190 and Emigrant Canyon Road. It's a pretty spot that more closely resembles a day-use area. Sites are small, close together, and exposed to the open desert. It's too small to serve as a base camp for several days, but it will do in a pinch. At 2,100 feet elevation and with no shade, it can be uncomfortably hot in summer, although cooler than the valley floor (but almost any place is cooler than the valley floor). Amenities include picnic tables, drinking water, and restrooms with flush toilets.

DIRECTIONS

Emigrant is located directly off paved Highway 190, approximately 21 miles east of

Panamint Springs, so it's easy to access and centrally located.

Wildrose

Cheerful and sunny **Wildrose Campground** (23 sites, first-come, first-served, year-round, free) is tucked away at the lower end of Wildrose Canyon. At 4,100 feet elevation, the camp sits at a good mid-level point to avoid the scorching temperatures of the valley floor in summer and the snow of the higher elevations. Unlike the seasonal campgrounds located at the higher elevations of the canyon, Wildrose is open year-round and rarely fills up. Its level sites don't offer privacy or shade, but it's a peaceful campground in a quiet and lovely section of the park. It's a great place to set up a base camp for exploring the Emigrant and Wildrose Canyon areas, with easy access to Skidoo, the Charcoal Kilns, Wildrose Peak, and Telescope Peak. Amenities include picnic tables, fire pits, potable water, and pit toilets; the campground is also accessible to small trailers.

DIRECTIONS

To get here from the north, take Emigrant Canyon Road south toward Wildrose Canyon from Highway 190 for approximately 21 miles, to the end of Emigrant Canyon Road. From the south, Trona Wildrose Road veers past it approximately 46 miles north of Trona. Trona Wildrose Road is prone to washouts, and the road was closed for most of 2014. Pay attention to park alerts, and check for road closures before planning your route.

Thorndike

Rocky and remote **Thorndike Campground** (6 sites, first-come, first-served, Mar.-Nov., free) is perched between the canyon walls high up in Wildrose Canyon. This campground lies between Wildrose Campground, downcanyon, and Mahogany Flat, at the top of the canyon, which means it can get overlooked. Since it's lightly visited, you should have no problem getting a spot; you might even have it all to yourself. The combination of steep canyon walls, a perch off the winding canyon road, and winds whipping downcanyon through gnarled juniper trees gives this place a wild and forgotten feel. However, the sheerness of the canyon walls cuts in on the daylight hours, so when the sun dips, it can get chilly. Bring firewood, as the nights can get surprisingly cold, even in summer. However, this can be a welcome relief when it's too hot at lower elevations.

You can stay in a tent cabin at the Panamint Springs Resort.

Almost all campsites are shaded—a rarity in Death Valley. Amenities include picnic tables, fire pits, and pit toilets; there is no drinking water available (the closest drinking water is at Wildrose Campground, about eight miles downcanyon). If you want to hike both Telescope Peak and Wildrose Peak, this is a great home base.

At 7,400 feet elevation, snow can make access impossible to vehicles from November to March.

DIRECTIONS
To get here from the north, take Emigrant Canyon Road south toward Wildrose Canyon from Highway 190 for approximately 21 miles, to the end of Emigrant Canyon Road at Wildrose Campground. At Wildrose Campground, take Wildrose Canyon Road another nine miles up the canyon. The pavement ends at seven miles, at the Charcoal Kilns. The gravel road is steep and rocky from here. A **high-clearance vehicle** is necessary; a 4WD vehicle is preferable when navigating snow, ice, or washouts. The road is not accessible to trailers. From the south, drive Trona Wildrose Road 46 miles north of Trona to the Wildrose Campground, and then drive an additional nine miles up Wildrose Canyon

Road. Keep in mind that Trona Wildrose Road is prone to washouts. If the road is closed, you might have to bypass it.

Mahogany Flat
Perched at the top of Wildrose Canyon, **Mahogany Flat Campground** (10 sites, first-come, first-served, Mar.-Nov., free) offers cool temperatures, sweeping views, and access to Telescope Peak, the highest mountain peak in the park. At 8,200 feet elevation, expect cool nights, which can be a lifesaver in the summer. Many people use this campground as a jumping-off point to hike Telescope Peak, since the trailhead starts just outside the campground. It gets some traffic because of the popularity of Telescope Peak, but you are still likely to find a spot.

Amenities include picnic tables, fire pits, and pit toilets; there is no drinking water available (the closest water is at Wildrose Campground, about nine miles down canyon). Snow may make the campground inaccessible November through March.

DIRECTIONS
To get here from the north, take Emigrant Canyon Road south toward Wildrose Canyon from Highway 190 for approximately 21

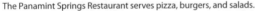

The Panamint Springs Restaurant serves pizza, burgers, and salads.

miles, to the end of Emigrant Canyon Road at Wildrose Campground. At Wildrose Campground, take Wildrose Canyon Road another 11 miles up the canyon to the end of the road at the campground. The road gets slightly steeper and rockier past Thorndike Campground. A **high-clearance vehicle** is necessary; a 4WD vehicle is better when navigating snow, ice, or washouts. From the south, drive Trona Wildrose Road 46 miles north of Trona to Wildrose Campground, and then drive an additional 11 miles up the Wildrose Canyon Road until it ends at the campground.

Backcountry Camping

Depending on where you go, backcountry camping could be your only option—or your best option.

In the Emigrant Canyon and Wildrose Canyon areas, developed campgrounds are the best bet; the most tempting backcountry choices here are off-limits. Backcountry camping is not allowed off Skidoo Road, Wildrose Canyon Road, or Aguereberry Point Road. These are all considered day-use only roads and are some of the only roads in the area.

WESTERN PANAMINT CANYONS

When exploring the western Panamint Canyons, backcountry camping is the only choice, unless you commute from Panamint Springs or Wildrose Canyon for day explorations only. Of course, this limits your fun. The Western Canyons, including **Surprise** **Canyon** and **Jail Canyon,** are popular backpacking and 4WD trails. Many of these canyons begin on Bureau of Land Management (BLM) land and cross into the jurisdiction of Death Valley National Park. When camping on BLM land, or for any backcountry camping, camp in a site that has already been disturbed (sometimes called a dispersed site or dispersed camping). To locate dispersed sites, look for pullouts or spurs off the road that are hard-packed and devoid of vegetation. These are not labeled as campsites, but if you know what to look for, you can have an enjoyable backcountry experience.

If you want to set up a main base camp or give yourself a fresh start for backpacking or exploring the 4WD trails in the canyons, the ghost town of **Ballarat** is a good place to start. There are no supplies aside from the cold soda and beer in the caretaker's icebox, but you will be strategically located to get your fill of old mining camps, rocky creeks, and sculpted canyon walls.

SALINE VALLEY

Saline Valley Warm Springs has semideveloped camping spots. These sites are used primarily by people visiting the springs. There are well-maintained pit toilets and outdoor shower stations with water piped from the hot springs. There are no fees for camping, and drinking water is not available. From Saline Valley Road, the primitive 6.8-mile road to the camp can be sandy and hard to follow.

Beyond the Boundaries

Lone Pine is located on U.S. 395 and acts as a western gateway to Death Valley, with a variety of **accommodations, restaurants, supplies,** and **gas.**

To the south, the intersections of Highway 14, U.S. 395, and Highway 178 form the **Indian Wells Valley.** Ridgecrest is your best bet for **gas, supplies,** and **services.** From here, Highway 178 heads north into the park.

East of Ridgecrest lies the **Searles Valley** and the long, dusty drive to the Trona Pinnacles.

LONE PINE

This charming Old West town serves as the portal to Mount Whitney, the highest peak in the contiguous United States. Buildings with Western facades line Main Street, with snow-covered Mount Whitney an impressive backdrop. Lone Pine is a tourist town, fully equipped with hotels and motels, restaurants, a grocery, and outdoor outfitter stores. There are bars, cafés, and shops for browsing.

The **Lone Pine Film Museum** (701 S. Main St., 760/876-9909, www.lonepine-filmhistorymuseum.org, 10am-5pm daily Nov.-Apr., 10am-4pm daily Apr.-Nov., $5) showcases the history of movies filmed in the nearby Alabama Hills. The museum has an interpretive handout guide to the area, or you can just wander through and enjoy the formations.

Accommodations

Built in 1923, the historic **Dow Villa Hotel** (310 S. Main St., 760/876-5521, www.dowvilla-motel.com, $69-173) is a refurbished period hotel with a pool and a spa. Stay in the original hotel or the motor court rooms, which were added later.

Lone Pine also has several basic budget motels, including the **Portal Motel** (425 S. Main St., 760/876-5930, www.portalmotel.com, from $59), **Trails Motel** (633 S. Main St., 760/876-5555, www.trailsmotel.com, from $59), and **Mt. Whitney Motel** (305 N. Main St., 760/876-4207, www.mtwhitneymotel.com, from $59). Chain hotels include the **Best Western Plus Frontier Motel** (1008 S. Main St., 760/876-5571, www. bestwesterncalifornia.com, from $80) and **Comfort Inn** (1920 S. Main St., 760/876-8700, www.comfortinn.com, from $80).

RV accommodations can be found at the **Boulder Creek RV Resort** (2550 U.S. 395, 760/876-4243, www.bouldercreekrvresort.com, $40). Summer is the busy season in Lone Pine, and hotels can fill ahead of time. Summer and holiday rates, both substantially more expensive, may also apply.

Food

Several restaurants along the main street serve a range of fare, including steaks, pizza, Chinese, and Mexican food. For breakfast, the **Alabama Hills Café** (111 W. Post St., 760/876-4675, 7am-2pm daily, $8-14) is a winner. This unassuming, tucked-away spot serves freshly baked bread and heaping plates of breakfast and lunch to fortify locals, hikers, and other visitors. The **Mt. Whitney Restaurant** (227 S. Main St., 760/876-5751, 6am-9pm daily winter, 6am-10pm daily summer, $7-24) gives a nod to Lone Pine's film heritage with its movie posters and memorabilia decor. It's a casual place, serving diner food and specializing in burgers and sandwiches.

The **Pizza Factory** (301 S. Main St., 760/876-4707, www,pizzafactory.com, 11am-9pm Sun.-Thurs., 11am-10pm Fri.-Sat., $7-28) is the go-to spot for pizza, sandwiches, and salads. The **Merry Go Round** (212 S. Main St., 760/876-4115, 4:30pm-8:30pm Mon.-Tues., 11am-2pm and 4:30pm-9pm Wed.-Fri., 4pm-9pm Sat.-Sun., $12-18) offers Chinese fare in a converted Merry-go-Round.

Getting There

Lone Pine lies directly on U.S. 395, 50 miles

Lone Pine

west of Panamint Springs. To get there, take Highway 190 west for 30 miles. Continue straight on Highway 136 for 17 miles until reaching U.S. 395. Turn north and drive 2 miles to the town of Lone Pine.

As you drive along Highway 136, you might see big, blue **Owens Lake** on your GPS map. But make no mistake; this has not been a viable lake for more than 100 years, since the California Aqueduct was built. The aqueduct funneled water from the bucolic Owens Lake to feed a thirsty Los Angeles (the movie *Chinatown* captures the political turmoil surrounding the water wars around this area).

Owens Lake was also an important part of the Cerro Gordo mining district. A barge called the *Bessie Brady* carted ore from the western port of Cartago along U.S. 395 to Swansea and Keeler on the northeastern side of the lake.

Alabama Hills

Lone Pine is right on the edge of the **Alabama Hills,** the scenic rocky Sierra Nevada foothills near Mount Whitney. It was named for mining prospectors sympathetic to the Confederate cause during the Civil War. The outstanding scenery attracted filmmakers beginning in the 1920s, and westerns, sci-fi movies, and other films have been shot here, making it a landscape that looks iconic and familiar to visitors. The area now known as **Movie Flats** is where most of the movies were filmed. Take a short hike through the Alabama Hills; the popular **Mobius Arch** is an easy 20-minute loop.

GETTING THERE
To get to the Alabama Hills from U.S. 395 in Lone Pine, turn west onto Whitney Portal Road and drive 2.7 miles to Movie Road. Turn right onto Movie Road and follow the many dirt roads through the area. A self-guided **tour map** is available online (www.theothersideofcalifornia.com).

INDIAN WELLS VALLEY
Ghost towns, some more living than others, and high concentrations of Native American rock art make this area worth digging into. Located on the southwestern edge of Death Valley, the Indian Wells Valley is roughly bounded by **Highway 14** to the west, **Trona Road** to the east, and **Highway 178** to the north. The major access point is the intersection of **U.S. 395** and Highway 178 in Inyokern. You'll travel through the Indian Wells Valley if you're coming from the south, but it's worth a detour from any direction.

Inyokern
INDIAN WELLS LODGE AND BREWING COMPANY
At the **Indian Wells Lodge and Brewing Company** (2565 Hwy. 14, Inyokern, 760/377-5989, www.mojavered.com, brewery 10am-5pm daily, restaurant 4:30pm-9pm Tues.-Sun.) kids will love the rows of novelty sodas—bacon soda, anyone?—and adults can enjoy the craft beers. The brewing company is positioned over an artesian spring and uses its water source wisely, brewing flavorful beers like the Mojave Red and Death Valley Pale Ale. There's a green lawn and picnic tables to sample a beer, have lunch, or give the kids a chance to run around. It's a perfect stop to break up the drive coming from the

south—get out of the wind and look over U.S. 395 and the surrounding desert. The restaurant is only open for dinner, but this can be a good stop for a real meal if you've been roughing it in Death Valley for a few days. They're not big on salads here, but they do the basic American entrées right.

GETTING THERE
Inyokern is located 70 miles south of Lone Pine, about a one-hour drive along U.S. 395. In Inyokern, Highway 14 leads southwest to Red Rock Canyon State Park, while Highway 178 cuts east to Ridgecrest, Trona, and the Trona Wildrose Road, a southern gateway to the Panamints. U.S. 395 continues south to the almost ghost town of Randsburg in 24 miles.

Ridgecrest
MATURANGO MUSEUM
About 20 miles north of Randsburg, the **Maturango Museum** (100 E. Las Flores Ave., Ridgecrest, 760/375-6900, www.maturango. org, 10am-5pm daily, $5) offers tours to one of the biggest and best-preserved groupings of Native American rock art in the country. The Big and Little Coso Canyon area, a National Historic Landmark, hosts a dizzying array of rock art. It's a shallow, rocky canyon with just the right kind of rocks for the wind to have varnished them with a dark smoky glaze over thousands of years. These rocks, covered with "desert varnish," are a prime canvas for petroglyphs, created by chipping into the rock.

Once you get over the initial awe of seeing so much ancient rock art all in one place, you can try to figure out what it all means. There's no definitive guide to the meanings, and many petroglyph symbols will probably remain great unsolved desert mysteries. What you will see are lots of bighorn sheep, hunting scenes, and elaborate pictures of shamans, rain, and other abstract symbols. These could have been part of shamanistic quests, religious ceremonies, or historic documentation. This is an amazing place, but it also happens to be located within the boundaries of the Naval Air

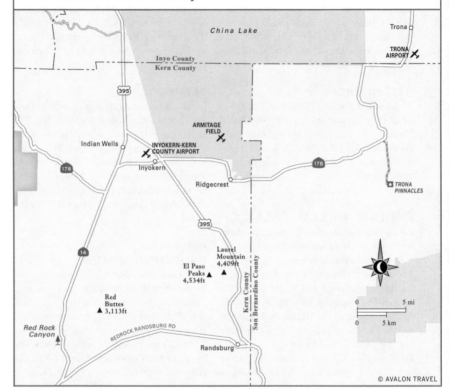

Indian Wells Valley

Weapons Station China Lake. It might seem counterintuitive, but this location has probably preserved the site; it's a sad fact that many well-known rock-art sites get vandalized.

The Maturango Museum holds **tours** most weekends in April and May, and these sell out. Check their website in late winter and early spring, and reserve a tour as soon as the schedule is posted. The tour is loosely guided by volunteers who have clearance to be on the base, but you'll be able to wander around and soak it in at your own pace.

GETTING THERE
The Maturango Museum is located off Highway 178 in Ridgecrest. From the junction of U.S. 395 and Highway 178 in Inyokern, follow Highway 178 east for 9.5 miles.

Randsburg
Randsburg is a time capsule of a ghost town that never died. It started as a gold mining camp in 1895, and the first post office opened in 1896. It's a perfect Western town with a saloon, a main street, a church, and cabins scattered over the hills. It's popular with the OHV set on weekend days in the fall and spring. Families and groups stop by for lunch or to stroll the tiny main street with an antiques shop and a general store. Randsburg is in the high Mojave Desert, so summer brings blazing heat and winter brings stinging cold.

RANDSBURG MINING DISTRICT
The historic mining towns of Randsburg, Johannesburg, and Red Mountain are all

clustered around U.S. 395 as part of the historic **Randsburg Mining District.** Randsburg is the most picturesque and visitor-friendly, but Johannesburg and Red Mountain are both a fascinating blend of old structures mixed in with the everyday. Red Mountain's closed saloon and general store are slowly giving up the ghost next to the highway. Johannesburg's cemetery, touching and handcrafted, rests in the shadow of the mine works on the hill. Atolia, Garlock, Cantil, and Saltdale are part of the chain of vanishing sites. You can learn more about these sites and others from a visit to the **Rand Desert Museum** (161 Butte Ave., Randsburg, 760/371-0965, www.randdesertmuseum.com, 10am-4pm Sat.-Sun., donation).

Off Redrock Randsburg Road, near the town of **Garlock,** William "Burro" Schmidt's **famous tunnel** to nowhere bores 0.5 mile through a granite ridge to connect his mining area with the smelter at the town of Mojave. Burro Schmidt got his well-earned name by inexplicably hand-digging the tunnel over a period of 38 years, even after a road was put in to connect the areas. Burro Schmidt is buried in the nearby Johannesburg Cemetery.

ACCOMMODATIONS AND FOOD

After a day of desert trails, the popular watering hole is the **White House Saloon** (168 Butte Ave., Randsburg, 760/374-2464, 11am-4pm Fri.-Sun., cash only). The smooth plank floors, long wooden bar, even the bartender and ice-cold pitchers of Mojave Red beer (a regional favorite) seem like they've been cast for the role. There is very basic bar food, but you don't come here for the food.

The **Randsburg General Store** (35 Butte Ave., Randsburg, 760/374-2143, www.randsburggeneralstore.com, 11am-4pm Mon. and Thurs.-Fri., 10am-5pm Sat.-Sun.), across the street, serves breakfast, lunch, and ice cream in a historic drug-store setting. The store also stocks basic supplies, maps and books.

The **Randsburg Inn** (166 Butte Ave., Randsburg, 760/374-2143, http://randsburginn.com, year-round, $65-105) is a tiny historic hotel that offers basic rooms, a full kitchen, and a wood-burning stove.

GETTING THERE

Randsburg is located west of U.S. 395, approximately 20 miles south of Ridgecrest. From U.S. 395, take the signed Redrock-Randsburg Road east for one mile.

Garlock is located on private property. The fenced remains of the town can be seen from Redrock Randsburg Road. The Burro Schmidt tunnel is on BLM land and can be reached via a dirt road off of Highway 14, suitable for high-clearance and 4WD vehicles. From the intersection of Redrock Randsburg Road and Highway 14, travel north about 14 miles. Turn right (east) onto a dirt road marked by a small wooden sign (the junction is unmarked from the other direction). Drive about 6.5 miles to a fork. Take the left fork and drive three miles to the tunnel.

Red Rock Canyon State Park

Red Rock Canyon State Park (Hwy. 14, Cantil, 661/946-6092, www.parks.ca.gov, $6) is a little slice of Utah in the California Desert. The red rock formations create a scenic drive through the area and a lovely place to hike. It's one of those unusual places that is easy to access but is as lovely as if you had hiked far from the highway. It's also a good place to set up a base camp to explore the Indian Wells region west of Death Valley.

CAMPING

The **Ricardo Campground** (50 sites, first-come, first-served, year-round, $25) features primitive campsites and miles of hiking trails through beautiful rock formations and cliffs. Sites are easily reached off the paved campground road and are spaced wide apart, tucked up against the red canyon cliffs. The campground has potable water, pit toilets, fire rings, and picnic tables.

GETTING THERE

Red Rock Canyon State Park is located near the intersection of Highway 14 and U.S. 395

Page 154

in the Mojave Desert. From Randsburg, head west on Redrock Randsburg Road for 20 miles to the intersection with Highway 14. Turn right (north) on Highway 14 and drive five miles to the park entrance.

THE SEARLES VALLEY

The Searles Valley is situated between the Slate and Argus Mountain Ranges, south of Panamint Valley and east of Ridgecrest and U.S. 395. Take Highway 178 east from the Kern River Valley and watch the landscape shift from California golden homestead to pioneer death trap. It has the draw of other-worldly rock formations and long stretches of austere desert. Coming from the rolling foothills of the Sierra Nevada Mountains, the land turns harsh and alien, beautiful in its own way.

The mining town of **Trona** is a little worse for the wear, but it is fascinating to look for the historic buildings mixed in with the new.

★ Trona Pinnacles

The **Trona Pinnacles** (www.blm.gov) are haunting and powerful. You can see them from the highway on the long dusty drive out, a draw to keep going. The pinnacles were formed through a geologic anomaly in which calcium-rich groundwater met ancient alkaline lake water over thousands of years to form tufa formations. What you see now is a ghost lake with alien spires. If you look hard, you can see where the water line used to be on the distant mountain range. It's the only hint of water you'll find out here.

GETTING THERE

The Trona Pinnacles are located on BLM land about 20 miles east of Ridgecrest and south of the historic and active mining town of Trona. Access the signed dirt road that leads to the Pinnacles from Highway 178 about 7.7 miles east of the intersection of Highway 178 and Trona-Red Mountain Road. The five-mile-long dirt road from Highway 178 to the Pinnacles is usually accessible to regular passenger vehicles, but the road may be closed during the winter months after a heavy rain.

PANAMINT SPRINGS
BEYOND THE BOUNDARIES

Camp along the impressive rock formations of Red Rock Canyon State Park.

Background

The Landscape

GEOGRAPHY

Death Valley is located in the northern Mojave Desert on the eastern side of California's Sierra Nevada Mountain Range. The Mojave (also spelled Mohave, the term used by the Mohave Tribal Nation) is a high desert area occupying a large swath of southeastern California and parts of southern Nevada, southwestern Utah, and northwestern Arizona. Death Valley National Park lies in the northeast section of the greater Mojave, mostly in California, with a small section, called the Nevada Triangle, in Nevada. Death Valley sits within the Great Basin, a hydrographic distinction that means all drainage of waterways is internal; no rivers lead to the sea.

During the series of ice ages from 1.8 million to 10,000 years ago, Death Valley was colder, with a climate more like British Columbia—glaciers and snowpacks in the Sierra Nevada Mountains drained into vast lakes and shallow drainage pools. When the climate shifted, it became hotter and more arid; the pools dried, leaving behind fossil lakes full of silt, clay, and minerals. Clear evidence of these plant-free playas can be seen in places like the **Racetrack, Badwater Basin,** and the **Trona Pinnacles.**

The evaporated lakes resulted in concentrated mineral beds that set the stage for mining activity. This area is known for its richness of mineral wealth, and it has a long and notorious mining history. Death Valley was settled by European Americans in the mid-19th century for its gold and silver despite harsh unknown territory and limited water sources. Mining operations eventually expanded to include borax, talc, gypsum, salt, and other minerals mined from these ancient mineral beds.

The "basin and range" topography is characterized by extremes in elevation: steep mountain ranges trending in the same direction, interspersed with deep valleys. The deepest of these is Death Valley, for which the park is named. During times of flood, water becomes a raging force as it hurtles through water-cut canyons and spills sediment at the canyon mouths in alluvial fan formations. These triangle-shaped spillages are prominent when driving through Death Valley, and are often the first obstacle to cross by car or on foot if you're trying to visit one of the valley's many fascinating canyons.

Wind, combined with other geologic processes, creates desert features such as sand dunes, desert varnish, and desert pavement. Desert varnish and desert pavement are unique to arid environments and are often found around alluvial fans. **Desert varnish** is a reddish-brown coating of clay manganese and iron oxides found on rocks. The varnish darkens over time and can be used to date rock formations. Native Americans used desert varnish as a canvas for petroglyphs, chipping it away to revealing the lighter-colored rock underneath. **Desert pavement** is a sturdy, compact rock surface of pebbles and broken rocks. One theory suggests that these rocks are left behind when the wind sweeps away smaller particles, while another attributes the distinct ground covering to the shrinking and swelling of clay soil, which pushes pebbles to the surface.

GEOLOGY

Throughout Death Valley, the earth's history is exposed in striking formations and tortured geologic features. A formation is a geologist's grouping of the stratified rock that forms the

Death Valley Dunes

First-time visitors to Death Valley may be surprised that the park is not a vast sea of sand. Sand dunes cover less than 1 percent of Death Valley National Park, but they are striking features, sometimes visible from long distances. Wind is a crucial factor in creating sand dunes, driving loose particles from dry riverbeds or lake beds, dry washes, and canyons until they reach a barrier such as the sheer mountains ringing the valley. The trapped sand piles up, migrating and shifting as the wind continuously sculpts these sand-scapes.

Dunes are categorized by shape, which tells you something about the way they were formed and their migration patterns. **Star dunes** are the highest, with ridges rising to a peak. The **crescent-shaped dunes** are more common, shaped by winds that blow constantly in the same direction. Prevailing winds that blow at an angle shape the **linear dunes,** characterized by their long, straight, or sometimes undulating lines.

These graceful, clean expanses compel us to climb them. Look carefully for signs of more complex life—delicate insect and animal tracks, and plants that grow from reserves of water hidden within dune systems. The following sand dune tour highlights each system's unique setting and features.

- The **Mesquite Flat Sand Dunes** (page 74) are visible from long distances along the valley floor near Stovepipe Wells, and are easily accessed from a parking area off Highway 190. This extensive dune system covers many acres, and includes star, linear, and crescent shapes.

- The **Ibex Dunes** (page 52), tucked away in the southeast corner of the park, offer isolation and easy hiking from the unmaintained dirt road that leads to the dunes. Hiking up the graceful sand ridges of the Ibex Dunes affords good views of the Saddle Peak Hills and a hidden talc mine. It's a great stop to pair with a visit to the lovely Saratoga Spring just a few miles away along the same road.

- The **Panamint Valley Dunes** (page 134) are swept up against the dark Cottonwood Mountains in the far upper reaches of the Panamint Valley. Although you can see them gleaming in the distance from Highway 190, the closest road stops more than three miles short, making them some of the remotest dunes in the park. The cross-country hike to reach them will all but guarantee you have these impressive dunes to yourself.

- If you find yourself in the Saline Valley, stop your car, get out, and walk less than a mile to reach the long, low **Saline Valley Dunes** (page 132). They're easy to pass by, but well worth stopping to get a closer look. Up close, they become low waves of sculpted sand hills, each rise giving way to another until you're immersed in the dunes. Follow your own footsteps to get back to your car.

- If sand dunes can be regal, the **Eureka Dunes** (page 99) earn that adjective. They are the tallest and most extensive dune system in the park, with the tallest of the dunes reaching 700 feet. The Eureka Dunes are also "singing dunes" or "booming dunes," one of only about 40 worldwide. From time to time they emit a low booming sound like a distant airplane, caused by the motion of moving sand grains. It's a long drive to the Eureka Valley in the northernmost reaches of the park, but well worth it. Camp in the primitive campsites at the foot of these dunes and make a destination of it.

landscape, as determined by age and duration. Formations can also be associated with geographic and climatic conditions. Death Valley has a complex set of at least **23 formations.** The oldest rocks in Death Valley are found in the steep Black Mountains above Badwater Basin, and are approximately 1.7 billion years old. Many of the rocks are ancient, but the stark topography, with its sheer rises and drops, is relatively recent.

Ancient Seas

In the Paleozoic Era (570 million years ago), the northern Mojave was a tidal area filled with shallow seas stretched along the coastline. Marine deposits built up over a span of millions of years. Some of these deposits are still visible, like the 700-million-year-old Noonday Dolomite in **Mosaic Canyon.** This quiet accumulation of sedimentary deposits in shallow waters drew to a close about 250 million years ago, and a much more cataclysmic era began, marked by colliding tectonic plates and magma plumes.

Volcanism

The Mesozoic Era (245-65 million years ago) marked a period of radical shifts in the landscape. As the Pacific plate became subducted under the North American plate, friction generated massive heat, melting rock and forming magma. The newly formed magma rose to the surface in a chain of volcanoes. The ocean was gradually pushed 200 miles west during the upheaval, leaving the northern Mojave Desert high, if not yet dry.

Deep magma plumes intruded the earth's crust and cooled, forming crystallized formations known as plutons. Granite is one of these plutonic rocks and is exposed in outcrops throughout sections of Death Valley, including the upper **Warm Spring Canyons** in the Panamint Mountains, **Hunter Mountain** in the Cottonwoods, and Emigrant Canyon around **Skidoo.** Volcanic activity continued to shape the landscape well beyond these dramatic shifts. Scattered volcanic debris is common in the valleys, and hot springs have been tapped in the Saline and Owens Valley. At Naval Air Weapons Station China Lake, on the southwest side of the park, the Navy harnessed the region's geothermal energy to create a clean power plant.

Basin and Range

Death Valley as we know it today started to gain its rough building blocks 65 million years ago in the Cenozoic Era, but it didn't take the topographic shape associated with the northern Mojave—high, sheer ranges perforated by deep basins—until much later. Scenic **Titus Canyon** gives us the earliest known records

of Cenozoic rock formations. The land then was probably broad and rolling with valleys, grasslands, lakes, and woodlands in a warm, wet climate. The fossil record reveals clear evidence of mammals, including rodents, tapirs, horses, and titanotheres, a bulky, horned animal that shares ancestry with the horse and rhino.

As these idyllic grasslands faded, tectonic movements formed the two main faults that define Death Valley. The **Northern Death Valley-Furnace Creek Fault** Zone follows the western side of the Amargosa Range, and the **Southern Death Valley Fault Zone** follows the western foot of the Black Mountains. These active faults form one of the longest running fault systems in California. Meltwater and precipitation filled the area with a series of shallow lakes; when these lakes evaporated, they left the mineral and salt-rich legacy that shaped the mining history of Death Valley. The crust is still dynamic. U.S. Geological Survey studies indicate that parts of Death Valley may still be rising or falling a foot every 500 years.

CLIMATE

Death Valley is one of the driest and hottest places in the western hemisphere, with scalding temperatures at the lower elevations in summer. In July 1913, Furnace Creek hit 134°F, the highest recorded atmospheric temperature on earth. The **summer average** is 115°F. Strangely, Death Valley's extreme heat is often a selling point—many visitors come specifically intent on experiencing it. There are no bodies of water or cloud cover to mitigate temperature, and the low-lying valleys trap heat. The same conditions can create bitter cold in **winter.** The same year that produced that record high also produced the record low of 15°F. Cold is more likely at the upper elevations, hit with strong winds and cold fronts from the Pacific Ocean. A temperature of 0°F is not uncommon, and Telescope Peak, the highest peak in the park at 11,049 feet, is snow-capped for a good part of the year.

Death Valley's arid climate is partly caused by the imposing Sierra Nevada Mountains, which tower more than 9,000 feet to the west. As storms roll in from the Pacific Ocean, they hit the western side of the Sierra Nevadas, wringing out most of their moisture before continuing on into the eastern desert. This rain shadow effect accounts for the 2 inches of annual rainfall in Death Valley, compared to as much as 60 inches of rain on the western side of the Sierra Nevadas. Four mountain ranges lie between the Pacific and Death Valley, each squeezing out the last bits of moisture from storm clouds as they head inland.

Death Valley holds dazzling topographic extremes within its boundaries, and temperatures and precipitation vary widely depending on the season and elevation. From the sizzling salt flats of Badwater Basin, 282 feet below sea level, to the snow-covered summit of Telescope Peak at 11,094 feet is only a distance of 15 miles. These drastic changes in elevation support a range of temperatures and diverse ecology. That means if it's 100°F at Badwater Basin, it may be 60°F at the top of Telescope Peak.

The good news is that it's possible to find a comfortable environment to visit, whether in summer or winter. **Spring** and **fall** are mostly temperate and pleasant, but unexpected weather—including monsoons and dust storms—can swoop in year-round, wreaking havoc in a short time. **Strong winds** and **sandstorms** occur frequently on the valley floor, and with little warning; these can last anywhere from a few minutes to a few days. Dust storms are formed by approaching cold fronts and can tear up anything not tied down, causing whiteout conditions. Rainstorms can trigger flash floods, picking up force in mountain canyons and causing washouts on the sunbaked desert floor.

ENVIRONMENTAL ISSUES
Nonnative Species
It takes a specially adapted plant or animal

to survive in Death Valley's severe climate. Most of the species that do are native, having adapted to Death Valley's specific conditions. A few nonnative species have stuck around, however, competing with native plants and animals for precious water resources.

TAMARISK
Originally from the eastern hemisphere, tamarisk trees were planted in the United States in the 1800s for ornamentation, shade, windbreaks, and erosion control. The trees were eventually planted in Death Valley by pioneers, the Civilian Conservation Corps, and even the National Park Service (NPS) in the early days. Tamarisk is resilient and looks lovely, but it's a major water suck in the northern Mojave Desert, where riparian environments are rare and fragile. You'll see tamarisk trees in areas where there is a substantial underground water supply; they crowd out native plants and animals and salinize the soil by dropping salty leaves. The bush variety, called salt cedar, has pink blooms in spring and gives riparian areas a lush look. The tree variety, Athel, adorn old mining camps like the well-watered **Ibex Spring Camp**, and add a picturesque quality to the old cabins. The NPS has made efforts to remove the plants from Saratoga Spring, Eagle Borax Works, Warm Spring Canyon, and other sites. Today, tamarisk abounds in riparian areas in the dry southwest, to the detriment of the native plants.

BURROS
Wild burros were introduced to Death Valley in the 1860s and used as pack animals when mining ruled the land. The "single-blanket jackass prospector," a phrase coined by the famous prospector Shorty Harris, relied on these animals to travel from strike to strike. Originally from the Sahara in Africa, burros are strong animals acclimated to life in the arid desert. They can also tolerate as much as 30 percent water loss by body weight and replenish it in five minutes of drinking. Inevitably some burros escaped or were

released when people moved on, and the wild burro population in Death Valley soared.

The NPS set a goal to remove all burros from within Death Valley National Monument's boundaries. In an enormous effort from 1983-1987, more than 6,000 burros were captured and put up for adoption. The NPS also built a 37-mile fence along the eastern border to keep wild burros from straying over from Nevada. In 1987 the NPS declared their efforts over, claiming that they had removed all wild burros from all the hidden nooks and crannies of the park. However, seven years later, in 1994, the national monument became a national park that included an additional million acres and inherited a whole new crop of burros. The **Saline Valley,** in particular, is home to several of the curious animals. They also stray into the relatively well-watered canyons on the western side of the Panamint Mountains. At this point many visitors feel that they are as much a part of the park as indigenous species, but ultimately they throw off the biological balance by competing with other animals, specifically bighorn sheep, for precious water resources.

Air Pollution

Air pollution is not always present in Death Valley, but when it does appear, it can diminish the spectacular views for which the park is known. Some of the air pollution is generated within the park when the wind whips up loose particles and dust from dry lake beds and the open desert. The largest source, however, is industrial and auto emissions in urban centers like Los Angeles, hundreds of miles away. **Spring** and **summer** days have the worst hazy air.

Night Sky

Death Valley National Park is one of three parks in the United States that the **International Dark-Sky Association** (www.darksky.org) has designated an International Dark Sky Park. It is so remote that it remains free of the light pollution of major cities or smaller urban areas. Even Las Vegas, more than 150 miles east, doesn't affect the inky, starry sky.

The spectacular night skies are one of the park's draws, and the NPS regards them as a natural treasure to be maintained. The NPS has reduced excessive outdoor lighting and has improved lighting facilities to reduce glow and glare. It maintains its commitment to protect natural darkness, and is one of the few places in the country where it is possible to experience the awe of truly dark skies. For those of us used to cities, the sight can be spectacular.

Wild burros run freely in parts of the Saline Valley, on the western side of the park.

Plants and Animals

PLANTS

The widely varying landscape of Death Valley forms biological islands to which specialized species of plants and animals have adapted. Sand dunes, desert wetlands, and high desert woodlands represent the wide array of habitat. Most wildlife can range and breed across landscapes, but plants remain in specific locations conducive to their survival. Water availability and temperature are strong influences.

Desert Lowlands

In the desert lowlands, plants must be able to adapt to heat, salt, and very little water. The lowest basins hover near or below sea level and include Death Valley, Saline Valley, and Panamint Valley. Dry lake beds, called playas, are remnants of Pleistocene-era lakes and have salt concentrations so high that they block plant growth. As salt levels lessen toward the edges, some plants are able to take root even in soils that are still relatively salty. **Pickleweed,** or picklebush, is one of most salt-tolerant species and can tolerate 6 percent salinity, twice the salinity of the ocean. A succulent shrub, pickleweed stores salt in its segmented, fleshy stems. A healthy crop of pickleweed can be found at Salt Creek, where it thrives along the muddy banks of this exposed desert stream.

Low-lying areas farther from the playa are less salt-heavy. As the salinity decreases, soil can support plants such as arrowweed or mesquite. **Mesquite** can tolerate 0.5 percent salinity. The plant has a long taproot, sometimes longer than 50 feet, and can anchor itself in sand dunes where other plants can't reach water, making it a great indicator of subsurface water; desert wells are often located near mesquite thickets. Mesquite is a wide-ranging species that played a vital role in Native American life for food, fuel, and housing.

Other plants that do not have a way to adapt to salinity or far-away water sources adapt by

developing mechanisms to cope with infrequent access to water. **Desert holly** shrivels up to reduce the rate of photosynthesis and its need for moisture. The leaves turn silvery to reflect more light.

Creosote is very common across the western hemisphere. This bush can continue photosynthesis after 30 months with no rain and withstands heat, cold, drought, and flooding. It has staggering longevity: One species has individuals dated to 11,700 years old. The first creosote bushes arrived in the Amargosa Desert east of Death Valley approximately 9,000 years ago, but did not reach the mountains until 5,000 years ago. Some of the creosote plants we see today may have been some of the first plants in the Mojave Desert.

The lower elevations of the northern Mojave also support about 20 species of desert **cactus.** They occur in hot lowland valleys from 1,000 to 9,500 feet to mix with the junipers and pinyons. The spines and ribs deflect heat and help preserve water, and the spines also deter animals from eating them.

Transition Elevations

The mid-level elevations, 1,300-5,900 feet, receive more rain and thus support more varied plantlife. Since the Mojave Desert's boundaries are not clear-cut, **Joshua trees** are often considered an indicator plant, signaling that the biological landscape has transitioned to the Mojave. Joshua trees are large, top-heavy yuccas with a spiky upper branch system that can reach more than 30 feet in height. They were named by Mormon settlers, who were reminded of the biblical story of Joshua reaching his arms up in prayer. Joshua trees grow in places that receive snowfall and take advantage of the small amounts of groundwater and deeper soil of these locations; they occur between lowland and higher-elevation vegetation, with the highest concentrations at 3,500 to 5,000 feet elevation. Joshua trees don't have growth rings, so they are hard to date; instead, they are measured by their size and growth rates, which are about 3 inches per year in the first 10 years and 1.5 inches (3.8 cm) per year after. Large, cream-white flowers bloom in spring and are pollinated by the yucca moth. Good places to see Joshua trees include Lee Flat along the Saline Valley South Pass, the Racetrack Valley Road, and Joshua Flats along the Big Pine Death Valley Road.

Wildflower season (mid-Feb.-mid-July) in the desert is a rare and elusive phenomenon; it doesn't happen every year. The perfect conditions have to be in place—well-timed rain intervals from Pacific storms between late fall and early spring, the right amount of warmth, and an easing up of the extreme drying desert winds. Wildflowers survive by sprouting only when these optimal conditions occur, then going out bright and fast, turning to seed again to lay dormant until another germination year. It's a wildly exultant time when the basins are filled with fragile, short-lived color.

The National Park Service provides a weekly **wildflower update** on its Facebook page (www.facebook.com/DeathValleyNP/info), pointing visitors to the best places to see wildflowers and describing their bloom status. Wildflower season runs from mid-February to mid-July and begins at the lower elevations, creeping up to the higher elevations as the season wears on. From mid-February to mid-April, wildflowers can be seen in the foothills and alluvial fans of the lower elevations such as those along the Badwater Road. From early April to early May, wildflowers may be found in the canyons and higher valleys like the Racetrack Valley. From May to mid-July, wildflowers pepper the higher mountain peaks and woodlands such as those of Wildrose and Telescope Peaks.

Desert Woodlands

Pinyon-juniper woodland marks the desert high-elevation tree line at around 6,000 feet. **Pinyons** and Utah **junipers** usually grow together in scrub forest on gravel or bedrock. This forest signals a change in water availability and elevation since it needs 9 or 10 inches of annual precipitation, a significant amount of water in the desert. Pinyon trees with mature pinecones have rich nutritious seeds—pine nuts, which were among the important food sources for indigenous people in northern Mojave. Wildrose Canyon and Wildrose Peak are good locations to see these woodlands.

Limber pine and **bristlecone pine** forests rise above the pinyon-juniper belt in the Inyo, Panamint, and part of the Grapevine Mountains. A good place to see this forest is Mahogany Flat, elevation 8,100 feet in the Panamint Mountains. A trail from here leads to Telescope Peak, the highest point in Death Valley National Park. Limber pines appear at about 9,000 feet. Bristlecone pines appear at about 10,000 feet. It is the oldest living tree on earth, and some individuals are thousands of years old. The oldest ring count approaches 5,000 years. Limber and bristlecone pines are gnarled and stark. Although they grow in cold, arid elevations not usually conducive to plantlife, these conditions may also help them. There are few fungi or insects, and forest fires sparked by lightning are uncommon since there is little ground cover.

ANIMALS

Death Valley's landscape often looks barren, but there is a surprising amount of wildlife diversity. Approximately 380 species of birds have been documented along with 51 species of mammals, and 41 species of reptiles and amphibians. Riparian environments, sand dunes, coniferous areas, and desert woodlands each have their own habitat. There are even six fish species in Death Valley. Five of these are not found anywhere else. The best places to see fish are freshwater marshes: Saratoga Spring, where you can find the Saratoga Spring pupfish, and Salt Creek, with the Salt Creek pupfish.

All animals in the northern Mojave have adapted to the harsh climate and have developed ways of avoiding the worst extremes and ways to conserve precious resources.

Most cold-blooded animals, snakes, lizards, tortoises, and reptiles hibernate in winter. In summer, some animals do the opposite, in a process called estivation. Metabolism lowers, and the animal, for example, the Mojave ground squirrel, lives on stored body fat from mid-summer until fall or winter. During mid-day some animals, like snakes and coyotes, retreat to shade or dens. Lowland animals are mostly nocturnal and hunt at night or at dawn. The beefy and distinctive Chuckwalla lizard stores extra water in the fatty tissues of its tail. Other animals get all or nearly all their water from plants.

Mammals

Bighorn sheep are often associated with the northern Mojave, but it is uncommon to see these elusive animals, although their droppings are abundant in canyons such as Ashford Canyon. They are well adapted to steep, rocky mountain passages and can survive in sparsely vegetated areas as long as they have access to water every few days. Bighorn sheep were common in the mid-19th century, but hunting and disease from domestic sheep drastically cut their numbers. The rise of feral burros introduced competition for vegetation and water. Burro reduction programs initiated

by the NPS and Bureau of Land Management (BLM) were geared toward protecting habitat for bighorn sheep.

The top-rung carnivore in the desert, the **mountain lion** or puma lives at upper elevations, preying on bighorn sheep and deer. The smaller cousins of these predators, **bobcats,** live at lower elevations and prey on smaller mammals and birds.

Birds

Some birds, like roadrunners, are here year-round, but for most others, Death Valley is a migratory stop from November through March. Birds congregate near water, like the Saline Valley freshwater marsh. Other birds migrate within the region. Ravens survive year-round in the hottest parts of Death Valley; they are intelligent and adaptable.

Desert Tortoise

An emblematic Mojave Desert animal, the desert tortoise lives 60 to 100 years. It hibernates in winter and estivates in summer, living in a 3- to 10-foot burrow underground, and forays out in fall and spring. It can store a quart of water. Desert tortoises have become increasingly rare, although as recently as the 1950s they were one of the most commonly

Death Valley supports a wide variety of bird life, including this great egret.

seen native animals in the Mojave. They have faced threats from habitat destruction and competition for food. Land development, livestock grazing, and off-highway-vehicle recreation destroys burrows; cars and recreational vehicles may crush tortoises. They were put on the federal threatened species list in 1990. You might be able to see a tortoise behind the Shoshone Inn in Shoshone Village or at the Jawbone Canyon rest area off U.S. 395.

Salt Creek Pupfish

A few animal species have become stranded in biological islands in the rare desert wetlands. During the late Pleistocene, Mojave pupfish filled the lakes and streams. They survived as the water shrank, becoming isolated from the network of water. Now each riparian environment has its own specialized pupfish, with the entire population of the species confined to one pool or creek.

Bats and Arthropods

Arthropods include insects, spiders, and scorpions. **Scorpions** look like a crustacean or a strange sea creature, evoking the region's watery history. **Bats** are predators of arthropods. All over the world, including the California deserts, bats have lost roosting and foraging areas. The thousands of abandoned mines in the Death Valley area make good roosting locations and make up for lost habitat. Open mine shafts can be dangerous, but wildlife biologists encourage property owners, including the federal government, to close off shafts with grated metal bars instead of filling them entirely with dirt.

History

NATIVE AMERICANS

During the end of the last glacial age, there were marshes and savannas in the desert lowlands, making them conducive to human settlement. Archaeological evidence from a number of sites confirms human habitation in the northern Mojave Desert for at least 11,000 years. There is evidence of camps near the shores of Lake Manly in Death Valley. As the lakes dried up and it became hotter and more inhospitable in the low-lying valleys, year-round human occupation dwindled. There is scarce evidence of human settlement between 4,500 and 7,500 years ago, a particularly arid period in natural history. From 4,500 years ago, the climate became more temperate, and hunter-gatherer cultures evolved in the region. They developed a way of life that allowed them to survive in this severe landscape.

When European Americans came on the scene in the 1800s, there were four cultural groups that had perfected a life in the difficult terrain in and around Death Valley: the **Kawaiisu** people to the south, the **Southern** Paiute, the **Owens Valley Paiute,** and **Western Shoshone** in Death Valley itself. The Shoshone were part of a larger Shoshone Nation that extended from western Wyoming to eastern Oregon, eastern California, and central Nevada. The groups moved seasonally between the desert floor and mountain camps, seeking favorable climate and seasonal plants. Winters were spent hunting and harvesting wild grasses and mesquite beans in the low desert valleys. In summer they moved to the cooler mountain elevations, where pinyon pine nuts were the staple. The group of Shoshone people at Furnace Creek in the heart of Death Valley called themselves Timbisha. Although the Spaniards had established coastal missions in California beginning in 1769, the European invasion of North America didn't begin to affect the groups living in the harsh interior, east of the Sierra Nevada Mountains, until the early 19th century. With mining and eventually tourism, an all-too familiar story of Native American displacement occurred with the Timbisha

Preserving Historic and Cultural Sites

Death Valley has been home to Native American people for thousands of years. Signs of their ancient culture, with its powerful connections to the land, are scattered across Death Valley, often blending in with the landscape. Stone alignments, rock walls, and rock art can be found in the **Greenwater Valley** area. Native American village sites are in the remote canyons of the **Saline Valley**. The secluded and rugged **Cottonwood Mountains** hide petroglyphs in deep mountain canyons.

Sadly, there is a code of silence that surrounds most of these sights due to the threat of **vandalism**. The only Native American rock art site readily disclosed in Death Valley is in the popular but rugged Titus Canyon at Klare Spring; as a result, this impressive panel of ancient petroglyphs has been badly vandalized.

Pioneer settlement and mining moved in on Native American territory, leaving historic traces throughout the lonely canyons and hills of Death Valley. Visit the **Ibex Spring Mining Camp,** a remote and scenic ghost camp in one of the lightly visited areas of the park. As you walk toward the camp, you might be struck by the isolation, the incongruousness of the palm trees against the barren rocky hills, the jagged cabins alone with the sun and wind. As you get closer, you may be struck by something else: a water tank riddled with bullet holes, or sheetrock cabin walls that looked like they've been punched in. It's still a fascinating spot, but the years of vandalism have taken their toll.

Death Valley is so vast that it's easy to go a day without seeing another soul. Because of its scale, many places in the park are lightly patrolled, and we as visitors are tasked with taking care of this monumental natural and cultural resources. Adding graffiti to an ancient petroglyph or thoughtlessly and illegally shooting up a mining camp may seem extreme, but these acts are shockingly common. Even less egregious behaviors, such as removing a rusted can from a ghost camp, for example, take a toll and chip away at historic sites. Along with the natural beauty of Death Valley, its historic and cultural sites tell the story of Death Valley and contribute to its fascination. Native American sites are still sacred to the Timbisha Shoshone people, who continue to have strong ties to the land. Do not disturb historic and cultural sites in any way. Leave them for others to discover and enjoy.

Shoshone people, who had called Death Valley home for thousands of years.

PIONEERS

After Lewis and Clark finished their exploratory journey through the West in 1806, fur trappers set up camp in the Rocky Mountains, beaver populations were soon exhausted, and traders began exploring farther west into the Great Basin region. A small group of traders led by Spaniard **Antonio Armijo** struck out to find a reliable route from New Mexico to California. Armijo traveled west from the present location of Las Vegas and followed the elusive desert river, the Amargosa, to the west and south. The Amargosa River flows mostly underground and disappears for good at the southern end of the Death Valley sink.

Armijo left the trail there, but he was the first European American to visit the desert basin that would become Death Valley. His trail became the Spanish Trail, used as a trading route and the original route for migrant pioneers coming to the area in the 1840s.

In 1840s the famous Death Valley 49ers were seeking a way to the Sierra Nevada Mountains where gold camps and wild speculation were beginning to boom. Tens of thousands of people flocked to the West, seeking their fortunes along the few established routes. The north-south route along the base of the Sierra Nevadas, the present-day U.S. 395, had been defined, but the area to the east was still unexplored. A group of 400 to 500 migrants in 110 wagons left from Salt Lake City under the guidance of Jefferson Hunt.

The plan was to follow the Spanish Trail. Partway into the trip, 20-year-old **Captain Orson Smith** convinced some of the members of the wagon train to leave the Spanish Trail and follow him on a shortcut to the goldfields. After only 25 miles into this so-called shortcut, the group encountered a deep canyon. Many of the party realized their mistake, cut their losses, and turned around to rejoin the initial group and successfully take the Spanish Trail to the Sierra Nevada Mountains. A smaller group of 27 wagons and 100 people somehow made it past this canyon and continued west across the desert, where they encountered the bleak, salty wildness of the Death Valley sink in December 1849.

This was unprecedented territory for non-native people, and they were faced with the extreme basin and range topography, with its sheer mountains and desolate lowlands. The groups continued to fracture into smaller and smaller units, feeling their way west through various rugged routes to the base of the Sierra Nevada. The **Pinney party** comprised 11 men traveling on foot. They ran low on food, and two men split off, eventually making their way to Owens Lake to be nursed back to health by the Paiute people. In 1862 the skeletons of nine men were found near the Death Valley Dunes, and were presumed to be the rest of the Pinney party.

The **Jayhawker party** consisted of 40 to 50 Illinois men. They split into smaller groups and made their way via various passes through the Panamint Mountains. Improbably, only two of the Jayhawker party died despite extreme hardship. Along the way they found rich silver-lead ore samples in the Panamint Range, which they packed out. One sample of exceptionally rich ore was made into a gun sight, and seekers for years returned to try to find the Lost Gunsight Lode, which has passed into Death Valley legend.

Possibly the most famous contingent of wanderers was the **Bennett-Arcane group,** comprising seven wagons and about 30 men, women, and children. After entering the salt flats, they turned south instead

One group of 49'ers forged this route to escape with their lives from Death Valley.

of following the Jayhawkers to the north. Exhausted and discouraged by the sheer Panamint Mountains, they eventually set up camp, most likely at today's Bennett's Well, off the West Side Road. Two men, William Lewis Manly and John Rogers, went for help, returning 26 days later to rescue the remaining group. In the interim another smaller group led by **Harry Wade** found their way southwest. Somehow only one member of the Bennett-Arcane group had died while awaiting rescue. As they walked over the southern Panamints with their lives, having long since abandoned and burned their wagons, one of the party supposedly turned and said, "Goodbye, death valley," naming North America's deepest basin.

COMPETING LAND-USE VISIONS

Death Valley and surrounding mountain ranges were signed into national monument status in 1933. More than 60 years later, in 1994, it was declared a national park, more than doubling the size of the protected lands. At 3.4 million acres—over 5,000 square miles—it is the biggest national park in the contiguous United States. The vastness and wide-open spaces of the northern Mojave Desert might make it seem like there's plenty of land to go around, but competing interests have often dictated the way the land is used. Miners, ranchers, off-road-vehicle recreation enthusiasts, the military, Native American groups, and conservationists have clashed in and around the northern Mojave Desert.

The Military

Military bases flank the park boundaries on two sides. **Naval Air Weapons Station China Lake** lies to the southwest, and **Fort Irwin National Training Center** to the northeast. Chosen for the vastness and seeming emptiness of the region, these military bases take up large swatches of the northern Mojave. Both were home to Native American groups for at least 15,000 years. When the China Lake facility's boundaries were established in 1943, it included one of the largest known concentrations of petroglyphs in the western hemisphere. The **Coso Rock Art District** in the Coso Range Canyons covers a 99-square-mile area with more than 50,000 documented petroglyphs. While the site no longer has easy public access, the Navy has a policy of stewardship toward cultural and natural sites located within the boundaries of the facility and allows for military-approved guided public tours of the rock art. Unlike the few well-known rock art sites in Death Valley, there is virtually no contemporary graffiti—being located inside a military base has arguably protected them.

Also located within the boundaries of the China Lake facility are the **Coso Hot Springs**, on the National Register of Historic Places. The springs were used by Native Americans dating back to the Coso people and later the Northern Paiute and Timbisha as a cultural and healing ritual site. Local Native American groups still have access to the springs for ceremonial purposes. In the

1920s a hot springs resort was built at Coso Hot Springs, and the ruins of this resort still stand. At times, visitors to Death Valley are reminded of the proximity of military operations. Especially in the Saline Valley, tucked against the western Inyo Mountains or the Eureka Dunes, high up in the northern Last Chance Range, it is possible for military planes to swoop in literally out of the blue to buzz the surreal mountain-scapes with maneuvers. Although both military centers have sought to expand their acreage into the surrounding desert, they operate under relatively clear mandates from Congress. Much of the current debate over land use is about areas outside their borders.

Mining

Death Valley's rich mineral resources were known from the time of the famous 1849 rush for gold, but most of the attention was focused on the western Sierra Nevada and the Comstock Lode in Nevada. The area around Death Valley didn't have its first mining heyday until the early 1870s, when the silver-mining town of Cerro Gordon in the Inyo Mountains grew into a sizeable silver-mining camp and drew attention to the area.

Panamint City sprouted up next, drawing hundreds of eager investors and miners to the silver veins in the Panamint Mountains. By 1874 Panamint City had swelled to a rowdy town of 2,000 people with a reputation for lawlessness and violence. By 1875 the boom was over. Small mining camps spread through the Panamints and other mountain ranges around Death Valley, appearing and being abandoned as the veins played out and people moved, along with their possessions and sometimes even buildings, to newer sites. The eastern side of Death Valley gained much attention after 1900 when towns like **Chloride City** and **Rhyolite** gained momentum. Rhyolite was the largest town in the Death Valley area with a population of 5,000 to 10,000 during its heyday, 1905 to 1911. The teens and 1920s saw interest in lead and copper mining, and mining efforts crept into remote places like the Racetrack Valley.

When Death Valley became a national monument in 1933, mining was briefly suspended, but Congress created a loophole to allow the continuation of mining claims. In the 1930s mining claims were at their highest as the depression brought people seeking alternative ways to eke out a living. These were small-time pocket miners, working small deposits of mineral that would support a few families. Gold fever had given way to more practical dreams. Talc and borax fever, for instance, though not nearly as romantic-sounding, had taken hold, and mining companies worked the land, maximizing technology to pull out even low-grade ore.

In 1971, when the third borax rush took off, attitudes toward the land had changed. In the 1800s people had swarmed the land for what they could eke out of it, but more than 100 years later most people saw that same land as something in need of protection. Mining practices had changed: Old mining practices had been relatively unobtrusive, and miners hand-dug pockets of ore, leaving the overall landscape intact. Newer methods included open-pit and strip-mining, which vastly degraded the landscape and changed its shape. Individuals seeking their fortunes had given way to mining corporations seeking wealth in highly visible locations within a national monument. Congress sought to get the number of mining claims within the monument's boundaries under control when it passed the Mining Act of 1976. Before the Mining Act, there were more than 4,000 claims in Death Valley; by the time Death Valley officially became a national park in 1994, there were fewer than 150. The last one, Billie Mine, a borax mine located along the Dante's View Road, closed in 2005.

Tourism

The economy of Death Valley began to transition from mining to tourism in the 1920s, and in 1933 Congress approved Death Valley

as a national monument. The first toll road designed for visitors was completed in 1926. It followed the contours of present-day Highway 190 from Towne Pass on the west side to Stovepipe Wells. The tourist village of Stovepipe Wells, briefly called Bungalow City, was completed in 1926.

The national monument designation protected the land, but Congress conveniently left a loophole for mining. The history of mining and tourism are inextricably intertwined in Death Valley history in many ways. The Pacific Coast Borax Company actually built some of the first lodging for visitors, completing the elegant Furnace Creek Inn in 1927 and investing money in the tourism potential of the land as mining claims played out.

Mining and tourism both began to boom in the middle of the 20th century, coexisting within the national monument. With mining claims somewhat regulated with the passage of the Mining Act of 1976, the park turned to other issues of conservation and public debate. Also in 1976, Congress attempted to create a plan that would encompass a wide range of land-use interests by establishing the California Desert Conservation Area on land managed by the BLM outside the park's boundaries.

The debate continued to rage until there was a sweeping attempt to shift priorities, in the form of the California Desert Protection Act of 1986. The legislation languished until 1994, when it was finally signed into existence. It added an additional million acres to the national monument to create the new and better-protected Death Valley National Park. It also added land and protected status to the newly created Joshua Tree National Park and the Mojave National Preserve. The act also acknowledged the claims of Native American groups, ordering a study to find reservation land for the Timbisha Shoshone people.

The Timbisha Shoshone People

Beginning with the arrival of the first

European American migrants in the mid-1850s, the Timbisha Shoshone people were displaced from their land and way of life as mining camps and towns sprung up and took control of water and other natural resources. They gradually acculturated, doing manual labor for road building, mining, ranching, and construction.

When Death Valley became a national monument in 1933, the focus for the land shifted toward conservation and tourism. Mining was also allowed, and mining claims continued to grow well into the 1970s. The only interest group completely left out of land management were the Timbisha Shoshone people, tied to the land through their lifestyle, religion, and history.

Following the national monument designation, the NPS built the Timbisha a 60-acre adobe village next to Furnace Creek, but they were forbidden to continue using the land for their subsistence lifestyle. Their first political triumph came on the heels of the Mining Act of 1976, which marked a shift in attitudes toward the land. In 1983 the Timbisha Shoshone gained formal federal recognition. When Death Valley became a national park in 1994, the act required a study to find them reservation land within their native region. In 2000 the **Timbisha Land Act** set aside 300 acres of homeland for the Timbisha Shoshone, along with provisions granting them access to national park lands for religious activities.

Wilderness

The wide-open spaces of the desert function as a canvas for the dreams and beliefs of the many people who visit and call it home. The vastness of Death Valley inspires a certain feeling of independence and solitude, and it is easy to embrace a feeling of open possibility, as opposed to the feeling that you are visiting an attraction. This might account for the competing visions about the way the land is used and protected.

During the 20th century, two increasingly divergent political viewpoints became clear. One contingent wanted to continue to eke out a living from the land with mining, ranching, and other economic activity. Others hold the idea that the scenic, geologic, ecological, and historic resources of the northern Mojave Desert need to be protected. These two points of view are not always mutually exclusive, but they represent two vastly different political perspectives, and continue to create political tension at Death Valley and the surrounding areas.

Within the park, debates continue over "Wilderness" designations, which have closed some 4WD roads. A Wilderness designation adds protection from land development, although roads still intersect it. Most of the park—95 percent—is **designated Wilderness.** Debates also continue over how historic sites like cabins should be maintained and who should be responsible. Some cabins and historic sites have been cared for by private citizens for years, and they feel a sense of ownership. Others, sadly, have not had the benefit of constant stewardship by anyone. A visit to a place like the Ibex Spring Camp makes it clear what the NPS is trying to prevent. Sheetrock walls are punched out, an old water tank is riddled with bullet holes, and weathered timbers have been pulled from cabins and used as fuel for bonfires.

Debates beyond the park's boundaries have become fiercer on land managed by the BLM in both California and Nevada, and mining and ranching battles on BLM land have received media coverage. In Death Valley National Park and beyond its boundaries, the northern Mojave Desert continues to inspire a fierce sense of independence, passion, and inspiration.

Essentials

Getting There

Death Valley National Park is at the southeastern side of central California, bordering Nevada on the east. A small portion of the park, the Nevada Triangle, is in Nevada. The closest major cities are Las Vegas, 140 miles southeast, and Los Angeles, 300 miles southwest. Most of the park is easily accessible year-round, although some higher-elevation locales may close due to snow during winter. Highway 190 is the major route that bisects the park; it is open year-round. It passes through the two main park hubs, Stovepipe Wells and Furnace Creek.

SUGGESTED ROUTES
West
U.S. 395 is the main route traversing the eastern side of California between the Sierra Nevada Mountains and the Nevada border. Routes to Death Valley via U.S. 395 work best for travelers coming from the north or west. From U.S. 395 there are two routes into the Death Valley Region.

Highway 190 runs east from the tiny town of Olancha, with a gas and café stop.

Highway 136 runs east from Lone Pine, a bigger town with hotels, restaurants, gas, and other services. Highway 136 joins Highway 190, which crosses into the park boundary at the Panamint Springs Resort, with its motel, restaurant, general store, gas, and campground. The resort has park information and can be used for exploring areas on the western side of Death Valley. The closest park hub is Stovepipe Wells, 30 miles east.

Southwest
Highway 14 cuts across the Mojave Desert from the Los Angeles area to join **Highway 178** in the town of Ridgecrest before heading northeast into the park. Ridgecrest is a moderate-size town on the edge of the Naval Air Weapons Station China Lake. It has most services, including hotels, restaurants, groceries, and outdoors stores. It's a good place to fill up on gas and grab any supplies you've forgotten.

Highway 178 enters the park and joins **Highway 190** just east of the Panamint Springs Resort, about 1.5 hours from Ridgecrest. The closest park hub is Stovepipe Wells, another 30 miles (30 minutes) northeast. Between Ridgecrest and Highway 190 where it enters the park, Highway 178 is prone to washouts; check road conditions before taking this route.

East
If you are using **Las Vegas** as your travel hub or entering Death Valley from the east, there are several eastern routes. Depending which route you take, travel time is 2-3.5 hours from Las Vegas.

U.S. 95 is a main route in Nevada that parallels both the state boundary and Death Valley. There are two points to enter Death Valley from U.S. 95. The first route leaves U.S. 95 south on **Highway 373** at Lathrop Wells, and then runs west, via a right turn at Death Valley Junction, onto **Highway 190** into the park. There is a gas station and a convenience store at Lathrop Wells, but no gas at Death Valley Junction.

North on U.S. 95 is the gateway town of Beatty, Nevada. From here, **Highway 374** leads south into the park. Beatty has lodging, restaurants, and gas and makes a good driving stop; it is also a good base camp for exploring the park.

Southeast
I-15 begins in San Diego and runs north,

passing about an hour east of Los Angeles. It is the main road between Southern California and Las Vegas. From Baker, which is a good gas and convenience-store stop, **Highway 127** runs north, intersecting with **Highway 190,** the main park route. This is the fastest route into the park from the Los Angeles area.

FROM LAS VEGAS

Las Vegas is the closest major city to Death Valley, less than three hours away. It has a major airport with flights from most U.S. cities, and offers car, RV, and 4WD vehicle rentals as well as equipment and supplies to prepare for your trip.

Car

I-15 intersects with U.S. 95 north of McCarran International Airport. To reach **Death Valley Junction** (2.5 hours, 140 miles) from Las Vegas, take U.S. 95 north for 88 miles to Lathrop Wells, Nevada. Turn left (south) onto Highway 373 and drive 24 miles southwest. Highway 373 becomes Highway 127 when it crosses into California. At the tiny outpost of Death Valley Junction, turn right (west) onto Highway 190 and continue west for 30 miles to the park hub at Furnace Creek.

From Las Vegas via **Beatty, Nevada** (2.5 hours, 160 miles), take U.S. 95 north for 116 miles. Turn left (south) onto Highway 374 and drive 19 miles southwest to Beatty Cutoff Road at the Hells Gate junction. Turn left onto Beatty Cutoff Road, and drive 10 miles south to Highway 190. Turn left onto Highway 190, and drive 11 miles south to Furnace Creek.

Air

McCarran International Airport (LAS, 5757 Wayne Newton Blvd., 702/261-5211, www.mccarran.com) is a major international airport positioned to serve Nevada and parts of Arizona and California. It's located near I-15 and U.S. 95 in Las Vegas. More than 20 commercial carriers land here, including Aeromexico, Air Canada, Alaska Airlines, American, British Airways, Delta, JetBlue,

Southwest, United, US Airways, and Virgin Atlantic.

Ground transportation is located outside Terminal 1's baggage claim area and on Terminal 3's Level Zero. If you're staying overnight in Las Vegas, group shuttles from the airport are available to many of the major hotel-resorts. **Taxis** are available from the airport and McCarran's Rent-A-Car Center. Some taxis do not take credit cards. Walk-up limo and SUV services are also available.

CAR RENTAL

Car rentals are located at the **McCarran Rent-A-Car Center** (7135 Gilespie St., 24 hours daily), three miles from the airport. Courtesy shuttles from the airport take you to the rental car center. The Center is located close to I-15 and I-215 as well as the Las Vegas Strip. A few rental-car agencies are not located within the rental center; make sure you double-check the location of your rental car.

Tours

Chartered day tours to Death Valley are available from Las Vegas. These tours often leave from popular hotels along the Las Vegas strip and take visitors to some of the park's highlights. Companies like **Incredible Adventures** (800/777-8464, www.incadventures.com) offer SUV and van tours.

RV Rental

Many RV rental agencies have offices in Las Vegas, including **Cruise America** (702/565-2224 or 800/671-8042, www.cruiseamerica.com), **Bates International** (702/737-9050 or 800/732-2283, www.batesintl.com), and **Sahara RV Center** (702/384-8818 or 800/748-6494, www.sahararv.com).

Smaller vehicles suit the Death Valley terrain better than big RVs, and they allow for more versatility in travel. Camper vans out of Las Vegas are available through companies that include **Escape Campervans** (877/270-8267 or 310/672-9909, www.escapecampervans.com).

Equipment Rental

REI (710 S. Rampart Blvd., 702/951-4488, www.rei.com), centrally located in Las Vegas's Boca Park, rents backpacks, sleeping bags, and camp stoves. One hour south, in Boulder City, **Desert Adventures** (1647A Nevada Hwy., Boulder City, 702/293-5026, www.kayaklasvegas.com) offers a wide selection of gear.

Accommodations and Food

There are many major hotel chains and accommodations convenient to the airport and highways. For that Vegas experience, the Las Vegas Strip is lined with casino resort hotels. The city is also a dining destination; many resort hotels have multiple restaurants to suit a variety of different tastes and price points, some with celebrity chefs to draw in crowds beyond the hotel guests. Luxury resorts include:

Stratosphere (2000 Las Vegas Blvd. S., 800/998-6937, www.stratospherehotel.com)

The Venetian (3355 Las Vegas Blvd. S., 702/414-1000, www.venetian.com)

Caesars Palace (3570 Las Vegas Blvd. S., 702/731-7110, www.caesarspalace.com)

Bellagio (3600 Las Vegas Blvd. S., 888/987-6667, www.bellagio.com)

The Palazzo (3325 Las Vegas Blvd. S., 702/607-7777, www.palazzo.com)

Las Vegas has kid- and family-friendly resorts as well:

Excalibur (Las Vegas Blvd. S., 800/879-1379, www.excalibur.com)

New York-New York (3790 Las Vegas Blvd. S., 866/815-4365, www.newyorknewyork.com)

Mandalay Bay Resort & Casino (3950 Las Vegas Blvd. S., 702/632-7777, www.mandalaybay.com)

Golden Nugget (E. Fremont St., 702/385-7111, www.goldennugget.com)

To steer clear of the clamor of the Strip, head toward the west side of town, close to Red Rock Canyon National Conservation Area:

JW Marriott Las Vegas (221 N. Rampart Blvd., 702/869-7777, www.marriott.com)

FROM LOS ANGELES

Approximately 300 miles south of Death Valley, Los Angeles has a major international airport with regular flights from U.S. and international cities. LA has all the civilization you could possibly need to prepare for your trip, including car, RV, and equipment rentals.

Car

The drive from Los Angeles to Death Valley takes about four hours, depending upon your destination within the park. You can plan your route via the western park entrance at Panamint Springs or the eastern entrance and Furnace Creek.

WESTERN ENTRANCE

Head north out of Los Angeles on U.S. 101 to Highway 170 and onto I-5. From I-5, take Highway 14, the Antelope Valley Freeway, north toward Palmdale and Lancaster. Drive 120 miles north to Indian Wells, where Highway 14 joins U.S. 395. Continue north on U.S. 395 for 42 miles to the town of Olancha. Turn right (east) onto Highway 190 and continue 45 miles to **Panamint Springs.** Stovepipe Wells lies 29 miles east of Panamint Springs; Furnace Creek is 53 miles east of Panamint Springs.

EASTERN ENTRANCE

Head east out of Los Angeles on I-10, the San Bernardino Freeway. After approximately 10 miles, around West Covina, follow signs for I-605 north. Follow I-605 north for approximately five miles, then take the exit onto I-210 east, the Foothill Freeway. Continue east on I-210 for 27 miles, then follow signs for I-15 north toward Barstow. Stay on I-15 north for 130 miles until its intersection with Highway 127 at the town of Baker. Take the Highway 127/Kelbaker Road exit toward Death Valley and drive north on Highway 127 for 87 miles to Death Valley Junction. Turn left (west) onto Highway 190 and drive another 30 miles west to **Furnace Creek.**

Air

Los Angeles International Airport (LAX,

1 World Way, 424/646-5252, www.lawa.org) is a major international airport and hub located about 16 miles southwest of downtown Los Angeles. It is one of the busiest airports in the world. The main airport serves the Los Angeles area with seven terminals, plus the Tom Bradley International Terminal (Terminal B).

Airport shuttles, hotel shuttles, long-distance vans, ride-share vans, and taxis can all be accessed at the lower Arrivals Level outside of the baggage claim area; median waiting platforms are marked by overhead signs. A **FlyAway Bus** service (no reservations, 24 hours daily) offers the best public transportation from LAX to destinations around the city, including Union Station (downtown), Van Nuys, Westwood, Santa Monica, and Hollywood.

CAR RENTAL

Approximately 40 car-rental companies operate at Los Angeles International Airport; all vehicle rental companies are located off-site. Several companies offer courtesy shuttles that pick up customers at the lower Arrivals Level of all terminals.

To reach other car rental agencies, take the LAX Bus C to reach the **Off-Airport Rental Car Terminal** to meet the rental car courtesy shuttle. Many of these rental car companies provide phone links inside or near the baggage claim areas on the lower Arrivals Level of the terminals so travelers can request a free shuttle pickup to reach the rental car sites. Check with your car rental agency when making a reservation to make sure you know how to get there.

RV Rental

A few RV rental agencies have offices in Los Angeles, including **Cruise America** (310/522-3870 or 800/671-8042, www.cruiseamerica.com). Camper van rentals are available through **Escape Campervans** (4858 W. Century Blvd., Inglewood, 877/270-8267 or 310 672-9909, www.escapecampervans.com), **Lost Campers** (8820 Aviation Blvd.,

Inglewood, 415/386-2693 or 888/567-8826, www.lostcampersusa.com), and **Juicy Rentals** (15318 Hawthorne Blvd., Lawndale, 800/650-4180, www.jucyrentals.com).

Equipment Rental

Adventure 16 (11161 W. Pico Blvd., 310/473-4575, www.adventure16.com) is located in West LA near the interchange of I-10 and I-405. They rent backpacks, sleeping bags, and tents, but rentals must be made in person. There are several REI locations around the Los Angeles area. The **REI Arcadia** (214 N. Santa Anita Ave., Arcadia, 626/447-1062, www.rei.com) is located east of Los Angeles, directly off I-210, and rents tents, camping stoves, and backpacks.

Accommodations and Food

There are many major hotel chains located near the airport, but if you want to make a night of it and get a taste of the city, head for vibrant downtown or iconic Hollywood.

Ace Hotel (929 S. Broadway, Downtown, 213/623-3233, www.acehotel.com/losangeles)

Hotel Figueroa (939 S. Figueroa St., Downtown, 213/627-8971, www.figueroahotel.com)

The Standard (550 S. Flower St., Downtown, 213/892-8080, www.standard-hotels.com)

Los Angeles Athletic Club (431 W. 7th St., Downtown, 213/625-2211, www.laac.com)

The Roosevelt Hotel (7000 Hollywood Blvd., Hollywood, 323/856-1970, www.thompsonhotels.com)

The Redbury (1717 Vine St., Hollywood, 323/926-1717, www.theredbury.com)

Los Angeles is known for its wide array of restaurants, which offer everything from-old school glamour to hip and casual.

Grand Central Market (317 S. Broadway, Downtown, 213/624-2378, www.grandcentralmarket.com) is a 1917 landmark food and retail emporium.

Guisados (541 S. Spring St., Suite 101, Downtown, www.guisados.co) serves casual tacos.

Baco Mercat (408 S. Main St., Downtown, 213/687-8808 bacomercat.com) is a western and eastern Mediterranean neighborhood hotspot.

Pizzeria Mozza (641 N. Highland Ave., Hollywood, 323/297-0101, www.pizzeriamozza.com) is a pizza enthusiast's temple.

Musso & Frank's (6667 Hollywood Blvd., Hollywood, 323/467-7788, www.mussoandfrank.com) is the oldest restaurant in Hollywood.

Loteria Grill (6627 Hollywood Blvd., Hollywood, 323/465-2500, www.loteriagrill.com) serves regional Mexican cuisine.

FROM PALM SPRINGS

Some visitors fly direct into Palm Springs, then head north along this remote and circuitous route to enter the park at its eastern access.

From Palm Springs, take Highway 111 west for 10 miles to merge onto I-10. Follow I-10 west for 40 miles until the junction with I-215. Take I-215 north for 15 miles and continue north as the freeway joins with I-15. In about 60 miles, I-15 crosses I-40 in Barstow. Keep left to stay on I-15 and continue another 62 miles north to Baker (a good place to fill your tank before heading into the park). At Baker, turn north onto Highway 127. You'll pass Tecopa in about 50 miles, or one hour; Shoshone lies 8 miles further. In another 27 miles, you'll reach Death Valley Junction; take Highway 190 west for 30 miles to the park hub at **Furnace Creek.**

It's also possible to take U.S. 395 north from I-15 near Victorville and enter the park from the south, via Ridgecrest and the Trona Road, or from the west via Olancha and Highway 190.

The total drive time will be about **4.5-5 hours** to cover the 300 miles from Palm Springs. In winter, chains may be required on the stretch of I-15 between Angeles and San Bernardino National Forests.

Getting Around

DRIVING

Death Valley's vast distances and lack of a park transportation system mean that you will likely spend a lot of time driving. Although heat-related issues are one of Death Valley's dangers, car accidents are the number one source of injury.

Roads

Death Valley has more than 1,000 miles of paved and dirt roads. When planning a trip, make sure you know what type of road you'll be traveling. **Graded dirt roads** are regularly maintained and usually passable in an ordinary passenger vehicle. **Dirt roads** are rougher but generally only require a high-clearance vehicle, like a small SUV. **Rough dirt roads** usually require a 4WD vehicle. For driving on extremely rough dirt roads, a short-wheelbase 4WD vehicle and expertise is required. These roads are no joke—slanted bedrock, boulders, and sheer drop-offs can make for a harrowing drive even for experienced drivers. *Do not attempt extremely rough dirt roads without expertise and the proper vehicle.*

These extreme situations aside, people have different comfort levels and are willing to push their cars to different performance levels. Use common sense to judge the situation, and be aware that backcountry roads can quickly become difficult and narrow with little possibility of turning around.

Roads can also change status. For example, a windstorm can cause sandy conditions and make a generally high-clearance-only road a 4WD road. Water can have a similar effect. The Harry Wade Exit Route generally only requires a high-clearance vehicle but can become a 4WD road when the Amargosa River

Death Valley Road Guide

ROAD	TYPE	ACCESS
Aguereberry Point Road	graded dirt road	high-clearance
Ashford Canyon Road	dirt road, rough dirt road	high-clearance first 2 miles, 4WD last mile
Badwater Basin Road	paved	passenger vehicle
Beatty Cutoff	paved	passenger vehicle
Big Pine Death Valley Road	graded dirt road	high-clearance
Chloride Cliff Road	dirt road, rough dirt road	high-clearance to Chloride City spur; 4WD thereafter
Cottonwood Canyon Road	rough dirt road	high-clearance first 8 miles, 4WD thereafter
Daylight Pass Road (Hwy. 374)	paved	passenger vehicle
Darwin Falls Road	graded dirt road	passenger vehicle to trailhead, 4WD thereafter
Echo Canyon Road	rough dirt road	high-clearance first 3 miles, 4WD thereafter
Greenwater Valley Road	graded dirt road	high-clearance
Hanaupah Canyon Road	rough dirt road	high-clearance first 5 miles, 4WD thereafter
Harry Wade Road (Harry Wade Exit Route)	rough dirt road	high-clearance, but may require 4WD
Hidden Valley Road	dirt road	high-clearance to Hunter Mountain; 4WD thereafter
Ibex Dunes Road (spur from Saratoga Spring Road)	dirt road	high-clearance to dunes, 4WD thereafter
Ibex Spring Road	dirt road	high-clearance

flows across it at certain times of the year, creating muddy conditions. In winter, be prepared for snow and ice at higher elevations. In summer, avoid remote roads at low elevation because of the possibility of mechanical failure.

Road conditions can change quickly in Death Valley due to floods, wind, snow, and other factors. In the event of a **flash flood,** even paved roads can be wiped out. Avoid canyon roads during rainy weather due to the possibility of flash floods. To keep updated on Death Valley's current road conditions, download the **Death Valley Morning Report** (www.nps.gov/deva/upload/Morning-Report.pdf); it's updated daily with current temperatures and road conditions. For very detailed road conditions and backcountry travel,

visit the **Death Valley Road Conditions** page on Facebook (www.facebook.com/DeathValleyRoadConditions).

Gas

Plan your fuel stops in advance and maintain a full tank before traveling long distances. Fuel is only available within the park at **Furnace Creek, Stovepipe Wells,** and **Panamint Springs.** There is no fuel available at Scotty's Castle. If you're planning a backcountry drive, make sure you have more than enough gas to get you there and back.

Outside the park the closest fuel stops are at **Beatty, Nevada,** on the east side, **Shoshone** to the southeast, and **Olancha, Lone Pine,** and **Big Pine** to the west. Many small communities around the park's boundaries do not have gas. Because of Death Valley's

ROAD	TYPE	ACCESS
Johnson Canyon Road	rough dirt road	high-clearance first 6 miles, 4WD thereafter
Lippincott Mine Road	rough dirt road	expert 4WD only
Lower Titus Canyon Road (to parking area and hiking access)	graded dirt road	passenger vehicle
Racetrack Valley Road	dirt road	high-clearance, but may require 4WD
Saline Valley Road	dirt road	high-clearance, but may require 4WD
Saratoga Spring Road	dirt road	high-clearance
Scotty's Castle Road	paved	passenger vehicle
Skidoo Road	dirt road	high-clearance
South Eureka Road	graded dirt road	high-clearance preferable
Steel Pass Road	rough dirt road	expert 4WD only
Titus Canyon Road	dirt road	high-clearance
Trona Wildrose Road	mostly paved	passenger vehicle
Warm Springs Road (Saline Valley)	dirt road	high-clearance; may be impassable after rain
Warm Spring Canyon Road	graded dirt road to rough dirt road	high-clearance first 10 miles to Warm Springs Camp, 4WD into Butte Valley, very rough 4WD over Mengel Pass
West Side Road	graded gravel road	high-clearance

remoteness, and its status as a tourism destination, gas prices are significantly cheaper outside the park. It's a good idea to fill up before entering Death Valley. Inside the park, Stovepipe Wells has the cheapest gas.

Maps and GPS

The National Park Service (NPS) strongly advises against navigating with a GPS receiver in Death Valley, and for good reason. Those who rely exclusively on GPS navigation can end up in life-threatening situations. When venturing beyond the paved park roads, use these tips to get safely around the park.

PARK MAPS

Always carry a basic park map and use it to get a general sense of the lay of the land. Park maps are included with every *Death*

Valley Visitor Guide and are available for free at the **Furnace Creek Visitors Center, Stovepipe Wells Ranger Station,** and **Scotty's Castle Visitors Center.** This map is accurate enough to get you around the paved park roads and major graded dirt roads. Panamint Springs is a privately owned resort, but they usually have free *Visitor Guides* in their general store. You can also download a *Visitor Guide* (www.nps.gov/deva/parknews/newspaper.htm) or a general-reference basic map (www.nps.gov/deva/planyourvisit) from the park website.

Unlike other national parks, Death Valley does not have entrance stations along its main roads. Begin your trip at one of the park hubs to pay your entrance fee, grab a map, and take advantage of the visitors center or other services.

DEATH VALLEY BACKCOUNTRY ROADS

For venturing into the backcountry, pick up a *Death Valley Backcountry Roads* map at one of the visitors centers or ranger stations. This map has slightly more detail than the basic park map, but its best feature is a list of backcountry roads with road descriptions, including the type of vehicle needed and the distances involved.

For more detailed planning and backcountry visits, I recommend Tom Harrison Maps' *Death Valley National Park Recreation Map*, which includes mileages, road conditions (paved, dirt, 4WD), and elevation. The NPS also recommends the National Geographic *Death Valley National Parks Illustrated* map. Both maps are available at visitors centers and ranger stations in the park where the Death Valley Natural History Association has kiosks.

RV TRAVEL

Having an RV can provide a great base camp in Death Valley's often windy, exposed landscape. But with the steep basin-and-range topography, you'll also need to plan your entrance route carefully.

The easiest RV route into the park is via **Highway 190** from the east via Death Valley Junction and Highway 127. It is also possible to enter via Beatty and Highway 374 (Daylight Pass Rd.). At the split on Daylight Pass Road, the Beatty Cutoff is suitable for RVs, but descends through some sharp, narrow curves. Highway 374 (Mud Canyon Rd.) also has some curves.

From the west, the mountain passes along Highway 190 toward Panamint Springs are steep and narrow. Through Towne Pass, there are grades of 7 to 9 percent; extra-long RVs are not recommended on this stretch. To enter from the west, follow **Highway 178** north from Ridgecrest to enter the park via the paved Trona Wildrose Road (subject to closure, so check road conditions) and Panamint Valley Road.

Once inside the park, the main roads—**Highway 190, Badwater Road** (Hwy. 178), and **Scotty's Castle Road**—are paved and easily drivable. However, other popular roads are not suitable for RVs or trailers: Titus Canyon Road, Skidoo Road, Upper Wildrose Canyon Road, Aguereberry Point Road, and Racetrack Valley Road. Some roads do not allow RVs and trailers over 25 feet in length: Artist's Drive, Dante's View Road, Emigrant Canyon Road, and Lower Wildrose Canyon Road.

RV sites are available at Furnace Creek, Texas Spring, Sunset, Mesquite Spring, Stovepipe Wells, and Panamint Springs, although only Furnace Creek, Stovepipe Wells, and Panamint Springs have full hookups. Beatty, Nevada, has RV accommodations and can be a good base camp. Shoshone, at the junction of Highways 127 and 178, also has RV accommodations.

TOURS

4WD Tours and Rentals

Nearly 1,000 miles of dirt and paved roads unravel across the park to the springs, dunes, mountains, canyons, and historic sights strewn across the immense landscape. Guided 4WD tours are available through **Farabee's Jeep Rentals** (Furnace Creek, 760/786-9872, www.farabeesjeeprentals.com, mid-Sept.-mid-May, $65-280 pp) to take you past some of the park's highlights as well as more remote locations. Wildflower tours are offered for a limited time during the spring, and custom tours are available for two or more people. Tours range two to eight hours.

Farabee's also rents 4WD vehicles, specializing in fully equipped Jeeps outfitted with sturdy off-road tires and 2-in-1 suspension lift to get you over boulders, washouts, and places that would otherwise seem crazy to attempt. The staff are knowledgeable and friendly; they have lots of helpful information about all those roads you might want to explore and will talk you through your planned route, giving you the latest on road conditions. A SPOT GPS tracking device is provided should you run into trouble.

Beware of GPS

Whether you are using a paper map, a GPS receiver, or a combination, at some point in exploring beyond the main paved roads, you may find that you're heading toward a dubious-looking road. Part of the reason that GPS navigation is so dangerous within Death Valley is that it does not always know the current state of the roads. The Death Valley region has been crisscrossed with roads throughout its time as a mining mecca. Many of these roads have fallen into disuse, and some have been actively closed by the NPS. However, they continue to exist in the map data that is used by GPS systems.

In addition, due to the extreme basin-and-range topography of Death Valley, very few roads traverse some of the steep mountain ranges in the park. Those that do are often rugged 4WD-only trails. GPS receivers are designed to calculate the shortest route from one place to another, which could send you on a difficult or dangerous path if you're trying to drive as the crow flies.

The NPS is actively working with GPS mapping companies like TomTom, Google, and Navteq to fix the navigation situation. For your safety, if you are heading toward a road that does not look passable, do not assume it will eventually work out. Do not proceed if the road does not look like something that is suitable for your car. Roads can quickly become impassible, with no place to turn around.

4WD or SUV rentals are also available through many of the major car-rental companies, but many of these are not intended for off-highway use; many car rental agencies write into their policies that cars must be kept on paved roads.

Horse Trail Tours

Except for walking or riding a burro loaded down with gold-prospecting equipment, riding a horse may be the most historically correct way to experience Death Valley. The Furnace Creek Ranch Resort offers guided trail rides through its **Furnace Creek Stables** (760/614-1018, www.furnacecreekstables.net, Oct.-May). One-hour guided horseback tours ($55 pp) take you across the valley floor, and two-hour rides ($70 pp) make a foray into the foothills of the Funeral Mountains with views of the valley. Sunset rides ($70 pp) and moonlight rides ($75 pp) are also available. Carriage rides (45 minutes, $30 adults, $15 under age 12) take visitors through the well-watered Furnace Creek golf course and date palm grove. Hay wagon rides ($20 pp) are available for small and large groups.

Recreation

HIKING

There are few developed and maintained hiking trails in Death Valley. Many trails follow old mining roads, canyons, or other natural features. A few popular trails in the Furnace Creek and Stovepipe Wells area are well-marked and easy to follow. Other trails require more research and preparation.

Michel Digonnet's books *Hiking Death Valley* and *Hiking Western Death Valley National Park* are the most comprehensive hiking guides written to date. The books include detailed information on accessing trailheads, trail length and conditions, history, and basic topo maps. These are a crucial resource for anyone interested in hiking beyond the most popular trails. Used in conjunction with the Tom Harrison Tom Harrison Maps' *Death Valley National Park Recreation Map*, these resources will get you very far.

For long day hikes, certain wilderness areas, or multiday backpacking trips, bring along the appropriate topo map in paper or electronic form. The company Trimble Outdoors offers an offline topo map app, **My Topo Maps Pro,** available for tablets. Maps for Death Valley National Park is available as a bundle. These electronic maps must be downloaded before your trip, as they will not be available in the park, where there is no Wi-Fi or cellular data access.

When hiking, wear light-colored clothing, sunscreen, sunglasses, and a hat with a wide brim. Layer your clothing to be prepared for changes in elevation. Carry plenty of water, and do not hike at low elevations during summer. Tell someone where you are going and when you expect to return. When hiking in remote locations, I leave a note in the window of my car listing my destination, date, and time.

BIKING

It's easy to be impressed by Death Valley's vastness, and it's possible to leave thinking that's the main selling point. With the right timing, a bike tour can be the perfect way to see some of the park's finer points. Bicycles are allowed on all park roads that are open to public vehicular traffic and on designated bike routes. Bikes are not allowed on closed roads (even if hiking is allowed), service roads, off-road, in wilderness areas, or on any trail. Riding single file is the rule.

The wide-open spaces and relatively light traffic make Death Valley a great place for road biking; however, biking requires a high level of planning, particularly for water. Water is not readily accessible, even along the main park highways; plan to carry extra water and to treat any backcountry springwater before drinking it. The Furnace Creek Visitors Center offers drinking water for refillable water bottles.

Summer in Death Valley is too hot for most activities, and physical exertion, especially at the lower elevations, can be dangerous. If you avoid the heat of the summer months, cycling can be ideal, with clear dry air, few cars, and a range of routes to fit all abilities. Plan cycling

routes for early morning or under the desert night sky. Avoid biking in canyons if there is a storm approaching. The NPS recommends sunglasses, proper clothing, and extra food and water for a safe trip.

Bicycle rentals are available at **Furnace Creek Ranch** (760/786-3371, www.furnacecreekresort.com). The bike-rental shop is next to the general store and offers mountain bikes with hourly ($15), half-day ($34), and full-day ($49) rates; kids ride for $5 per hour.

BACKCOUNTRY CAMPING

Death Valley has more than 3 million acres of wilderness and more than 1 million visitors per year, giving everyone plenty of space to stretch out. With a little planning, it's possible to snag a gorgeous scenic camping spot with as much privacy as you could want, all for the price of admission to the park.

The desert is fragile, but by adhering to some basic rules, you can leave the least impact, preserving it for others. Backcountry camping is permitted **at least two miles from paved roads;** try to camp in places that have previously been used for camping. Hard-packed or gravel ground is the most resistant to impact. Avoid walking in water, trampling vegetation, and walking on delicate soil surfaces. Camping is prohibited along several of the park's major dirt roads. Check out the park's website (www.nps.gov/deva) for a complete list of prohibited camping areas and guidelines.

RANGER PROGRAMS

There are a variety of ranger programs offered in **winter** and **spring** (Nov.-Apr.), including ranger-guided canyon walks and ranger talks. The schedule varies and is available online (www.nps.gov/deva) and in the visitors center. Regular programs include the twice-monthly **Moon and Star Programs,** which take advantage of full and new moons for guided walks. Winter **Paleontology Tours** are daylong guided hikes to fragile paleontological sites that are normally closed to the public; these tours are available on a very limited basis, by reservation and lottery only. **Indoor and Outdoor Evening Programs** (Thurs.-Sun.) explore a range of topics in archaeology, geology, natural history, and human history. Other guided walks, activities, and demonstrations are offered on such diverse subjects as bird-watching and stone tool making.

Travel Tips

There is **no cell phone reception** in Death Valley National Park, with the exception of Furnace Creek. Depending on your provider, you may also luck into a tiny window of cell service at unpredictable moments. Do not rely on your cell phone for communication.

Cell service is unpredictable to nonexistent in many areas around the park. On the western side of the park, there is cell service in the town of Lone Pine and along U.S. 395. On the eastern side of the park, there is cell service in the town of Beatty and along U.S. 95. Many individual businesses provide wireless Internet for guests.

INTERNATIONAL TRAVELERS

The closest gateway city for international travelers to fly into is **Las Vegas.** The drive from Las Vegas to Death Valley takes two to three hours along paved highway roads that are open year-round. Along the way, you will cross the state line from Nevada to California, but there are no stops, checkpoints, or special concerns along this route.

Visas and Passports

Visitors from most other countries must have a valid passport and a visa to enter the United States. You may qualify for the Visa Waiver Program if you hold a passport from one of the following countries: Andorra, Australia, Austria, Belgium, Brunei, Czech Republic, Denmark, Estonia, Finland, France, Germany, Greece, Hungary, Iceland, Ireland, Italy, Japan, Latvia, Liechtenstein, Lithuania, Luxembourg, Malta, Monaco, the Netherlands, New Zealand, Norway, Portugal, San Marino, Singapore, Slovakia, Slovenia, South Korea, Spain, Sweden, Switzerland, Taiwan, and the United Kingdom. To qualify, apply online with the **Electronic System for Travel Authorization** (http://esta.cbp.dhs.gov/esta) and make sure you have a return plane ticket to your country of origin dated less than 90 days from your date of entry. Holders of Canadian passports do not need visas or visa waivers. To learn more about visa and passport requirements, visit http://travel.state.gov.

In most countries, the local U.S. embassy or consulate should be able to provide a **tourist visa.** The average fee for a visa is US$160. While a visa may be processed as quickly as 24 hours on request, plan at least a couple of weeks, as there can be unexpected delays, particularly during the busy summer season (June-Aug.).

Los Angeles is home to **consulates** from many countries around the globe. If you should lose your passport or find yourself in some other trouble while visiting California, contact your country's offices for assistance. To find a consulate or embassy, check online (www.state.gov) for a list of all foreign countries represented in the United States. A representative will be able to direct you to the nearest consulate.

Customs

Before entering the United States from another country by air, you'll be required to fill out a customs form. Check with the U.S. embassy in your country or the **U.S. Customs and Border Protection** (www.cbp.gov) for an updated list of items you must declare. If you require medication administered by injection, you must pack syringes in a checked bag; syringes are not permitted in carry-ons coming into the United States. Also, pack documentation describing your need for any narcotic medications you've brought with you. Failure to produce documentation for narcotics on request can result in severe penalties in the United States. For information about current regulations on domestic flights, visit the **Transportation Security Administration website** (www.tsa.gov).

If you are driving into California along I-5 or another major highway, prepare to stop at **Agricultural Inspection Stations** a few miles inside the state line. You don't need to present a passport or a driver's license; instead, you must be prepared to present any fruits and vegetables you have in the vehicle. California's largest economic sector is agriculture, and a number of the major crops grown here are sensitive to pests and diseases. In an effort to prevent known pests from entering the state and endangering crops, travelers are asked to identify all the produce they're carrying in from other states or from Mexico. If you are carrying produce, it may be confiscated on the spot. You'll also be asked about fruits and veggies on the U.S. Customs form that you fill out on the plane before reaching the United States.

Money

California and Nevada businesses use the **U.S. dollar** ($). Most businesses also accept the major credit cards Visa, MasterCard, Discover, and American Express. ATM and debit cards work at many stores and restaurants, and ATMs are available at banks and in some local businesses like convenience or grocery stores. Within Death Valley, ATMs are limited. Currency exchange offices are available at any international airport.

Visiting the National Parks

Death Valley National Park draws many international travelers year-round who often add in trips to other nearby national parks, including **Yosemite, Sequoia and Kings Canyon,** and **Joshua Tree.** While these national parks appear relatively close on a map, they span a wide range of climates, distances, and geography. If you're planning a trip to multiple destinations, your itinerary should consider the following factors for safe and efficient travel.

SEASONAL ACCESS

All national parks are open year-round, but depending on the time of year, certain areas and roads may have limited access—or no access—as well as limited services. The season for parks in the **Sierra Nevada Mountains** (Yosemite, Sequoia and Kings Canyon) generally runs **April-October.** The most popular time to visit is summer. During winter, heavy snows often close mountain roads for months at a time.

Desert parks (Death Valley, Joshua Tree) operate on a reverse schedule—their season runs **October-April.** During summer, the heat at low elevations makes activities such as hiking dangerous and may prompt road closures. Winter is generally a good time to visit Death Valley and other desert areas, although snow can cause road closures even in desert mountains.

ROAD CONDITIONS

When planning your visit, be aware that maps may not show road conditions. For example, most roads that run east-west across the rugged Sierra Nevada Mountains **do not provide through-access in winter**— including **Highway 120,** the main route through Yosemite National Park.

Also consider the type of road when planning a route. On a map, many backcountry or unpaved roads may look like they provide a shortcut, but rough road conditions may make the trip longer than it appears—or make it dangerous, depending on the state of the road. Stay on paved park roads. If you do plan to travel in the backcountry, make sure you are properly prepared.

ACCESS FOR TRAVELERS WITH DISABILITIES

Death Valley may be known for its ruggedness, but it is still possible to experience many of the park's natural wonders and historic sites without going into rough backcountry or traveling on a trail that does not meet ADA standards.

An **Access Pass** (www.nps.gov) is available for free to U.S. citizens or permanent residents with permanent disabilities. Passes can be obtained at a visitors center or ranger station in Death Valley. The pass is part of the National Parks and Federal Recreational Lands Pass Series and can be used to cover entrance fees at 2,000 other locations, including national forests and national wildlife refuges.

All museums, visitors centers, and contact stations within the park abide by ADA-compliant guidelines and are accessible to all visitors. This includes the Furnace Creek Visitors Center, the Borax Museum at Furnace Creek, Scotty's Castle Visitors Center and Museum, and the Stovepipe Wells Ranger Station. In addition, the grounds at Scotty's Castle are accessible to all visitors. **Tours of Scotty's Castle** can be accommodated with a wheelchair lift; only one person may be accommodated per tour. Please let a ranger know when making a reservation if you will need the lift.

Most **developed campgrounds** within the park have accessible sites and accessible restrooms, including Furnace Creek and Sunset Campgrounds in the Furnace Creek Area, Stovepipe Wells Campground, Emigrant Campground in the Panamint Springs area (which does not accommodate RVs or campers), and Mesquite Spring in the Scotty's Castle Area. For the most scenic and pleasant accessible camping, Mesquite Spring is the best bet. Most sites are paved, widely spaced, and flat—even those not designated as ADA compliant. There are accessible restrooms with flush toilets.

Throughout the park, **accessible restrooms** with flush toilets are located at the Furnace Creek Visitors Center, Stovepipe Wells General Store, Scotty's Castle Visitors Center, Grapevine Ranger Station, and Emigrant Campground picnic area. Pit toilets, located at many sights and campgrounds throughout the park, are also accessible, including those at Badwater Basin and the Eureka Dunes.

There is only one accessible hiking trail in the park: the **Salt Creek Trail** in the Stovepipe Wells area. A small parking area leads to a boardwalk trail that covers a one-mile loop alongside Salt Creek. Outside the park boundaries, the **Ash Meadows National Wildlife Refuge** has wheelchair-accessible boardwalk trails. Although accessible trails are limited in the area, there are many sights and drives available to visitors with physical disabilities.

TRAVELING WITH CHILDREN

Death Valley can be a fun place for kids. The Mesquite Flat and Eureka Dunes give them a place to run or dig in the sand. Mosaic Canyon, Golden Canyon, and Natural Bridge offer the chance to do some canyon exploring. Salt Creek is full of tiny fish. Stovepipe Wells and Furnace Creek Ranch both have family-friendly lodgings with swimming pools to give everyone a break in the midday heat. When sightseeing, pack extra snacks and make sure children are properly hydrated and slathered with sunscreen. Kids will appreciate the Wild West experience in ghost towns and mining areas, but be sure to keep a very careful eye on children—there are exposed mining shafts in the park, old mining equipment and structures can have sharp or rusty edges, and rusty cans and broken glass can be found at historic sites.

The **Junior Ranger Program** is designed for children ages 5 to 13 and offers a structured way for kids to learn about the park and enjoy a sense of stewardship. Pick up a copy of the Junior Ranger booklet at any Visitors Center; have the kids complete age-appropriate activities, do a park project, and attend a ranger program.

Accessible Death Valley

These recommended destinations include drives and sights easily seen from parking areas as well as two ADA-accessible trails. Roads are paved or graded dirt, and in most cases there are no formal parking spaces.

- **Ash Meadows National Wildlife Refuge:** Graded dirt roads throughout the refuge lead to wheelchair-accessible boardwalks through the Mojave's largest remaining oasis. Roads should be accessible for any vehicle, including a van with a lowered floor; however, road conditions are always subject to change.

- **Badwater Basin:** A paved road leads to a paved parking area, where a wheelchair ramp allows access to the salt flats.

- **Devil's Golf Course:** A graded dirt road leads to a small parking area with close-up views of strange salt formations.

- **Dante's View:** A paved road leads to a parking area and a spectacular overlook of Death Valley.

- **Mesquite Sand Dunes:** A paved road to the parking area offers close-up views of these dunes.

- **Eureka Dunes:** A graded dirt road leads to the foot of spectacular sand dunes.

- **Ubehebe Crater:** A paved road leads to a small parking area at the edge of a colorful volcanic crater.

- **Trona Pinnacles:** A graded dirt road leads to haunting tufa rock formations left over from an ancient lake bed.

- **Artist's Drive:** A short, scenic drive on a paved road with beautiful views of colorful hills.

TRAVELING WITH PETS

If possible, leave your pets at home when visiting Death Valley. Pets are allowed in the park, but they are not allowed on any trails or more than 100 feet from a road or picnic area. Pets are allowed in campgrounds, but again are not allowed to stray more than 100 feet. There is a limit of four pets per site in campgrounds. Pets cannot be left unattended at any time, especially in a vehicle. High temperatures can be extreme and could quickly harm a pet locked in a car, even with the windows cracked. Dogs must be on a leash no longer than six feet at all times. Wild coyotes in the park could be potentially dangerous to pets that are off-leash.

SENIOR TRAVELERS

Seniors age 62 and older can purchase an **Interagency Access Pass** (www.nps.gov, $10) at any visitors center or ranger station in Death Valley. The pass is part of the National Parks and Federal Recreational Lands Pass Series and can be used to cover entrance fees at 2,000 locations, including national forests, national wildlife refuges, and Death Valley National Park. If you already have a Golden Age or Golden Access Pass, both are good for entry into the park. Elsewhere in Death Valley, the Interagency Senior Pass qualifies you for discounted tour rates for Scotty's Castle tours.

- **Titus Canyon Road:** This one-way, 27-mile road may not be appropriate for a van with a lowered floor. Carefully consider this drive, check road conditions, and proceed with caution.

- **Scotty's Castle:** Paved roads, parking areas, and wheelchair-accessible grounds. House tours can be accommodated with a wheelchair lift.

- **Harmony Borax Works:** A graded dirt road leads to a small parking area. The road should be accessible for any vehicle, including a van with a lowered floor; however, road conditions are always subject to change.

- **Charcoal Kilns:** A graded dirt road leads to a parking area. The road should be accessible for any vehicle, including a van with a lowered floor; however, road conditions are always subject to change.

- **Warm Springs Camp:** A graded dirt road. Depending on road conditions, this drive may not be appropriate for a van with a lowered floor. Carefully consider this drive, check road conditions, and proceed with caution.

- **Goldfield:** A paved road leads to the small Nevada mining town. There are dirt roads throughout the town.

- **Ballarat:** A graded dirt road leads to the mostly abandoned mining town and a general store run by a caretaker. The road should be accessible for any vehicle, including a van with a lowered floor; however, road conditions are always subject to change.

- **Rhyolite:** A graded dirt road should be accessible for any vehicle, including a van with a lowered floor; however, road conditions are always subject to change.

- **Salt Creek:** A graded dirt road leads to a parking area; a wheelchair-accessible boardwalk traverses a one-mile loop along the banks of Salt Creek. The road should be accessible for any vehicle, including a van with a lowered floor; however, road conditions are always subject to change.

HEALTH AND SAFETY
Heat
Heat is the biggest health threat in Death Valley. The hottest conditions occur at the lower elevations during summer. Furnace Creek and the valley floor south toward Badwater Basin log the highest temperatures in the park and can be dangerously hot **May-October.** Many visitors choose to visit Death Valley in summer, and it is possible to do so safely if you take some precautions. *Avoid hiking or other outdoors exertion at low elevations during summer.* In summer, confine hiking to high elevations, or, go out early in the morning or late in the evening; stick to paved roads for touring at low elevations. When hiking or exploring outdoors, wear a wide-brimmed hat, sunglasses, and proper sun protection.

Lightweight, light-colored breathable clothing can offer better protection than sunscreen—wear both.

Contrary to popular belief, Death Valley is not hot everywhere all the time. Its arid desert climate, however, does create extremes in temperature. Many upper mountain elevations are prone to ice and snow in winter. Telescope Peak, the highest point in the park, is snow-capped most of the year. Hike at higher elevations in summer and lower elevations in winter.

Dehydration
It's crucial to drink plenty of water, especially during physical activity. Signs of heat exhaustion include **dizziness, nausea,** and

Desert Survival Tips

Death Valley's vast spaces, remote roads, and weather extremes can create potentially risky situations, but traveling is not any more dangerous than in other national parks if you are prepared for the unique environment. Know what weather to expect and where you're going, and be prepared for the unexpected.

TELL SOMEONE WHERE YOU ARE GOING
Whether you're hiking, driving, or a combination, make sure you tell someone where you are going and when to expect your return. Death Valley covers a huge area, and in the event that you are stranded, the search effort can be pinpointed. For hiking or backcountry camping, obtain a voluntary backcountry permit from the ranger station.

BRING SUPPLIES
Temperatures can fluctuate 40 degrees between day and night. Bring a sleeping bag or emergency blanket even if you do not plan to be out overnight. Pack appropriate clothing for a range of temperatures, and be prepared for cold temperatures at night. Always bring extra water and extra nonperishable food that does not have to be cooked. GPS navigation is notoriously unreliable in the park. Be prepared with a paper map or an electronic offline map and a charger. Cell phones do not work in the park. Be prepared to survive until help arrives if you are stranded.

VEHICLE BREAKDOWNS
Sharp rocks, long bumpy roads, and heat can cause your vehicle to break down. Always drive with a full-size spare tire. A fix-a-flat tire kit may also be helpful. Getting two flat tires is not an unheard of situation on Death Valley's back roads. If you are stranded, stay with your car until help arrives. It is much easier to spot a big metal car that flashes in the sunlight than a person walking. Also, it is dangerous to overexert yourself in the heat of Death Valley, so hiking out to safety is not generally the best option. Be prepared with extra supplies including food, water, and warm clothes.

WIND STORMS
The wind can be a relentless companion in Death Valley, especially in spring, with nights generally windier than days. Wind can be a minor irritant or it can seriously impact your visit and create potentially dangerous situations. At times, wind can descend in the form of a windstorm preceded by a cold front. There may be very little warning, and a dark cloud may be the only indication that a windstorm is approaching. Always stake tents and secure other camp belongings such as camp chairs. Windstorms can create whiteout conditions with serious visibility limitations. If you are driving, use headlights and be prepared to pull over if visibility becomes limited to the degree that driving is dangerous.

headaches. If these occur, get into the shade and drink plenty of water or sports drinks.

Drink at least one gallon (four liters) per day, or more depending on your level of physical activity. Always carry extra water—at least five gallons extra if you are traveling in the backcountry. If you run out of water, all water in the park is potable. Water is available at visitors centers, ranger stations, and museums and at most campgrounds, including Furnace Creek, Sunset, and Texas Spring in the Furnace Creek area; Stovepipe Wells; Mesquite Spring in the Scotty's Castle area; and Emigrant and Wildrose Campgrounds in the Panamint Springs area.

Wildlife
Death Valley has its share of venomous animals, though they are rarely life-threatening to humans. The desert **tarantula** and giant desert hairy **scorpion** produce toxins sufficient to immobilize a small animal. To a

human, their bite may be comparable to a bee sting.

The **Mojave rattlesnake** (also called Mojave green) is known to be one of the most venomous and deadly of North American species. These snakes tend to hunt at night in rocky areas and open vegetation, like Joshua tree flats or creosote scrub. The **sidewinder** and **Panamint rattlesnake** are also venomous. The sidewinder likes sandy hills and dunes; you may see its distinctive J-shaped trail in the sand. It loops along so that only two points of its body have to touch the hot sand. The Panamint rattlesnake prefers rocky slopes and mountain areas. Fortunately, rattlesnakes announce their presence by rattling their tails. If you hear a rattle, stop moving and slowly back away from the sound. The best way to avoid getting bitten by any animal is to give them their space—never put your hands and feet where you cannot see. For a rattlesnake bite, seek immediate treatment at the nearest hospital or emergency room.

the Mojave rattlesnake

Resources

Suggested Reading

Death Valley's history, strange geography, and potential for solitude and adventure have inspired enthusiasts, scholars, and travelers to chisel out hundreds of books about this region. The list below offers a few suggestions to help navigate a trip to Death Valley, or better understand this unusual place.

INTRODUCTORY GUIDES

Atchison, Stewart. *Death Valley: Splendid Desolation*. Mariposa, CA: Sierra Press, 2009. A photographic introduction to Death Valley's landscape, human and geologic history, plants, and animals.

Naylor, Roger. *Hottest Place on Earth*. Tucson: Rio Nuevo Publishers, 2013. A conversational blend of history, photography, and fun facts, this guide introduces the potential visitor to Death Valley's main attractions, ghost towns, roads, and hikes.

Tweed, William C., and Lauren Davis. *Death Valley and the Northern Mojave: A Visitor's Guide*. Los Olivos, CA: Cachuma Press, 2003. An introduction to Death Valley and the northern Mojave including geology, climate, plants and animals, Native American history, mining history, and the advent of tourism. Colorful photography and region-specific information will entice the first-time visitor or anyone interested in the area.

HIKING AND EXPLORATION

Bryan, T. Scott, and Betty Tucker-Bryan. *The Explorer's Guide to Death Valley National Park*. Boulder, CO: University Press of Colorado, 2009. This classic travel guide includes geological, human, and natural history. It's best-known for detailed descriptions of roads to scenic and historic destinations, and is extremely useful for touring Death Valley's backcountry routes.

Digonnet, Michel. *Hiking Death Valley: A Guide to Its Natural Wonders and Mining Past*. Palo Alto, CA: Michel Digonnet, 2012. The most comprehensive hiking guide to Death Valley to date, this book is indispensable for exploring the region. Detailed trail directions and topo maps are included.

Digonnet, Michel. *Hiking Western Death Valley National Park: Panamint, Saline, and Eureka Valleys*. Palo Alto, CA: Michel Digonnet, 2009. A comprehensive hiking guide focused on western Death Valley's geologic and cultural history, with detailed trail directions and maps. A must-have.

HISTORY

Crum, S. J. *The Road on Which We Came: A History of the Western Shoshone*. Salt Lake City: University of Utah Press, 1994. Most histories of Death Valley focus on its mining history. This book, written by an enrolled tribe member, offers a comprehensive Native American history of the Great Basin Shoshone.

Green, Linda W., and John A. Latschar. *Historic Resource Study: A History of Mining in Death Valley National Monument.* Denver: National Park Service, 1981. A historic resource study conducted by the National Park Service to assess the cultural value of mining sites in Death Valley in relation to land conservation goals. Contains interesting history of mining sites in and around the Death Valley region.

Lingenfelter, R. E. *Death Valley and the Amargosa: A Land of Illusion.* Berkeley, CA: University of California Press, 1986. The classic history of Death Valley, spanning a century from the 1830s, when the first Europeans opened a trail through the area, to 1933, when Death Valley became a national monument. Focuses on Death Valley's mining history and also discusses Native American history and Death Valley's journey from mining to tourism.

Lingenfelter, R. E. *Death Valley Lore: Classic Tales of Fantasy, Adventure, and Mystery.* Reno: University of Nevada Press, 1988. Historical collection of accounts of Death Valley gleaned from the popular media of the late 19th and early 20th century when adventurers, prospectors, and explorers flocked to the land.

Palazzo, Robert P. *Ghost Towns of Death Valley.* Charleston, SC: Arcadia Publishing, 2014. Brief histories and historical photographs of Death Valley ghost towns, including buildings and local characters.

Rothman, Hal K., and Char Miller. *Death Valley National Park: A History.* Reno: University of Nevada Press, 2013. An environmental and human history of Death Valley National Park. Details the region's path to preservation and debates over land use in the northern Mojave Desert from the perspective of Native American groups, miners, ranchers, the military, tourists, wilderness advocates, and the National Park Service.

MAPS

Tom Harrison Recreation Maps. *Death Valley National Park.* San Rafael, CA: Tom Harrison, 2014. Shaded relief 1:250,000 topographic map with contour lines and vegetation. The only detailed map that includes mileage between road junctions; extremely useful for general navigation and backcountry travel.

National Geographic Trails Illustrated Maps. *Death Valley National Park.* Evergreen, CO: National Geographic Maps, 2014. A detailed 1:165,000 topographic map with trail and backcountry road information. UTM grids for use with GPS units.

NATURE AND GEOGRAPHY

Grayson, Donald. *The Great Basin: A Natural Prehistory.* Oakland, CA: University of California Press, 2011. A detailed environmental and human history of the Great Basin geographic watershed region that encompasses Death Valley. The book takes a multidisciplinary approach through history, geology, and archaeology to look at the rich and diverse ecosystems in the Great Basin.

Mackay, Pam. *Mojave Desert Wildflowers,* 2nd ed. Guilford, CT: Falcon Guides, 2013. A detailed guide to wildflowers of the Mojave Desert region. Contains background on geography, climate, topography, geology, and environmental issues. Colorful photographs and plant descriptions are useful in identifying hundreds of plants.

Sharp, Robert P., and Allen F. Glazner. *Geology Underfoot in Death Valley and Owens Valley.* Missoula, MT: Mountain Press Publishing, 1997. This guide is designed to come to the rescue of the curious desert visitor or amateur geologist staring at an impressive pile of rocks, wondering how on earth it was formed. Written in guide format, the book details the geologic history of Death Valley and Owens Valley to the east.

Steward, Jon Mark. *Mojave Desert Wildflowers*. Albuquerque: Jon Stewart Photography, 1998. Simple and elegant, this guide gets straight to the point with full-page color photographs and corresponding information that makes identifying wildflowers easy and straightforward.

Internet Resources

DEATH VALLEY
Death Valley National Park
www.nps.gov/deva
The park's official website is a great place to start planning a trip to Death Valley. It has information on where to stay (campgrounds, hotels, links to reservations) and what to visit. Visitor Guides, backcountry road guides, and other information can be downloaded from the website. It also has helpful advice on weather, road conditions, and other tips for travelers to the desert.

Death Valley National History Association
www.dvnha.org
The Death Valley National History Association has retail outlets for books and gifts on Death Valley in the park's visitors centers. They also offer their excellent selection through their website's online store. The site also includes information on the association's programs and events.

Recreation.gov
www.recreation.gov
In Death Valley National Park, only Furnace Creek Campground accepts reservations; make them at this website.

BEYOND THE BOUNDARIES
Alabama Hills
www.blm.gov
The Alabama Hills span over 30,000 acres of public land and are known for their beautiful scenery as well as their film history. They have been the setting for many westerns and other movies, beginning in the 1920s. The Bureau of Land Management website provides a description of the area, directions, and a downloadable "Movie Road" touring brochure.

Ancient Bristlecone Pine Forest
www.fs.usda.gov
The U.S. Forest Service website provides crucial information on park hours, seasons, and directions as well as a phone number to check road conditions. It gives an overview of the pine groves and hikes in the area.

Ash Meadows National Wildlife Refuge
www.fws.gov/refuge/ash_meadows
The refuge's website offers tips to help plan your visit, including weather and visitors center hours as well as information about the desert oasis habitat.

Beatty
www.beattynv.info
This "gateway to Death Valley" town website devotes several pages to visitor information, including dining and lodging in Beatty. It also links to sites for nearby attractions like the ghost town of Rhyolite.

Lone Pine
www.lonepinechamber.org
The Lone Pine website provides a good catalog of restaurants and hotels in town with contact information and links to individual business websites.

Randsburg
www.randsburg.com
This website is a good resource for exploring the town and surrounding areas. It includes a listing of Randsburg businesses with contact

numbers as well as links to regional maps, wilderness areas, and nearby attractions, including historic mining sites and ghost towns.

Red Rock Canyon State Park
www.parks.ca.gov
The state park website offers basic planning information including park hours and regulations, facilities, and campground information.

Shoshone
www.shoshonevillage.com
A charming gateway town on the southeastern edge of Death Valley, Shoshone has basic visitor services. The town's website includes descriptions and contact information for all local businesses. It also includes helpful links to nearby wilderness destinations, attractions, and land-use organizations.

Index

E

Eagle Borax Spring: 38
Eagle Borax Works: 38
Echo Canyon: 24, 33
Eichbaum, Herman William: 76
Emigrant Canyon: 20, 121, 125-127; map 126
environmental issues: 159-160
Eureka Dunes: 19, 99-100
Eureka Dunes Dry Camp: 99
Eureka Dunes Road: 95
Eureka Mine: 125
Eureka Valley: 94, 98-100; map 99
Eye of the Needle: 33

F

Fall Canyon: 79-80, 85; map 80
Farabee's Jeep Rentals: 24, 178
fauna: 162-164
flora: 161-162
four-wheel drive roads: 24, 176-177
Funeral Mountains: 49, 85
Furnace Creek and Amargosa Range: 26-67; maps
    29, 30, 59
Furnace Creek Bicycle Path: 47-48
Furnace Creek Inn: 17, 54-55, 57
Furnace Creek Ranch: 34
Furnace Creek Stables: 179
Furnace Creek Village: 17, 20, 34; map 35
Furnace Creek Visitors Center: 20, 31-32

G

Garlock: 153
gas: 16, 32, 72, 95, 122-123, 176-177
geography: 156
Geologist's Cabin: 34
geology: 156-158
ghost towns: 23
Goldbelt Spring Mining District: 107
Golden Canyon: 17, 21, 35, 39-41; map 41
Goldfield (Nevada): 114-115
Gold Hill: 33
Gold Hill Mill: 39
Gold Point: 23, 113-114
Goldwell Open Air Museum: 18, 77
golf: 49
Gower Gulch: 35, 39-41
GPS: 177, 179
Grandstand, The: 19, 101, 103
Grapevine Mountains: 85
Greenwater Valley Road: 48-49
Grotto Canyon: 85

H

Hanaupah Canyon: 33, 43-44, 46; map 44
Hanaupah Canyon Road: 43

Hanaupah Spring: 43
Happy Burro Chili and Beer: 18, 88
Harmony Borax Works: 35
Harry Wade Exit Route: 49
health and safety: 185-187
Hidden Valley Road: 107
Highway 120: 182
Highway 190: 143
Highway 266: 113
hiking: general discussion: 21-22, 179-180;
    Furnace Creek and Amargosa Range 35, 39-47,
    51-52, 53-54, 65-66; Panamint Springs and
    the Saline Valley 125, 134-143, 153; Scotty's
    Castle and Eureka Valley 98, 99, 103-107, 112,
    113; Stovepipe Wells and the Nevada Triangle
    76, 78-84
Hole-in-the-Wall Road: 48
Homestake Dry Camp: 96, 106
horseback riding: 179
Hungry Bill's Ranch: 21, 33, 44-46; map 45

I

Ibex Dunes: 52-53
Ibex Spring: 50-52; map 51
Ibex Spring Camp: 33
Ibex Spring Road: 49, 50-51
Indian Wells Lodge and Brewing Company: 151
Indian Wells Valley: 151-154; map 152
international travelers: 181-182
Inyokern: 151
Inyo Mine Camp: 23, 24, 33
Inyo Mountain Wilderness Area: 144
itineraries: 17-25

JKL

Jeep rentals: 178
John Muir Wilderness: 112-113
Johnson Canyon: 21, 22, 45
Johnson Canyon Road: 45
Klare Spring: 76
landscape: 156-160
Lane Mill: 79
Las Vegas: 17, 172-173
Leadville: 76
Lee Flat Joshua Tree Forest: 129, 131
Lida: 113
Limekiln Spring: 139
Lippincott Mine: 106-107
Lippincott Mine Road: 96, 106-107
Little Hebe Crater: 98
lodging: 14
Lone Pine: 149-151; map 150
Lone Pine Film Museum: 149
Los Angeles: 173-175
Lost Burro Mine: 19, 23, 100

T

Teakettle Junction: 19, 102-103
Tecopa: 24, 64-67
Tecopa Hot Springs: 64-65
Tecopa Hot Springs County Park: 65
Telescope Peak: 21, 140-141; map 142
Titus Canyon Road: 18, 20, 72-73, 75-76, 84
Tonopah (Nevada): 115-116
Tonopah Historic Mining Park: 115
Trail Canyon: 48
Trio Mill Site: 136
Trona: 154
Trona Pinnacles: 154
Trona Wildrose Road: 122, 143-144
Tucki Mountain: 85
Tule Spring: 38
20-Mule Team Canyon: 36, 48

UVWXYZ

Ubehebe Crater: 19, 98-99
Ubehebe Mine: 103-104
Ubehebe Mine Camp: 105
Ubehebe Peak: 19, 21, 103; map 105
Upper Monarch Canyon: 85
Upper Warm Springs: 133
U.S. 95: 114-116

visas and passports: 181
visitor centers: 15, 31-32, 94, 96-97
Wacouba Road: *see* Big Pine-Death Valley Road
Warm Spring Canyon: 23, 24, 33-34, 39
Warm Springs Camp: 23, 33, 39
Warm Springs Road: 133
Water Canyon: 140
waterfalls: Furnace Creek and Amargosa Range
    66; Panamint Springs and the Saline Valley
    134, 135-136, 137, 138
Waterfall Trail: 66
weather: 158-159
West Side Road: 32-33, 37-39, 46, 47
Western Panamint Canyons: 121
wildlife refuge: 60
wildlife/wildlife-watching: 74-75, 162-164, 186-
    187
Wildrose Campground: 21, 121, 125, 146
Wildrose Canyon: 20, 121, 125-127; map 126
Wildrose Charcoal Kilns: 20, 125
Wildrose Peak: 20, 21-22, 141, 143; map 143
Wildrose Peak Trail: 125
Willow Spring: 34
Wilson Spring: 45
World Beater Mine: 124
Wyoming Mine: 140
Zabriskie Point: 17, 21, 35, 39-41

List of Maps

Also Available

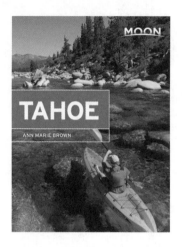

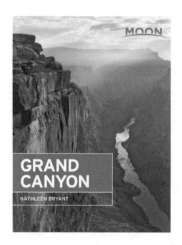

MAP SYMBOLS

≡≡≡	Expressway	○	City/Town	✈	Airport	⚲	Golf Course
━━━	Primary Road	◉	State Capital	✗	Airfield	🅿	Parking Area
═══	Secondary Road	⊛	National Capital	▲	Mountain	⛢	Archaeological Site
- - - -	Unpaved Road	★	Point of Interest	✦	Unique Natural Feature	⛪	Church
────	Feature Trail	•	Accommodation			⛽	Gas Station
- - - - -	Other Trail	▼	Restaurant/Bar	🕅	Waterfall		Glacier
············	Ferry	■	Other Location	♠	Park		Mangrove
═══	Pedestrian Walkway	▲	Campground	❶	Trailhead		Reef
▥▥▥	Stairs			⛷	Skiing Area		Swamp

CONVERSION TABLES

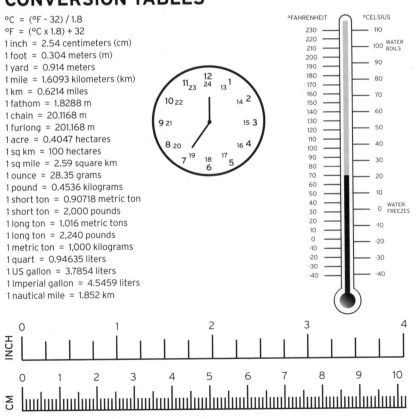

°C = (°F - 32) / 1.8
°F = (°C x 1.8) + 32
1 inch = 2.54 centimeters (cm)
1 foot = 0.304 meters (m)
1 yard = 0.914 meters
1 mile = 1.6093 kilometers (km)
1 km = 0.6214 miles
1 fathom = 1.8288 m
1 chain = 20.1168 m
1 furlong = 201.168 m
1 acre = 0.4047 hectares
1 sq km = 100 hectares
1 sq mile = 2.59 square km
1 ounce = 28.35 grams
1 pound = 0.4536 kilograms
1 short ton = 0.90718 metric ton
1 short ton = 2,000 pounds
1 long ton = 1.016 metric tons
1 long ton = 2,240 pounds
1 metric ton = 1,000 kilograms
1 quart = 0.94635 liters
1 US gallon = 3.7854 liters
1 Imperial gallon = 4.5459 liters
1 nautical mile = 1.852 km

MOON DEATH VALLEY NATIONAL PARK
Avalon Travel
an imprint of Perseus Books
a Hachette Book Group company
1700 Fourth Street
Berkeley, CA 94710, USA
www.moon.com

Editor and Series Manager: Sabrina Young
Copy Editor: Christopher Church
Production and Graphics Coordinator: Darren Alessi
Cover Design: Faceout Studios, Charles Brock
Moon Logo: Tim McGrath
Map Editor: Albert Angulo
Cartographers: Brian Shotwell, Albert Angulo, Lohne & Wright
Indexer: Greg Jewett

ISBN-13: 978-1-63121-009-9
ISSN: 2378-802X

Printing History
1st Edition — September 2015
5 4 3 2

Front cover photo: Badwater, Death Valley National Park © Tomas Kaspar / Alamy
Title page photo: © istockphoto.com
All other photos © Jenna Blough except page 6 (bottom) © Lloyd Tanner, (top left) © Laina Babb; page 26 (bottom) © Laina Babb; page 187 © Steve Byland/123rf.com

Printed in Canada by Friesens